D0964747

Also by the author:
   Bastard Out of Carolina
   Trash
   The Women Who Hate Me

Skin

dorothy allison

Talking About Sex, Class & Literature

Firebrand
Books
Ithaca, New York

Selections from this book have appeared, some in earlier or amended versions, in the following books and periodicals: *American Voice; Critical Condition/Women on the Edge of Violence* edited by Amy Scholder; *Forum: Leatherfolk* edited by Mark Thompson; *New York Native; New York Times Book Review; Pleasure and Danger* edited by Carol Vance; *San Francisco Focus; Sisters, Sexperts, Queers* edited by Arlene Stein; *Village Voice;* and *ZYZZYVA.*

Book and cover design by Debra Engstrom
Cover photograph by Jill Posener
Typesetting by Bets Ltd.

Printed in the United States on acid-free paper by McNaughton & Gunn

10 9 8 7 6 5 4 3 2 1

Library of Congress Cataloging-in-Publication Data

Allison, Dorothy
    Skin : talking about sex, class & literature / Dorothy Allison.
      P. cm.
    ISBN 1-56341-045-1 (acid-free paper) — ISBN 1-56341-044-3
    (pbk. : acid-free paper)
      1. Allison, Dorothy—Biography.   2. Women authors, American—20th century—Biography.   3. Lesbians—United States—Literary collections.   4. Southern States—Social life and customs.
      5. Feminists—United States—Biography.   6. Lesbians—United States—Biography.   I. Title.
    PS3551.L453Z475   1994
    814'.54—dc20   94 15071
                                                    CIP

814.54
ALL
9/94

Acknowledgments

This book was a long time coming together—more than a decade. It could not have been accomplished without the help and inspiration of Alix Layman, Joy Johannessen, Nancy Bereano, Jewelle Gomez, Amber Hollibaugh, Frances Goldin, Sydelle Kramer, Elly Bulkin, Diane Sabin, Pat Califia, Amy Scholder, my students who have taught me so much these last few years, and more friends and critics than I can name here. I must also acknowledge the welcome interruptions of my son, Wolf Michael. While none of my friends are responsible for my errors, Wolf—an avid keyboard fan—will answer for the typos.

For the women of my family

Contents

Context

One summer, almost ten years ago, I brought my lover down to Greenville to visit my aunt Dot and the rest of my mama's family. We took our time getting there, spending one day in D.C. and another in Durham. I even thought about suggesting a side trip over to the Smoky Mountains, until I realized the reason I was thinking about that was that I was afraid. It was not my family I feared. It was my lover. I was afraid to take my lover home with me because of what I might see in her face once she had spent some time with my aunt, met a few of my uncles, and tried to talk to any of my cousins. I was afraid of the distance, the fear, or the contempt that I imagined could suddenly appear between us. I was afraid that she might see me through new eyes, hateful eyes, the eyes of someone who suddenly knew fully how different we were. My aunts' distance, my cousins' fear, or my uncles' contempt seemed much less threatening.

I was right to worry. My lover did indeed see me with new eyes, though it turned out that she was more afraid of my distancing myself from her than of her fear and discomfort coming between us. What I saw in her face after the first day in South Carolina was nothing I had expected. Her features were marked with a kind of tenuous awe, confusion, uncertainty, and shame. All she could say was that she hadn't been prepared. My aunt Dot had welcomed her, served ice tea in a tall glass, and made her sit in the best seat at the kitchen table, the one near the window where my uncle's cigarette smoke wouldn't bother her. But my lover had barely spoken.

"It's a kind of a dialect, isn't it," she said to me in the motel that night. "I couldn't understand one word in four of anything your aunt said." I looked at her. Aunt Dot's accent was pronounced, but I had never thought of it as a dialect. It was just that she hadn't ever been out of Greenville County. She had a television, but it was for the kids in the living room. My aunt lived her life at that kitchen table.

My lover leaned into my shoulder so that her cheek rested against my collar bone. "I thought I knew what it would be like—your family, Greenville. You told me so many stories. But the words..." She lifted her hand palm up into the air and flexed the fingers as if she were reaching for an idea.

"I don't know," she said. "I thought I understood what you meant when you said 'working class' but I just didn't have a context."

I lay still. Although the motel air conditioner was working hard, I could smell the steamy moist heat from outside. It was slipping in around the edges of the door and windows, a swampy earth-rich smell that reminded me of being ten years old and climbing down to sleep on the floor with my sisters, hoping it would be a little cooler there. We had never owned an air conditioner, never stayed in a motel, never eaten in a restaurant where my mother did not work. Context. I breathed in the damp metallic air-conditioner smell and remembered Folly Beach.

When I was about eight my stepfather drove us there, down the road from Charleston, and all five of us stayed in one room that had been arranged for us by a friend of his at work. It wasn't a motel. It was a guesthouse, and the lady who managed it didn't seem too happy that we showed up for a room someone else had already paid for. I slept in a fold-up cot that kept threatening to collapse in the night. My sisters slept together in the bed across from the one my parents shared. My mama cooked on a two-burner stove to save us the cost of eating out, and our greatest treat was take-out food—

fried fish my stepfather swore was bad and hamburgers from the same place that sold the fish. We were in awe of the outdoor shower under the stairs where we were expected to rinse off the sand we picked up on the beach. We longed to be able to rent one of the rafts, umbrellas, and bicycles you could get on the beach. But my step-father insisted all that stuff was listed at robbery rates and cursed the men who tried to tempt us with it. That didn't matter to us. We were overcome with the sheer freedom of being on a real vacation in a semi-public place all the time where my stepfather had to watch his temper, and of running everywhere in bathing suits and flip-flops.

We were there a week. Twice my stepfather sent us to the beach while he and Mama stayed in the room. We took the opportunity to follow other families around, to listen to fathers praising their sons and watch mothers blushing with pride at how people looked at their girls. We listened to accents and studied picnic menus. Everyone was strange and wonderful, on vacation.

My stepfather lost his temper only once on that trip. He was hor-rified at the prices in the souvenir shops and made us keep our hands in our pockets.

"Jew bastards will charge me if you break anything," he cursed.

I flinched at his words and then realized that the man behind the counter heard him. I saw his blush and outrage as his eyes fol-lowed my stepfather's movement toward the door. Then I saw his eyes flicker over to me and my sisters, registering the same contempt with which he had looked at my stepfather. Heat flamed in my neck and I wanted to apologize—to tell him we were not like our stepfather —but I could do nothing. I couldn't speak a word to him in front of my stepfather, and if I had, why would he have believed me? Remember this, I thought. Don't go deaf and blind to what this feels like, remember it. I gritted my teeth and kept my head up, looked that man in the face and mouthed, "I'm sorry," but I could not tell if he understood me.

What context did he have for people like us?

After my lover fell asleep that first night in Greenville, I lay awake a long time thinking. My lover was a Yankee girl from a good family, who had spent the summers of her childhood on the Jersey Shore. I had gone there with her, walked with her on the beaches of her memory, wide and flat and grey-white, so clean I felt intimidated. Seeing where she had grown up, meeting some of her family, I had understood her better, seen where some of her fear came from, and her pride. What had she understood about me today? I wondered.

I turned my head to the side to look at her asleep, her mouth soft against my skin. Her hair was dark and shiny, her teeth straight and white. I wondered what she would have thought of Folly Beach, the poor man's Jersey Shore, or of us if she could have seen us there. I burned with old shame and then stubbornly shook it off.

Context is so little to share, and so vital.

A Question of Class

The first time I heard, "They're different than us, don't value human life the way we do," I was in high school in Central Florida. The man speaking was an army recruiter talking to a bunch of boys, telling them what the army was really like, what they could expect overseas. A cold angry feeling swept over me. I had heard the word *they* pronounced in that same callous tone before. *They,* those people over there, those people who are not us, they die so easily, kill each other so casually. They are different. *We,* I thought. *Me.*

When I was six or eight back in Greenville, South Carolina, I had heard that same matter-of-fact tone of dismissal applied to me. "Don't you play with her. I don't want you talking to them." Me and my family, we had always been *they.* Who am I? I wondered, listening to that recruiter. Who are my people? We die so easily, disappear so completely—we/they, the poor and the queer. I pressed my bony white trash fists to my stubborn lesbian mouth. The rage was a good feeling, stronger and purer than the shame that followed it, the fear and the sudden urge to run and hide, to deny, to pretend I did not know who I was and what the world would do to me.

My people were not remarkable. We were ordinary, but even so we were mythical. We were the *they* everyone talks about—the ungrateful poor. I grew up trying to run away from the fate that destroyed so many of the people I loved, and having learned the habit

13

of hiding, I found I had also learned to hide from myself. I did not know who I was, only that I did not want to be *they*, the ones who are destroyed or dismissed to make the "real" people, the important people, feel safer. By the time I understood that I was queer, that habit of hiding was deeply set in me, so deeply that it was not a choice but an instinct. Hide, hide to survive, I thought, knowing that if I told the truth about my life, my family, my sexual desire, my history, I would move over into that unknown territory, the land of they, would never have the chance to name my own life, to understand it or claim it.

Why are you so afraid? my lovers and friends have asked me the many times I have suddenly seemed a stranger, someone who would not speak to them, would not do the things they believed I should do, simple things like applying for a job, or a grant, or some award they were sure I could acquire easily. Entitlement, I have told them, is a matter of feeling like we rather than they. You think you have a right to things, a place in the world, and it is so intrinsically a part of you that you cannot imagine people like me, people who seem to live in your world, who don't have it. I have explained what I know over and over, in every way I can, but I have never been able to make clear the degree of my fear, the extent to which I feel myself denied: not only that I am queer in a world that hates queers, but that I was born poor into a world that despises the poor. The need to make my world believable to people who have never experienced it is part of why I write fiction. I know that some things must be felt to be understood, that despair, for example, can never be adequately analyzed; it must be lived. But if I can write a story that so draws the reader in that she imagines herself like my characters, feels their sense of fear and uncertainty, their hopes and terrors, then I have come closer to knowing myself as real, important as the very people I have always watched with awe.

I have known I was a lesbian since I was a teenager, and I have spent a good twenty years making peace with the effects of incest and physical abuse. But what may be the central fact of my life is that I was born in 1949 in Greenville, South Carolina, the bastard daughter of a white woman from a desperately poor family, a girl who had left the seventh grade the year before, worked as a waitress, and was just a month past fifteen when she had me. That fact, the inescapable impact of being born in a condition of poverty that this society finds shameful, contemptible, and somehow deserved, has had dominion over me to such an extent that I have spent my life trying to overcome or deny it. I have learned with great difficulty that the vast majority of people believe that poverty is a voluntary condition.

I have loved my family so stubbornly that every impulse to hold them in contempt has sparked in me a countersurge of pride—complicated and undercut by an urge to fit us into the acceptable myths and theories of both mainstream society and a lesbian-feminist reinterpretation. The choice becomes Steven Spielberg movies or Erskine Caldwell novels, the one valorizing and the other caricaturing, or the patriarchy as villain, trivializing the choices the men and women of my family have made. I have had to fight broad generalizations from every theoretical viewpoint.

Traditional feminist theory has had a limited understanding of class differences and of how sexuality and self are shaped by both desire and denial. The ideology implies that we are all sisters who should only turn our anger and suspicion on the world outside the lesbian community. It is easy to say that the patriarchy did it, that poverty and social contempt are products of the world of the fathers, and often I felt a need to collapse my sexual history into what I was willing to share of my class background, to pretend that my life both as a lesbian and as a working-class escapee was constructed by the patriarchy. Or conversely, to ignore how much my life was shaped by growing up poor and talk only about what incest did to my identity as a woman and as a lesbian. The difficulty is that I can't ascribe everything that has been problematic about my life simply and easily to the patriarchy, or to incest, or even to the invisible and much-denied class structure of our society.

In my lesbian-feminist collective we had long conversations about the mind/body split, the way we compartmentalize our lives to survive. For years I thought that that concept referred to the way I had separated my activist life from the passionate secret life in which I acted on my sexual desires. I was convinced that the fracture was fairly simple, that it would be healed when there was time and clarity to do so—at about the same point when I might begin to understand sex. I never imagined that it was not a split but a splintering, and I passed whole portions of my life—days, months, years—in pure directed progress, getting up every morning and setting to work, working so hard and so continually that I avoided examining in any way what I knew about my life. Busywork became a trance state. I ignored who I really was and how I became that person, continued in that daily progress, became an automaton who was what she did.

I tried to become one with the lesbian-feminist community so as to feel real and valuable. I did not know that I was hiding, blending in for safety just as I had done in high school, in college. I did not recognize the impulse to forget. I believed that all those things I did not talk about, or even let myself think too much about, were not important, that none of them defined me. I had constructed a life, an identity in which I took pride, an alternative lesbian family in which I felt safe, and I did not realize that the fundamental me had almost disappeared.

It is surprising how easy it was to live that life. Everyone and everything cooperated with the process. Everything in our culture—books, television, movies, school, fashion—is presented as if it is being seen by one pair of eyes, shaped by one set of hands, heard by one pair of ears. Even if you know you are not part of that imaginary creature—if you like country music not symphonies, read books cynically, listen to the news unbelievingly, are lesbian not heterosexual, and surround yourself with your own small deviant community

—you are still shaped by that hegemony, or your resistance to it. The only way I found to resist that homogenized view of the world was to make myself part of something larger than myself. As a feminist and a radical lesbian organizer, and later as a sex radical (which eventually became the term, along with pro-sex feminist, for those who were not anti-pornography but anti-censorship, those of us arguing for sexual diversity), the need to belong, to feel safe, was just as important for me as for any heterosexual, nonpolitical citizen, and sometimes even more important because the rest of my life was so embattled.

The first time I read the Jewish lesbian Irena Klepfisz's poems,* I experienced a frisson of recognition. It was not that my people had been "burned off the map" or murdered as hers had. No, we had been encouraged to destroy ourselves, made invisible because we did not fit the myths of the noble poor generated by the middle class. Even now, past forty and stubbornly proud of my family, I feel the draw of that mythology, that romanticized, edited version of the poor. I find myself looking back and wondering what was real, what was true. Within my family, so much was lied about, joked about, denied, or told with deliberate indirection, an undercurrent of humiliation or a brief pursed grimace that belied everything that had been said. What was real? The poverty depicted in books and movies was romantic, a backdrop for the story of how it was escaped.

The poverty portrayed by left-wing intellectuals was just as romantic, a platform for assailing the upper and middle classes, and from their perspective, the working-class hero was invariably male, righteously indignant, and inhumanly noble. The reality of self-hatred and violence was either absent or caricatured. The poverty I knew was dreary, deadening, shameful, the women powerful in ways not generally seen as heroic by the world outside the family.

My family's lives were not on television, not in books, not even comic books. There was a myth of the poor in this country, but it

---

*A Few Words in the Mother Tongue: Poems, Selected and New (Eighth Mountain Press: Portland, Oregon, 1990)

did not include us, no matter how hard I tried to squeeze us in. There was an idea of the good poor—hard-working, ragged but clean, and intrinsically honorable. I understood that we were the bad poor: men who drank and couldn't keep a job; women, invariably pregnant before marriage, who quickly became worn, fat, and old from working too many hours and bearing too many children; and children with runny noses, watery eyes, and the wrong attitudes. My cousins quit school, stole cars, used drugs, and took dead-end jobs pumping gas or waiting tables. We were not noble, not grateful, not even hopeful. We knew ourselves despised. My family was ashamed of being poor, of feeling hopeless. What was there to work for, to save money for, to fight for or struggle against? We had generations before us to teach us that nothing ever changed, and that those who did try to escape failed.

My mama had eleven brothers and sisters, of whom I can name only six. No one is left alive to tell me the names of the others. It was my grandmother who told me about my real daddy, a shiftless pretty man who was supposed to have married, had six children, and sold cut-rate life insurance to poor Black people. My mama married when I was a year old, but her husband died just after my little sister was born a year later.

When I was five, Mama married the man she lived with until she died. Within the first year of their marriage Mama miscarried, and while we waited out in the hospital parking lot, my stepfather molested me for the first time, something he continued to do until I was past thirteen. When I was eight or so, Mama took us away to a motel after my stepfather beat me so badly it caused a family scandal, but we returned after two weeks. Mama told me that she really had no choice: she could not support us alone. When I was eleven I told one of my cousins that my stepfather was molesting me. Mama packed up my sisters and me and took us away for a few days, but again, my stepfather swore he would stop, and again we went back after a few weeks. I stopped talking for a while, and I have only vague memories of the next two years.

My stepfather worked as a route salesman, my mama as a waitress, laundry worker, cook, or fruit packer. I could never understand, since they both worked so hard and such long hours, how we never had enough money, but it was also true of my mama's brothers and sisters who worked hard in the mills or the furnace industry. In fact, my parents did better than anyone else in the family. But eventually my stepfather was fired and we hit bottom—nightmarish months of marshals at the door, repossessed furniture, and rubber checks. My parents worked out a scheme so that it appeared my stepfather had abandoned us, but instead he went down to Florida, got a new job, and rented us a house. He returned with a U-Haul trailer in the dead of night, packed us up, and moved us south.

The night we left South Carolina for Florida, my mama leaned over the backseat of her old Pontiac and promised us girls, "It'll be better there." I don't know if we believed her, but I remember crossing Georgia in the early morning, watching the red clay hills and swaying grey blankets of moss recede through the back window. I kept looking at the trailer behind us, ridiculously small to contain everything we owned. Mama had packed nothing that wasn't fully paid off, which meant she had only two things of worth: her washing and sewing machines, both of them tied securely to the trailer walls. Throughout the trip I fantasized an accident that would burst that trailer, scattering old clothes and cracked dishes on the tarmac.

I was only thirteen. I wanted us to start over completely, to begin again as new people with nothing of the past left over. I wanted to run away from who we had been seen to be, who we had been. That desire is one I have seen in other members of my family. It is the first thing I think of when trouble comes—the geographic solution. Change your name, leave town, disappear, make yourself over. What hides behind that impulse is the conviction that the life you have lived, the person you are, is valueless, better off abandoned, that running away is easier than trying to change things, that change itself is not possible. Sometimes I think it is this conviction—more seductive than alcohol or violence, more subtle than sexual hatred or gender injustice—that has dominated my life and made real change so painful and difficult.

Moving to Central Florida did not fix our lives. It did not stop my stepfather's violence, heal my shame, or make my mother happy. Once there, our lives became controlled by my mother's illness and medical bills. She had a hysterectomy when I was about eight and endured a series of hospitalizations for ulcers and a chronic back problem. Through most of my adolescence she superstitiously refused to allow anyone to mention the word *cancer*. When she was not sick, Mama and my stepfather went on working, struggling to pay off what seemed an insurmountable load of debts.

By the time I was fourteen, my sisters and I had found ways to discourage most of our stepfather's sexual advances. We were not close, but we united against him. Our efforts were helped along when he was referred to a psychotherapist after he lost his temper at work, and was prescribed drugs that made him sullen but less violent. We were growing up quickly, my sisters moving toward dropping out of school while I got good grades and took every scholarship exam I could find. I was the first person in my family to graduate from high school, and the fact that I went on to college was nothing short of astonishing.

We all imagine our lives are normal, and I did not know my life was not everyone's. It was in Central Florida that I began to realize just how different we were. The people we met there had not been shaped by the rigid class structure that dominated the South Carolina Piedmont. The first time I looked around my junior high classroom and realized I did not know who those people were—not only as individuals but as categories, who their people were and how they saw themselves—I also realized that they did not know me. In Greenville, everyone knew my family, knew we were trash, and that meant we were supposed to be poor, supposed to have grim low-paid jobs, have babies in our teens, and never finish school. But Central Florida in the 1960s was full of runaways and immigrants, and our mostly white working-class suburban school sorted us out not by income and family background but by intelligence and aptitude tests. Suddenly I was boosted into the college-bound track, and while there was plenty of contempt for my inept social skills, pitiful wardrobe, and slow drawling accent, there was also something I had never experienced before: a protective anonymity, and a kind of grudging respect and curiosity about who I might become. Because they did not see poverty and hopelessness as a foregone conclusion for my life, I could begin to imagine other futures for myself.

In that new country, we were unknown. The myth of the poor settled over us and glamorized us. I saw it in the eyes of my teachers, the Lion's Club representative who paid for my new glasses, and the lady from the Junior League who told me about the scholarship I had won. Better, far better, to be one of the mythical poor than to be part of the *they* I had known before. I also experienced a new level of fear, a fear of losing what had never before been imaginable. Don't let me lose this chance, I prayed, and lived in terror that I might suddenly be seen again as what I knew myself to be.

As an adolescent I thought that my family's escape from South Carolina played like a bad movie. We fled the way runaway serfs might have done, with the sheriff who would have arrested my stepfather the imagined border guard. I am certain that if we had remained in South Carolina, I would have been trapped by my family's heritage of poverty, jail, and illegitimate children—that even being smart, stubborn, and a lesbian would have made no difference.

My grandmother died when I was twenty, and after Mama went home for the funeral, I had a series of dreams in which we still lived up in Greenville, just down the road from where Granny died. In the dreams I had two children and only one eye, lived in a trailer, and worked at the textile mill. Most of my time was taken up with deciding when I would finally kill my children and myself. The dreams were so vivid, I became convinced they were about the life

I was meant to have had, and I began to work even harder to put as much distance as I could between my family and me. I copied the dress, mannerisms, attitudes, and ambitions of the girls I met in college, changing or hiding my own tastes, interests, and desires. I kept my lesbianism a secret, forming a relationship with an effeminate male friend that served to shelter and disguise us both. I explained to friends that I went home so rarely because my stepfather and I fought too much for me to be comfortable in his house. But that was only part of the reason I avoided home, the easiest reason. The truth was that I feared the person I might become in my mama's house, the woman of my dreams—hateful, violent, and hopeless.

It is hard to explain how deliberately and thoroughly I ran away from my own life. I did not forget where I came from, but I gritted my teeth and hid it. When I could not get enough scholarship money to pay for graduate school, I spent a year of rage working as a salad girl, substitute teacher, and maid. I finally managed to find a job by agreeing to take any city assignment where the Social Security Administration needed a clerk. Once I had a job and my own place far away from anyone in my family, I became sexually and politically active, joining the Women's Center support staff and falling in love with a series of middle-class women who thought my accent and stories thoroughly charming. The stories I told about my family, about South Carolina, about being poor itself, were all lies, carefully edited to seem droll or funny. I knew damn well that no one would want to hear the truth about poverty, the hopelessness and fear, the feeling that nothing I did would ever make any difference and the raging resentment that burned beneath my jokes. Even when my lovers and I formed an alternative lesbian family, sharing what we could of our resources, I kept the truth about my background and who I knew myself to be a carefully obscured mystery. I worked as hard as I could to make myself a new person, an emotionally healthy radical lesbian activist, and I believed completely that by remaking myself I was helping to remake the world.

For a decade, I did not go home for more than a few days at a time.

When in the 1980s I ran into the concept of feminist sexuality, I genuinely did not know what it meant. Though I was, and am, a feminist, and committed to claiming the right to act on my sexual desires without tailoring my lust to a sex-fearing society, demands that I explain or justify my sexual fantasies have left me at a loss. How does anyone explain sexual need?

The Sex Wars are over, I've been told, and it always makes me want to ask who won. But my sense of humor may be a little obscure to women who have never felt threatened by the way most lesbians use and mean the words *pervert* and *queer.* I use the word queer to mean more than lesbian. Since I first used it in 1980 I have always meant it to imply that I am not only a lesbian but a transgressive lesbian—femme, masochistic, as sexually aggressive as the women I seek out, and as pornographic in my imagination and sexual activities as the heterosexual hegemony has ever believed.

My aunt Dot used to joke, "There are two or three things I know for sure, but never the same things and I'm never as sure as I'd like." What I know for sure is that class, gender, sexual preference, and prejudice—racial, ethnic, and religious—form an intricate lattice that restricts and shapes our lives, and that resistance to hatred is not a simple act. Claiming your identity in the cauldron of hatred and resistance to hatred is infinitely complicated, and worse, almost unexplainable.

I know that I have been hated as a lesbian both by "society" and by the intimate world of my extended family, but I have also been hated or held in contempt (which is in some ways more debilitating and slippery than hatred) by lesbians for behavior and sexual practices shaped in large part by class. My sexual identity is intimately constructed by my class and regional background, and much of the hatred directed at my sexual preferences is class hatred—however much people, feminists in particular, like to pretend this is not a factor. The kind of woman I am attracted to is invariably the kind of woman who embarrasses respectably middle-class, politically aware lesbian feminists. My sexual ideal is butch, exhibitionistic, physically aggressive, smarter than she wants you to know, and proud of being called a pervert. Most often she is working class, with an aura of danger and an ironic sense of humor. There is a lot of contemporary lip service paid to sexual tolerance, but the fact that my sexuality is constructed within, and by, a butch/femme and leather fetishism is widely viewed with distaste or outright hatred.

For most of my life I have been presumed to be misguided, damaged by incest and childhood physical abuse, or deliberately indulging in hateful and retrograde sexual practices out of a selfish concentration on my own sexual satisfaction. I have been expected to abandon my desires, to become the normalized woman who flirts with fetishization, who plays with gender roles and treats the historical categories of deviant desire with humor or gentle contempt but never takes any of it so seriously as to claim a sexual identity based on these categories. It was hard enough for me to shake off demands when they were made by straight society. It was appalling when I found the same demands made by other lesbians.

One of the strengths I derive from my class background is that I am accustomed to contempt. I know that I have no chance of becoming what my detractors expect of me, and I believe that even the attempt to please them will only further engage their contempt, and my own self-contempt as well. Nonetheless, the relationship between the life I have lived and the way that life is seen by strangers has constantly invited a kind of self-mythologizing fantasy. It has always been tempting for me to play off of the stereotypes and misconceptions of mainstream culture, rather than describe a difficult and sometimes painful reality.

I am trying to understand how we internalize the myths of our society even as we resist them. I have felt a powerful temptation to write about my family as a kind of morality tale, with us as the heroes and middle and upper classes as the villains. It would be within the romantic myth, for example, to pretend that we were the kind of noble

Southern whites portrayed in the movies, mill workers for generations until driven out by alcoholism and a family propensity for rebellion and union talk. But that would be a lie. The truth is that no
one in my family ever joined a union.

Taken to its limits, the myth of the poor would make my family
over into union organizers or people broken by the failure of the unions.
As far as my family was concerned union organizers, like preachers,
were of a different class, suspect and hated however much they might
be admired for what they were supposed to be trying to achieve. Nominally Southern Baptist, no one in my family actually paid much attention to preachers, and only little children went to Sunday school.
Serious belief in anything—any political ideology, any religious system,
or any theory of life's meaning and purpose—was seen as unrealistic. It was an attitude that bothered me a lot when I started reading
the socially conscious novels I found in the paperback racks when
I was eleven or so. I particularly loved Sinclair Lewis's novels and
wanted to imagine my own family as part of the working man's
struggle.

"We were not joiners," my aunt Dot told me with a grin when
I asked her about the union. My cousin Butch laughed at that, told
me the union charged dues, and said, "Hell, we can't even be persuaded to toss money in the collection plate. An't gonna give it to
no union man." It shamed me that the only thing my family wholeheartedly believed in was luck and the waywardness of fate. They
held the dogged conviction that the admirable and wise thing to do
was keep a sense of humor, never whine or cower, and trust that luck
might someday turn as good as it had been bad—and with just as
much reason. Becoming a political activist with an almost religious
fervor was the thing I did that most outraged my family and the Southern working-class community they were part of.

Similarly, it was not my sexuality, my lesbianism, that my family saw as most rebellious; for most of my life, no one but my mama
took my sexual preference very seriously. It was the way I thought
about work, ambition, and self-respect. They were waitresses, laundry

workers, counter girls. I was the one who went to work as a maid, something I never told any of them. They would have been angry if they had known. Work was just work for them, necessary. You did what you had to do to survive. They did not so much believe in taking pride in doing your job as in stubbornly enduring hard work and hard times. At the same time, they held that there were some forms of work, including maid's work, that were only for Black people, not white, and while I did not share that belief, I knew how intrinsic it was to the way my family saw the world. Sometimes I felt as if I straddled cultures and belonged on neither side. I would grind my teeth at what I knew was my family's unquestioning racism while continuing to respect their pragmatic endurance. But more and more as I grew older, what I felt was a deep estrangement from their view of the world, and gradually a sense of shame that would have been completely incomprehensible to them.

"Long as there's lunch counters, you can always find work," I was told by my mother and my aunts. Then they'd add, "I can get me a little extra with a smile." It was obvious there was supposed to be nothing shameful about it, that needy smile across a lunch counter, that rueful grin when you didn't have rent, or the half-provocative, half-pleading way my mama could cajole the man at the store to give her a little credit. But I hated it, hated the need for it and the shame that would follow every time I did it myself. It was begging, as far as I was concerned, a quasi-prostitution that I despised even while I continued to rely on it. After all, I needed the money.

"Just use that smile," my girl cousins used to joke, and I hated what I knew they meant. After college, when I began to support myself and study feminist theory, I became more contemptuous rather than more understanding of the women in my family. I told myself that prostitution is a skilled profession and my cousins were never more than amateurs. There was a certain truth in this, though like all cruel judgments rendered from the outside, it ignored the conditions that made it true. The women in my family, my mother included, had sugar daddies, not johns, men who slipped them money because they needed it so badly. From their point of view they were nice to those men because the men were nice to them, and it was never so direct or crass an arrangement that they would set a price on their favors. Nor would they have described what they did as prostitution. Nothing made them angrier than the suggestion that the men who helped them out did it just for their favors. They worked for a living, they swore, but this was different.

I always wondered if my mother hated her sugar daddy, or if not him then her need for what he offered her, but it did not seem to me in memory that she had. He was an old man, half-crippled, hesitant and needy, and he treated my mama with enormous consideration and, yes, respect. The relationship between them was painful, and since she and my stepfather could not earn enough to support the family, Mama could not refuse her sugar daddy's money. At the same time the man made no assumptions about that money buying anything Mama was not already offering. The truth was, I think, that she genuinely liked him, and only partly because he treated her so well.

Even now, I am not sure whether there was a sexual exchange between them. Mama was a pretty woman, and she was kind to him, a kindness he obviously did not get from anyone else in his life. Moreover, he took extreme care not to cause her any problems with my stepfather. As a teenager, with a teenager's contempt for moral failings and sexual complexity of any kind, I had been convinced that Mama's relationship with that old man was contemptible. Also, that I would never do such a thing. But the first time a lover of mine gave me money and I took it, everything in my head shifted. The amount was not much to her, but it was a lot to me and I needed it. While I could not refuse it, I hated myself for taking it and I hated her for giving it. Worse, she had much less grace about my need than my mama's sugar daddy had displayed toward her. All that bitter contempt I felt for my needy cousins and aunts raged through me and burned out the love. I ended the relationship quickly, unable to forgive

myself for selling what I believed should only be offered freely—
not sex but love itself.

When the women in my family talked about how hard they
worked, the men would spit to the side and shake their heads. Men
took real jobs—harsh, dangerous, physically daunting work. They
went to jail, not just the cold-eyed, careless boys who scared me with
their brutal hands, but their gentler, softer brothers. It was another
family thing, what people expected of my mama's people, mine. "His
daddy's that one was sent off to jail in Georgia, and his uncle's another. Like as not, he's just the same," you'd hear people say of boys
so young they still had their milk teeth. We were always driving down
to the county farm to see somebody, some uncle, cousin, or name-
less male relation. Shaven-headed, sullen, and stunned, they wept
on Mama's shoulder or begged my aunts to help. "I didn't do nothing,
Mama," they'd say, and it might have been true, but if even we didn't
believe them, who would? No one told the truth, not even about how
their lives were destroyed.

One of my favorite cousins went to jail when I was eight years
old, for breaking into pay phones with another boy. The other boy
was returned to the custody of his parents. My cousin was sent to
the boys' facility at the county farm. After three months, my mama
took us down there to visit, carrying a big basket of fried chicken,
cold cornbread, and potato salad. Along with a hundred others we
sat out on the lawn with my cousin and watched him eat like he hadn't
had a full meal in the whole three months. I stared at his near-bald
head and his ears marked with fine blue scars from the carelessly
handled razor. People were laughing, music was playing, and a tall,
lazy, uniformed man walked past us chewing on toothpicks and watching us all closely. My cousin kept his head down, his face hard with
hatred, only looking back at the guard when he turned away.

"Sons-a-bitches," he whispered, and my mama shushed him.
We all sat still when the guard turned back to us. There was a long
moment of quiet, and then that man let his face relax into a big wide

grin.

"Uh-huh," he said. That was all he said. Then he turned and walked away. None of us spoke. None of us ate. He went back inside soon after, and we left. When we got back to the car, my mama sat there for a while crying quietly. The next week my cousin was reported for fighting and had his stay extended by six months. My cousin was fifteen. He never went back to school, and after jail he couldn't join the army. When he finally did come home we never talked, never had to. I knew without asking that the guard had had his little revenge, knew too that my cousin would break into another phone booth as soon as he could, but do it sober and not get caught. I knew without asking the source of his rage, the way he felt about clean, well-dressed, contemptuous people who looked at him like his life wasn't as important as a dog's. I knew because I felt it too. That guard had looked at me and Mama with the same expression he used on my cousin. We were trash. We were the ones they built the county farm to house and break. The boy who was sent home was the son of a deacon in the church, the man who managed the hardware store.

As much as I hated that man, and his boy, there was a way in which I also hated my cousin. He should have known better, I told myself, should have known the risk he ran. He should have been more careful. As I grew older and started living on my own, it was a litany I used against myself even more angrily than I used it against my cousin. I knew who I was, knew that the most important thing I had to do was protect myself and hide my despised identity, blend into the myth of both the good poor and the reasonable lesbian. When I became a feminist activist, that litany went on reverberating in my head, but by then it had become a groundnote, something so deep and omnipresent I no longer heard it, even when everything I did was set to its cadence.

By 1975 I was earning a meager living as a photographer's assistant in Tallahassee, Florida. But the real work of my life was my lesbian-feminist activism, the work I did with the local women's center and the committee to found a women's studies program at Florida State University. Part of my role, as I saw it, was to be a kind of evangelical lesbian feminist, and to help develop a political analysis of this woman-hating society. I did not talk about class, except to give lip service to how we all needed to think about it, the same way I thought we all needed to think about racism. I was a determined person, living in a lesbian collective—all of us young and white and serious—studying each new book that purported to address feminist issues, driven by what I saw as a need to revolutionize the world.

Years later it's difficult to convey just how reasonable my life seemed to me at that time. I was not flippant, not consciously condescending, not casual about how tough a struggle remaking social relations would be, but like so many women of my generation, I believed absolutely that I could make a difference with my life, and I was willing to give my life for the chance to make that difference. I expected hard times, long slow periods of self-sacrifice and grinding work, expected to be hated and attacked in public, to have to set aside personal desire, lovers, and family in order to be part of something greater and more important than my individual concerns. At the same time, I was working ferociously to take my desires, my sexuality, my needs as a woman and a lesbian more seriously. I believed I was making the personal political revolution with my life every moment, whether I was scrubbing the floor of the childcare center, setting up a new budget for the women's lecture series at the university, editing the local feminist magazine, or starting a women's bookstore. That I was constantly exhausted and had no health insurance, did hours of dreary unpaid work and still sneaked out of the collective to date butch women my housemates thought retrograde and sexist never interfered with my sense of total commitment to the feminist revolution. I was not living in a closet: I had compartmentalized my own mind to such an extent that I never questioned why I did what I did. And I never admitted what lay behind all my feminist convictions—a class-constructed distrust of change, a secret fear that someday I would be found out for who I really was, found out and thrown out. If I had not been raised to give my life away, would I have made such an effective, self-sacrificing revolutionary? The narrowly focused concentration of a revolutionary shifted only when I began to write again. The idea of writing stories seemed frivolous when there was so much work to be done, but everything changed when I found myself confronting emotions and ideas that could not be explained away or postponed until after the revolution. The way it happened was simple and unexpected. One week I was asked to speak to two completely different groups: an Episcopalian Sunday school class and a juvenile detention center. The Episcopalians were all white, well-dressed, highly articulate, nominally polite, and obsessed with getting me to tell them (without their having to ask directly) just what it was that two women did together in bed. The delinquents were all women, 80 percent Black and Hispanic, wearing green uniform dresses or blue jeans and workshirts, profane, rude, fearless, witty, and just as determined to get me to talk about what it was that two women did together in bed.

I tried to have fun with the Episcopalians, teasing them about their fears and insecurities, and being as bluntly honest as I could about my sexual practices. The Sunday school teacher, a man who had assured me of his liberal inclinations, kept blushing and stammering as the questions about my growing up and coming out became more detailed. I stepped out into the sunshine when the meeting was over, angry at the contemptuous attitude implied by all their questioning, and though I did not know why, so deeply depressed I couldn't even cry.

The delinquents were another story. Shameless, they had me blushing within the first few minutes, yelling out questions that were part curiosity and partly a way of boasting about what they already knew. "You butch or femme?" "You ever fuck boys?" "You ever want to?" "You want to have children?" "What's your girlfriend like?" I finally broke up when one very tall, confident girl leaned way over and called out, "Hey, girlfriend! I'm getting out of here next weekend. What you doing that night?'' I laughed so hard I almost choked. I laughed until we were all howling and giggling together. Even getting frisked as I left didn't ruin my mood. I was still grinning when I climbed into the waterbed with my lover that night, grinning right up to the moment when she wrapped her arms around me and I burst into tears.

That night I understood, suddenly, everything that had happened to my cousins and me, understood it from a wholly new and agonizing perspective, one that made clear how brutal I had been to both my family and myself. I grasped all over again how we had been robbed and dismissed, and why I had worked so hard not to think about it. I had learned as a child that what could not be changed had to go unspoken, and worse, that those who cannot change their own lives have every reason to be ashamed of that fact and to hide it. I had accepted that shame and believed in it, but why? What had I or my cousins done to deserve the contempt directed at us? Why had I always believed us contemptible by nature? I wanted to talk to someone about all the things I was thinking that night, but I could not. Among the women I knew there was no one who would have understood what I was thinking, no other working-class woman in the women's collective where I was living. I began to suspect that we shared no common language to speak those bitter truths.

In the days that followed I found myself remembering that afternoon long ago at the county farm, that feeling of being the animal in the zoo, the thing looked at and laughed at and used by the real people who watched us. For all his liberal convictions, that Sunday school teacher had looked at me with the eyes of my cousin's long-ago guard. I felt thrown back into my childhood, into all the fears I had tried to escape. Once again I felt myself at the mercy of the important people who knew how to dress and talk, and would always be given the benefit of the doubt, while my family and I would not.

I experienced an outrage so old I could not have traced all the ways it shaped my life. I realized again that some are given no quarter, no chance, that all their courage, humor, and love for each other is just a joke to the ones who make the rules, and I hated the rule-makers. Finally, I recognized that part of my grief came from the fact that I no longer knew who I was or where I belonged. I had run away from my family, refused to go home to visit, and tried in every way to make myself a new person. How could I be working class with a college degree? As a lesbian activist? I thought about the guards at the detention center. They had not stared at me with the same picture-window emptiness they turned on the girls who came to hear me, girls who were closer to the life I had been meant to live than I could bear to examine. The contempt in their eyes was contempt for me as a lesbian, different and the same, but still contempt.

While I raged, my girlfriend held me and comforted me and tried to get me to explain what was hurting me so bad, but I could not. She had told me so often about her awkward relationship with her own family, the father who ran his own business and still sent her checks every other month. She knew almost nothing about my family, only the jokes and careful stories I had given her. I felt so alone and at risk lying in her arms that I could not have explained anything at all. I thought about those girls in the detention center and the stories they told in brutal shorthand about their sisters, brothers, cousins, and lovers. I thought about their one-note references to those they had lost, never mentioning the loss of their own hopes, their own futures, the bent and painful shape of their lives when they would finally get free. Cried-out and dry-eyed, I lay watching my sleeping girlfriend and thinking about what I had not been able to say to her. After a few hours I got up and made some notes for a poem I wanted to write, a bare, painful litany of loss shaped as a conversation between two women, one who cannot understand the other, and one who cannot tell all she knows.

It took me a long time to take that poem from a raw lyric of outrage and grief to a piece of fiction that explained to me something I had never let myself see up close before—the whole process of running away, of closing up inside yourself, of hiding. It has taken me most of my life to understand that, to see how and why those of us who are born poor and different are so driven to give ourselves away or lose ourselves, but most of all, simply to disappear as the people we really are. By the time that poem became the story "River of Names,"* I had made the decision to reverse that process: to claim my family, my true history, and to tell the truth not only about who I was but about the temptation to lie.

By the time I taught myself the basics of storytelling on the page, I knew there was only one story that would haunt me until I understood how to tell it—the complicated, painful story of how my mama had, and had not, saved me as a girl. Writing *Bastard Out of Carolina*** became, ultimately, the way to claim my family's pride and tragedy, and the embattled sexuality I had fashioned on a base of violence and abuse.

The compartmentalized life I had created burst open in the late 1970s after I began to write what I really thought about my family. I lost patience with my fear of what the women I worked with, mostly lesbians, thought of who I slept with and what we did together. When schisms developed within my community; when I was no longer able to hide within the regular dyke network; when I could not continue to justify my life by constant political activism or distract myself by sleeping around; when my sexual promiscuity, butch/femme orientation, and exploration of sadomasochistic sex became part of what was driving me out of my community of choice—I went home again. I went home to my mother and my sisters, to visit, talk, argue, and begin to understand.

Once home I saw that as far as my family was concerned, lesbians were lesbians whether they wore suitcoats or leather jackets. Moreover, in all that time when I had not made peace with myself, my family had managed to make a kind of peace with me. My girl-

---

* *Trash* (Firebrand Books: Ithaca, New York, 1988)
**Dutton: New York, 1992

friends were treated like slightly odd versions of my sisters' husbands, while I was simply the daughter who had always been difficult but was still a part of their lives. The result was that I started trying to confront what had made me unable really to talk to my sisters for so many years. I discovered that they no longer knew who I was either, and it took time and lots of listening to each other to rediscover my sense of family, and my love for them.

It is only as the child of my class and my unique family background that I have been able to put together what is for me a meaningful politics, to regain a sense of why I believe in activism, why self-revelation is so important for lesbians. There is no all-purpose feminist analysis that explains the complicated ways our sexuality and core identity are shaped, the way we see ourselves as parts of both our birth families and the extended family of friends and lovers we invariably create within the lesbian community. For me, the bottom line has simply become the need to resist that omnipresent fear, that urge to hide and disappear, to disguise my life, my desires, and the truth about how little any of us understand—even as we try to make the world a more just and human place. Most of all, I have tried to understand the politics of *they*, why human beings fear and stigmatize the different while secretly dreading that they might be one of the different themselves. Class, race, sexuality, gender—and all the other categories by which we categorize and dismiss each other—need to be excavated from the inside.

The horror of class stratification, racism, and prejudice is that some people begin to believe that the security of their families and communities depends on the oppression of others, that for some to have good lives there must be others whose lives are truncated and brutal. It is a belief that dominates this culture. It is what makes the poor whites of the South so determinedly racist and the middle class so contemptuous of the poor. It is a myth that allows some to imagine that they build their lives on the ruin of others, a secret core of shame for the middle class, a goad and a spur to the marginal working class, and cause enough for the homeless and poor to feel no constraints on hatred or violence. The power of the myth is made even more apparent when we examine how, within the lesbian and feminist communities where we have addressed considerable attention to the politics of marginalization, there is still so much exclusion and fear, so many of us who do not feel safe.

I grew up poor, hated, the victim of physical, emotional, and sexual violence, and I know that suffering does not ennoble. It destroys. To resist destruction, self-hatred, or lifelong hopelessness, we have to throw off the conditioning of being despised, the fear of becoming the *they* that is talked about so dismissively, to refuse lying myths and easy moralities, to see ourselves as human, flawed, and extraordinary. All of us—extraordinary.

An earlier version of this essay appeared in *Sisters, Sexperts, Queers*, edited by Arlene Stein (Penguin/Plume: New York, 1993).

Never Expected to Live Forever

The meeting had gone well but run late. Coming back, my girlfriend and I were tired, joking and talking to stay alert, taking the fastest way home. I heard the boy come up behind us, and I knew immediately that something was wrong. For a minute I tried to think of what I could say, words that were distracting, sympathetic. He stopped all that when he whispered over my shoulder, "I don't want to hurt you."

"Oh shit." I took a deep breath and kept walking. All I had with me was a couple of subway tokens and a notebook, nothing that would satisfy a serious thief. The guy ran around in front of us and pointed his coat pocket at me.

"I said I don't want to hurt you."

I stood frozen, looking at him, a young fine-featured dark-faced man. That was a very nice coat he was wearing. It was, in fact, the nicest coat I'd seen in days, tweed and tailored and impressive even in the dim light of the street. For that matter, so was he—an altogether handsome, slender young man with delicate features and a soft tenor voice. How could someone who looked like that and dressed in that kind of coat point his pocket at me?

"Come on," I said, trying to joke with him. I glanced back and saw that my girlfriend had quietly tucked her purse inside her coat.

"I'm not fooling."

He couldn't have been more than twenty and he seemed very nervous, giving quick looks up and down the street to see if anyone was coming. I caught my girlfriend's eye again. She looked back at me. It was the kind of look that said, "Hey, we're in this together." I took another deep breath and tried not to start shaking. All right, I thought, and remembered the last time I had been this scared.

I got through college by the grace of the National Merit Scholarship fund, a local mop factory, and the Roberts Dairy Company. The fund paid the tuition, while the mop factory and the dairy store let me work evenings, weekends, and holidays to pay for the rest. For three years I spent every Christmas and Easter selling cigarettes, beer, and milk products at the drive-in dairy store, earning a flat holiday bonus of twenty-five dollars a shift. There were tips, too, since many people thought it a shame I had to be there to sell them their eggnog and butter. One Christmas, a lady even gave me a fruitcake—one I'd swear she bought at another dairy store down the street. "You have a Merry Christmas!" she insisted after buying a coffee ring she probably gave to whoever she'd paid for the fruitcake.

The dairy store was a good job even though I regularly worked sixteen-hour shifts. The owners didn't care how much I studied or talked out loud just so long as I kept the milk, beer, and cigarette racks full. "And don't do nothing stupid," they told me, talking about how often those little stores got held up. "Somebody sticks you up, you just hand the money over. It's never as much money as your hospital bills would be."

For three years I was lucky. The store was broken into twice, but both times they came in the stockroom while I was busy up front. The thieves got a lot of beer and milk. I never even saw their faces. One night, though, a skinny-faced man came in to tell me his partner had a shotgun.

"Give me the money," he whispered. All I could see in the car outside was a woman whose face was even skinnier than his. It looked like there was someone in the backseat, but it could have been kids for all I could tell. I thought a minute and then gave him the money. "Thank you," he said politely. When he drove away, I saw they'd taped over the license plate. Ray, the guy who relieved me that night, said I should have made them show me the gun. Then he lifted his shirt so I could see his own.

"An't nobody gonna rob me," he insisted, and rubbed that gun barrel like it was the closest friend he had.

"You know Ray carries a gun?" I asked the manager.

"Yeah, but that's his business. He got pistol-whipped once and now I can't get him to leave it at home. 'Course he'll probably shoot himself before he shoots some thief."

I shook my head, unable to imagine shooting somebody over a few hundred dollars and a case of milk. But that summer night when the four boys walked in, I had a moment of desperately wishing Ray were there.

"I don't want to shoot you." The pistol in that child's hand was silver, very small and very shiny in the fluorescent light. He was shorter than I was, maybe five-feet-two-inches tall. I looked in his face and realized he had to be no more than fifteen. His skin was shiny with sweat, and the hand with the gun was shaking terribly.

"Don't make me shoot you lady."

The other three were about his age, just as short, just as scared. They were filling their pockets with cigarettes. One of them went in the back and came out with my purse and the bank deposit. Another one emptied the cash register, while the third decided to use a grocery bag for the rest of the cigarettes. One of them started to laugh, and the one with the gun started to grin. I stood still, trying to look like none of it was any of my business.

"What you looking at?"

He waved the silver gun and my stomach heaved. People had died all around me when I was a child, but I had always tried to convince myself that I could survive anything. Now I felt sweat break out all over my body. He brought the silver gun up and put the barrel right between my eyes. When it touched my forehead, it burned.

I bit my tongue to keep from throwing up.

"You looking at me?"

I couldn't breathe. I thought, I haven't even graduated college yet. I looked at his belt buckle. Snakes and wild dogs, one of my aunts had told me once, don't take your eyes off of them. But I could not look up at this child with his cold silver gun. He would kill me. He would kill me because I was scared and stupid and unable to think what to do. I opened my mouth and made myself lift my shoulders and my eyebrows in the same motion.

"Shitfire," I said and laughed. I didn't know where that laugh came from. "I'm so scared," I said. "I an't looking at nothing. I couldn't see Jesus if he came in here to talk to me right now."

The child laughed. He wiggled the gun. Now it felt like a cube of ice scoring my skin.

"You want to see Jesus?" The boy was talking to the others. I felt one of them come up behind me.

I laughed again and made myself shrug again, that comic exaggerated shrug. I remembered the time my aunt Dot hit her husband with a cane-backed chair, calmly and methodically doing what she thought she had to do. I would do what I had to do, I told myself.

"I just want to see morning," I told the boy. He laughed at me.

The one who had come up behind me put his arms around me and started undoing the buttons on the front of my dress. He put his hands inside. Fire and ice. I became very calm and wondered if I should let myself throw up. Would it help?

"Don't you want to go for a ride with us?"

"No."

"Oh come on. Come go for a ride with us."

I planted my feet. I imagined that I weighed three thousand pounds, that my feet were sunk in cement. The one with the gun tugged at my arm. I rocked but didn't move. The only thing I was sure of at that moment was that I was going nowhere.

"Come on. Come on."

"Quit fooling around."

He pulled the gun back, cocked it. I can't die, I thought, and made myself keep my eyes on the floor. I heard a clicking noise and then they were running, laughing and yelling and gone. I looked out the front of the big glass double doors to the street. Cars were passing by, lights were shining, and soft damp smells of swamp and tar were blowing in. I tried to move but couldn't. I was wet all over, standing in a puddle of my own sweat, unable to move or shout. "Jesus," I said out loud. "Thank you, Jesus."

By the time the police came I was sitting with a roll of paper towels, wiping myself dry and practicing how I was going to quit that job. The young policeman who took my statement congratulated me on staying alive. He said, "I wouldn't let a woman in my family work this job." I shrugged for him the way I had for those boys.

The manager kept saying, "But they're gone. Why do you have to quit?" I just laughed and made him pay me off. I knew if I stayed they'd be back, and next time they'd pull me away with them, give me a chance to be the featured character in a *True Crime* magazine story. "No," I told him, "I won't come back tomorrow. I'm not coming back at all."

I took a job as a salad girl in a kitchen, a job that had no contact with the public or handled any cash. "You could do better than this," the man who ran the line told me, but I just shrugged. For a solid year, I screamed every time someone came up behind me without warning. For more than a year, I got nauseous every time I saw someone who looked like any of those four boys. I even bought a rifle from Sears, Roebuck & Company but took it back when I realized it scared me more than nervous fifteen-year-old boys with tiny silver pistols.

When I spoke to my aunt Dot that year I told her about the robbery, told her, "I never expected to survive to be grown. For damn sure, I don't want to have some child kill me for a few hundred dollars and a feel of my tits."

"I said I don't want to hurt you." The boy in the tweed coat sounded hoarse. He was getting impatient. He gestured with his coat pocket again.

"I believe you," I told him. I looked him right in the eye. "But I an't got a thing to give you," I said. I turned my bag up and poured my papers and notebook all over the sidewalk.

"We've just been out to a meeting," I said to him, "and all I brought was a notebook. I'm not crazy, man, if I had anything, I'd give it to you." I pulled at my pockets, pushed at my papers. He frowned and waved his pocket at me. For a moment I thought I saw a glint of silver, thought I heard a cop say disgustedly, "I didn't ask what color it was, I asked what kind it was." No, it was a pocket, only a pocket with a hand in it.

"I don't carry cash with me to meetings. I an't even got another subway token."

"Don't tell me that."

I looked back at my girlfriend, wondered if I looked as frozen up as she did. Probably.

Our mugger shrugged in his coat.

"Shit."

He looked so disgusted, I almost sympathized with him. It was a cold night to be prowling the street. Maybe he'd been planning just this one effort and then home to a warm bed. I shrugged back at him but couldn't quite bring myself to say I was sorry. I took another deep breath and tried not to smile too wide.

"Shit," he said again, and stalked away from us.

I looked over at my girlfriend. She was very pale, her eyes huge and wide. Neither of us moved. We just watched him walk to the end of the street. At the corner he turned back to us, took his hand out of his pocket and waved.

"Have a nice day," he yelled and was gone.

"Have-a-nice-day?" My girlfriend stared after him dumbfounded. She looked like she couldn't decide whether to be outraged or relieved. "HAVE-A-NICE-DAY?!"

"Have a nice day," I giggled back and shook my head. "Incredible." We grabbed each other's hands and started running.

"HAVE A NICE DAY!"

I stopped at the corner and looked left and right. Up the next block I saw a tweed coat moving fast away from us. It was our well-tailored mugger. For a moment I almost jumped back so that he wouldn't see me, but then stood where I was and watched him, that slender stiff-necked young man moving fast. At the next corner he turned, looked back, paused and took his hand out of his pocket. I could just see his smile and the gun in his hand shining silver in the light from the streetlamp over his head. I watched him tuck it away inside the coat and cut up across the intersection toward the dark far side of the street.

"Jesus," I whispered, and felt all the rigidity flow out of my bones. I never expected to survive. Maybe I was right.

Some of the material in this essay first appeared in 1983 in the *New York Native* in an article entitled "Robbed."

Gun Crazy

When we were little, my sister and I would ride with the cousins in the back of my uncle Bo's pickup truck when he drove us up into the foothills where we could picnic and the men could go shooting. I remember standing up behind the cab, watching the tree branches filter the bright Carolina sunshine, letting the wind push my hair behind me, and then wrestling with my cousin, Butch, until my aunt yelled at us to stop.

"Ya'll are gonna fall out," she was always screaming, but we never did.

Every stop sign we passed was pocked with bullet holes.

"Fast flying bees," Uncle Jack told us with a perfectly serious expression.

"Hornets with lead in their tails," Bo laughed.

My mama's youngest brother, Bo, kept his guns, an ought-seven rifle and a lovingly restored old Parker shotgun, wrapped in a worn green army blanket. A fold of the blanket was loosely stitched down a third of its length to make a cloth bag, the only sewing Bo ever did in his life. He kept his cleaning kit—a little bag of patches and a plastic bottle of gun oil—in the blanket pouch with the guns. Some evenings he would spread the blanket out in front of the couch and sit there happily cleaning his guns slowly and thoroughly. All the while he would sip cold beer and talk about what a fine time a man could have with his weapons out in the great outdoors. "You got to sit still, perfectly still," he'd say, nod, and sip again, then dab a little more gun oil on the patch he was running through the rifle barrel.

"Oh, you're good at that," someone would always joke.

"The man an't never shot an animal once in his life," Bo's wife, Nessa, told us. "Shot lots of bottles, whiskey bottles, beer bottles, coke-cola bottles. The man's one of the great all-time bottle destroyers."

I grinned. Stop signs and bottles, paper targets and wooden fences. My uncles loved to shoot, it was true, but the only deer they ever brought home was one found drowned in a creek and another that Uncle Jack hit head-on one night when he was driving his Pontiac convertible with the busted headlights.

"Let me help you," I begged my uncle Bo one night when he had pulled out his blanket kit and started the ritual of cleaning his gun. I was eleven, shy but fearless. Bo just looked at me over the angle of the cigarette jutting out of the corner of his mouth. He shook his head.

"I'd be careful," I blurted.

"Nessa, you hear this child?" Bo yelled in the direction of the kitchen and then turned back to me. "An't no such thing as careful where girls and guns are concerned." He took the cigarette out of his mouth and gave me another of those cool, distant looks. "You an't got no business thinking about guns."

"But I want to learn to shoot."

He laughed a deep throaty laugh, coughed a little, then laughed again. "Girls don't shoot," he told me with a smile. "You can do lots of things, girl, but not shooting. That just an't gonna happen."

I glared at him and said, "I bet Uncle Jack will teach me. He knows how careful I can be."

Bo shook his head and tucked the cigarette back in the corner of his mouth. "It an't about careful, it's about you're a girl. You can whine and wiggle all you wont. An't nobody in this family gonna teach you to shoot." His face was stern, his smile completely gone. "That just an't gonna happen."

When I was in high school my best girlfriend was Anne, whose mama worked in the records division at the local children's hospital. One Sunday Anne invited me to go over to the woods out behind the mental hospital, to a hollow there where we could do some plinking.

"Plinking?"

"You know, plinking. Shooting bottles and cans." She pushed her hair back off her face and smiled at me. "If there's any water we'll fill the bottles up and watch it shoot up when the glass breaks. That's my favorite thing."

"You got a gun?" My mouth was hanging open.

"Sure. Mama gave me a rifle for my birthday. Didn't I tell you?"

"I don't think so." I looked away, so she wouldn't see how envious I felt. Her mama had given her a gun for her sixteenth birthday! I had always thought Anne's mama was something special, but that idea was simply amazing.

Anne's mama refused to cook, smoked Marlboros continuously, left the room any time any of her three children mentioned their dead father, and drank cocktails every evening while leaning back in her Lazy-Boy lounge chair and wearing dark eyeshades. "Don't talk to me," she'd hiss between yellow stained teeth. "I got crazy people and drunken orderlies talking at me all day long. I come home, I want some peace and quiet."

"My mama thinks a woman should be able to take care of herself," Anne told me.

"Right," I agreed. "She's right." Inside, I was seething with envy and excitement. Outside, I kept my face smooth and noncommittal. I wanted to shoot, wanted to shoot a shotgun like all my uncles, pepper stop signs and scare dogs. But I'd settle for a rifle, the kind of rifle a woman like Anne's mama would give her sixteen-year-old daughter.

That Sunday I watched closely as Anne slid a bullet into the chamber of her rifle and sighted down the gully to the paper target we had set up thirty feet away. Anne looked like Jane Fonda in *Cat Ballou* after she lost her temper—fierce, blonde, and competent. I swallowed convulsively and wiped sweaty palms on my jeans. I would have given both my big toes to have been able to stand like that, legs apart, feet planted, arms up, and the big rifle perfectly steady as the center circle target was fissured with little bullet holes.

Anne was myopic, skinny, completely obsessed with T.E. Lawrence, and neurotically self-conscious with boys, but holding that rifle tight to her shoulder and peppering the target, she looked different—older and far more interesting. She looked sexy, or maybe the gun looked sexy, I wasn't sure. But I wanted that look. Not Anne, but the power. I wanted to hold a rifle steady, the stock butting my shoulder tightly while I hit the target dead center. My mouth went dry. Anne showed me how to aim the gun a little lower than the center of the target. "It shoots a little high," she said. "You got to be careful not to let it jump up when it fires." She stood behind me and steadied the gun in my hands. I put the little notch at the peak of the barrel just under the target, tightened my muscles, and pulled the trigger. The rifle still jerked up a little, but a small hole appeared at the outer edge of the second ring of the target.

"Goddamn!" Anne crowed. "You got it, girl." I let the barrel of the rifle drop down, the metal of the trigger guard smooth and warm under my hand.

You got to hold still, I thought. Perfectly still. I sighted along the barrel again, shifting the target notch to the right of the jars Anne had set up earlier. I concentrated, focused, felt my arm become rigid, stern and strong. I pulled back on the trigger slowly, squeezing steadily, the way in the movies they always said it was supposed to be done. The bottle exploded, water shooting out in a wide fine spray.

"Goddamn!" Anne shouted again. I looked over at her. Her glasses had slipped down on her nose and her hair had fallen forward over one eye. Sun shone on her sweaty nose and the polished whites of her teeth. She was staring at me like I had stared at her earlier, her whole face open with pride and delight.

Sexy, yeah. I pointed the barrel at the sky and let my mouth widen into a smile.

"Goddamn," I said, and meant it with all my heart.

Shotgun Strategies

I'm forty-three years old now. Twenty years ago I went to my first consciousness-raising group—an extraordinarily important event for me. I have talked about that day many times since, but what I have rarely discussed is how desperate I was, almost at the point where I was ready to give up. I was practically suicidal, madly in love with yet another completely bitchy mean little girl who was not giving me anything I needed, and working myself near to death with long hours at the Social Security Administration. I was working longer hours helping to publish a feminist magazine, volunteering in the childcare center, and answering phones at the rape crisis hot line. I was feeling those six-meetings-a-week-don't-need-to-sleep-anyway blues.

I went into that Sunday afternoon lesbian CR group, sat down, and everybody started talking—mostly about other women who were not there with whom they had recently broken up. But one of the women, the one sitting in the beanbag chair across from me, spoke about her father. Whispered that she really needed to tell people how much she hated him, how she dreamed every night of going home to kill him. She dreamed in powerful, agonizing detail of a double-barrel shotgun, blue gun metal and wooden stock. She dreamed of breaking down that gun and packing it in a bag, holding it close to her body until she could take it out when he was right in front of

her once again. She needed to say that the dreams had become so
vivid, they were the only things she still looked forward to.

Listening to her, I remembered my own dreams of a gun just
like hers, blue-metal powerful and cold. I leaned forward to hear every word she said and did not say, to see the strain in her neck and
the way her hands pulled at each other, the pain and rage plain in
everything. She was as close to breaking as I felt myself, as desperate and alone. I wanted to touch her, not like a lover, but like family,
to offer comfort and love and hope. Instead, I offered her the one
unfailing gift of my family—bitter humor. I gave a little laugh and
said, "I'll do yours, if you'll do mine." I was joking, but I was also
half-serious. And then I told her I'd had the same dreams.

It was the first time I had told anyone I wanted to kill my stepfather.

That was the beginning for me of being able to talk about how
I had grown up. I had been taught never to tell anyone outside my
family what was going on, not just because it was shameful, but because it was physically dangerous for me to do so. I had been repeat-
edly warned throughout my childhood that if I ever revealed what
went on in our house, they would take me away. I would wind up
in juvenile detention and spend the rest of my life in and out of jail.
It did not matter that what was being done to me was rape and that
I had never asked for it. It did not matter because I was who I was,
the child of my family, poor and notorious in the county where we
lived, poor and hopeless. Oh, I had dreamed of killing the man, but
little girls do not kill their fathers and get away with it. I was taught
to be very quiet, very polite in public, to talk to the Sunday school
ladies with good diction, to work to get that scholarship and get the
hell out of my home. That is exactly what I did.

I got away so successfully that I convinced myself only poor men
beat their daughters, only poor men rape their daughters, and only
poor women let them. I believed that grown-up middle-class girls
were different creatures, that sexual abuse didn't happen in their
families. That was another reason not to tell. But the woman in the

beanbag chair wasn't just middle class. She was a failed upper-class kid, a runaway. In talking to me about her life, though, she was telling me about mine. She told us when she was a girl, she used to fight with her little brother about who was going to have to sleep closer to the door. That was something my sisters and I had done until I left home and they had to deal with our stepfather alone. She talked about sleeping over with girlfriends, not because she wanted to be friends or even to make love, but because then she wasn't sleeping at home. She talked about how the sex was the least of it, though it was always the part that everyone else wanted to know about. Far worse was the daily ongoing contempt.

That was my life she was talking about, a world removed from the place and the family where she had grown up, but my life just the same. Both of us had grown up believing that being beaten is normal, that being backhanded is ordinary, that being called names is a regular part of life. That everyone does it, that they just don't talk about it in public. We both had thought ourselves freaks. Monsters. What we discovered talking to each other—and eventually there were four or five others discovering this together—is that we were cut from the same cloth. For all of us, the family had been a prison camp: a normal everyday horror, fully known and hidden.

I didn't start writing—or rather I didn't start keeping my writing —until 1974, when I published a poem. Everything I wrote before then, ten years of journals and short stories and poems, I burned, because I was afraid somebody would read them. Always in the back of my mind there was my mother's whisper: "They'll send you to detention. You'll wind up in the county home and your life will be over. You don't want to do that."

Even now, all these years later, I dream I am a thirteen-year-old girl locked behind bars, her pussy hurting, not knowing how to talk to anyone. Sometimes I still dream that I go down to Florida with a shotgun, broken down and packed in a suitcase.

When I set out to write my novel, *Bastard Out of Carolina*, I wanted to do two things: to recreate the family that I deeply loved and was not saved by, and to put in print everything I understood that happens in a violent family where incest is taking place. I wanted to show people that everyday life is everyday life, even if you are being beaten and raped; that mostly they come to get you at night, or when your mama is working late; and that the biggest part of the struggle as a child is about trying to believe you are not the monster you are being told you are. You need to know that you are a real person, that this thing happening to you is not something you are making happen—because when I was a child I thought I was doing it. I thought that if only I were a little better, a little smarter, a little meaner, a little faster, or maybe even a better Christian, none of those terrible things would be happening. So I wrote as strong a story as I could about a young girl who is slowly being convinced that she is a monster, and who is not saved by those she loves most.

What has always been missing for me, both in reading books about incest and in talking to other survivors, is how I felt about my mother. I don't need to tell anyone what my stepfather did to me as a child. I have worked through enough of the violence I survived that it is no longer a necessity for me to talk about it as much, other than to bluntly state the facts, to refuse to be ashamed of my childhood or who I became through surviving it. I have to be matter-of-fact about what happened to me for my own sanity, in order not to deny myself, not ever to surrender to the constant pressure to do that. So I try to be straightforward about being a survivor of incest and violent contempt, but the things I still need to figure out, to talk about, are not the obvious issues, those most readily accessible.

Rather than the details of sexual abuse, it is the questions of family and loss and betrayal I want to examine. I need to understand and talk about my mother, about the choices she was forced to make, the impossible grief of her struggle to create a family and care for her daughters. How, I ask, can love and betrayal become so deeply intertwined?

I come at my mother's life from my own, remembering that I

loved my little sisters but wanted them to sleep closest to the door. I look at my life, remembering being a child who loved my mother absolutely, and hated her every time she was late coming home from work. Every time she was an hour and a half late and I had to survive that hour and a half alone—at five, seven, nine, and eleven—I raged at her. I truly loved my mother, but I could not, as a child, understand why she did not take us out of there, go anywhere, live in any condition other than the one in which we were trapped. I knew absolutely that my mother loved me and my sisters, and that she did everything she could understand to do to try to save us. But I also know that my mother had no idea what was going on in our home: partly because she was telling lies to herself to stay sane, partly because we were lying to her to save her and ourselves, and partly because the world had lied to her and us about the meaning of what was happening. The world told us that we were being spanked, not beaten, and that violent contempt for girl children was ordinary, nothing to complain about. The world lied, and we lied, and lying becomes a habit.

I have promised myself to break the habit of lying, to try to make truth everyday in my life, but it is not simple. Piecing out lies and truth is sometimes excruciatingly complicated, particularly for writers. I make fiction, construct it, intend it to have an impact, an effect, to quite literally change the world that lied to my mother, my sisters, and me. The fiction I make comes out of my life and my beliefs, but it is not autobiography, not even the biomythography that Audre Lorde* championed. What I have taught myself to do is to craft truth out of storytelling.

My sisters do not remember all of our childhood, and one of the roles I have played in our family is being the one who gives it back to them. A problem that arises with my fiction is that sometimes I take small pieces of things that happened to us and move very far away from them, and sometimes my sisters don't know the difference between the story I made up and our lives. What I had to do

---

*Zami, A New Spelling of My Name (Crossing Press: Freedom, California, 1983)

in the year after I finished my novel was sit down with my little sister and go through some of it. I had to say, "That page is true. It didn't happen to me, though, it happened to you." And I do not know anything that has been as hard as that. When my little sister and I finally used the word *incest*, and talked about the worst thing, the everyday hatred we breathed in as girls, she told me she wouldn't allow any man "like that" to be alone with her girls. I had to say to her that it isn't just men, and it isn't just men "like that." I had to talk to her about the women I had found after I left home, women who breathed out hatred as steadily as the worst man we had ever known. I had to say that the world is a bigger, meaner, more complicated place than anyone ever told us, and the tools for dealing with it are real, but we have to invent them for ourselves, make them up as we go along.

One of the reasons I write is to make up my own rules, discover my own tools, in order to show my sisters a few of the things I have learned. And in so doing to create a conversation between us so that I can get back from them the things they can teach me.

Another reason I write is because of that woman in the bean-bag chair, the one who did not live my life but who did. Not too long ago I received a letter from her. She lives in Iowa with her daughter, and in that letter she told me she doesn't dream about shotguns anymore. She just thinks about it now and again in the daylight.

This essay is derived from a panel discussion, "Self-Revelation: Writing as Transformation," held at the LAB in San Francisco in Spring 1993. The panel included Cheryl Brodie, Christine Cobaugh, Sapphire, and Sue Martin. A section of the talk appeared in *Critical Condition: Women on the Edge of Violence,* edited by Amy Scholder (City Lights Books: San Francisco, 1993).

What Do We See?
What Do We Not See?

I moved North in 1979 and immediately became a whole new person in my family's eyes, taking on the glamour and magic of the legendary New York City. My mama thought that my move there was the most impressive thing I'd done in ten years. While she enjoyed my fiction, she tempered her enthusiasm with, "Well, you've always told stories." It had something to do with her practical bent. When she found out that the story I was so proud of publishing had earned me all of $21.85, she asked me if maybe they wouldn't have paid me more if I'd made it longer. I told her it wasn't a case of getting paid by the word, that I had actually only gotten a share of a literary grant the magazine had received.

"Well," Mama said, "maybe after you've been in New York City a little longer you'll find the magazines that pay real money."

My sister was more to the point when she called the second month after I'd arrived. "Have you got a job?" she asked.

"Sure, I'm working with computers."

"Oh," she sighed with relief. "I thought you'd just run up there with no kind of plan or anything. Computers are good. There's probably always work with computers."

I didn't tell her I had lucked into the job, that I had, in fact, moved with no plan at all, just a confidence in my own ability to hustle.

My little sister turned respectable a few years ago, after a legendary misspent youth. She talked her boyfriend into a methadone program, married him, got a job at an electronics firm, and wound up a suburban married lady with the mortgage in her name. Since then, I've had to be more careful how I talk to her, and I'm still surprised she hasn't taken up with some Christian fundamentalist sect. What she has taken up is fundamentalist capitalism. She preaches to me about the wisdom of hard work, payroll deductions, and household insurance. I've been known to lose track of our conversations just when she's making some particular point about a new savings plan she's going to use for their tax refund, and it's not because what she's saying doesn't make sense. It's the fact that this is the same sister who used to walk in on me and my girlfriends in bed, and who, at the time, was such a stoned-out hippie that she never figured out what we were doing. Every time she talks so reasonably, I flash back to her wild flying braids and big glazed pupils shining bland and innocent past my girlfriend's hurried struggles to get her jeans back on, and every time it cracks me up. My sister is convinced that in spite of the fact that I'm five years older, and a big city queer to boot, somehow I will never be a serious person.

She gave me one surprise in that phone call. She told me, "I knew it. I always knew you'd move to New York City." She sounded so sure of herself that I had to challenge her.

"I'm not sure I'm going to stay. The winters up here are murder. All this concrete gets cold and stays cold. And it's damp—I think the mildew problem is worse than in Tallahassee."

"You weren't happy in Tallahassee," she said flatly, which startled me. I hadn't been particularly happy in Tallahassee, but that wasn't anything my little sister would have known about. She spent less than twenty-three hours in that city on what was supposed to be a week-long visit. The shock of the lesbian collective where I was living with its twelve women, two children, five cats, and two boa constrictors was something she'd talked about for years.

"We've always known you'd have to move to New York City."

Have to?

"Oh, yeah," I'd said, finally catching on. "All of us queers eventually move to the evil city."

"OH YOU!" She'd sounded righteously angry. "You think that's all anybody thinks about. It's not just that you're...." She hesitated. My mama used the word, although with a slight emphasis to show the effort, but my sister never did. "That you're the way you are—"

"A lesbian," I filled in for her.

"ALL RIGHT, a lesbian." The blush was almost audible. "That's only part of it. You were always different. All that reading, writing, that political stuff—that's what people up there do. There's just more people like you up there," she finished.

I'm not sure she's right. I really think most people up North are like my sister, nice straight family types dutifully calling their queer relatives on their birthdays and gently suggesting the joys of settled family life. Of course, my sister has never gone that far. She's always been as much into the myth of the evil city as I ever was, and she was hot to come North for a visit, to check out the nightlife and see what big city Yankees are like. My sisters and my mother were forever pumping me about city life.

"Do you see television stars on the subway?"

"I don't think they ride it, but I did see a woman in leopard skin tights and a red leather bodice."

"No shit!?"

My most tacky act was to buy a series of picture postcards and fill them in with notes and arrows. *I work two blocks from this theater. ... We live a mile and a half from this bridge.... Rode my bicycle in this park.... Got threatened by a drunk near here.* My mama loved those cards.

What she liked better, of course, were the lotto tickets I sent her every few weeks. At irregular intervals she'd even have a dream, or just get a number in mind, and call me up, sure she was about to become rich. She was quite convinced that she was meant to win the New York State Lottery. It's that magical thinking my whole family has always prized. After her trip to Las Vegas didn't produce the winnings she'd predicted, Mama began taking an interest in lottery tickets from various states. For years she got lotto tickets from places she couldn't imagine actually visiting.

Mama finally did get to see the evil city. She and her best friend, Mab, came up to visit me after a brief try at the Atlantic City slot machines. We did the usual things, like take the Circle Line bus tour, ride the subway, and walk Broadway staring at all the people and theater marquees. I even took them to the Lone Star Café for dinner. Mama wasn't impressed with the music, and she thought the beans were poorly seasoned, but she got caught up in the show that took place on the sidewalk outside. I did too; it was more interesting than the guitar players with their Brooklyn accents and honky-tonk lyrics.

A drunk had cruised the windows for a while and then settled into a chair near the front of the place with no intention of paying the cover. The waitresses tried to humor him into paying or leaving, but he was having none of it. He surrounded himself with cane-backed chairs and insisted on his "rights as a citizen of the city." Twenty minutes later two very calm city cops were leaning on those chairs and talking to him quietly.

Mama remarked that if we'd been down in Orlando, one of the cops would have had him in a chokehold and out the door in a flash. These quiet, matter-of-fact, polite policemen were not part of her mythology of New York City. We all had another beer and watched the drama off and on. The cops and the citizen talked on, sometimes quietly, sometimes loudly. Finally, with a mutual grimace, the cops started pulling away the chairs. The drunk started screaming and trying to hook his arms and legs around the furniture. Everyone else moved away, and the cops managed to get him by the arms and legs and carry him out.

Through the side windows where we were sitting, Mama, Mab, and I saw the manager give the cops a hand. The man was laid down on the sidewalk. A patrol car pulled up. It was a quiet scene, no sound reaching us through the glass. The drunk started struggling, throwing punches up at the policemen, his mouth moving in shouts we couldn't hear. His fist connected with the neck of the policeman above him. I watched the cop stagger back for a second, then looked over to my mama who was pushing her hair out of her eyes and shaking her head slowly.

"That boy's gonna get hurt."

Mab had turned away to watch the next band set up. The waitresses were busy moving chairs back and seating people. Only my mama and a few people outside were watching the man on the sidewalk. One of the policemen was kneeling on the small of the drunk's back. The other had twisted his left arm up over his head so that his wrist was pointed down to his shoulder blades. The drunk's mouth was open. He could have been screaming. The policeman very deliberately, very carefully punched that twisted elbow. The arm went loose, the drunk arched, then went limp. Mama's mouth fell open. A man standing in the aisle beside us said, "Son-of-a-bitch!"

"He broke it," my mama said. "I think he broke his arm."

"What?" Mab said, standing up to look out on the now placid scene—the quiet cops and the limp drunk.

"No," I said, "not the arm, the shoulder. He dislocated his shoulder."

Mama stared at me. "You know a lot about it." She looked around the tables almost angrily. "We should either go, or you should sit down."

It was then that I realized I was half out of my chair and that my fist was curled on the window jam pushing at the glass. I sat back down. My mama moved her plate out of the way and reached over to take my hand. "I've seen worse," she said. "Did I ever tell you about the time I saw some men break a counterstool over that boy's back in Greenville? And he hadn't done anything." She squeezed my hand very hard, looking at me intently. I could see she had no intention of letting go until I relaxed. She expected me to do something stupid.

Another patrol car pulled up. In a moment there were six policemen standing over the now passive drunk as he cradled his useless arm. I shook my hair back and squeezed back on my mama's hand. "Well, you wanted to see the City," I told her. "Now you'll have a story to tell everybody back at the luncheonette."

"Sure," she smiled, letting go of my hand. "I'll tell everybody how the restaurants in New York City can't season a plate of pinto beans."

The title of this essay is taken from "What Do We See?" by Muriel Rukeyser in *The Collected Poems of Muriel Rukeyser* (McGraw-Hill: New York, 1982). An earlier version appeared in the *New York Native* on May 17, 1981 as "Living in the Evil City."

Neighbors

I used to live in what was called a transitional neighborhood. It was recognizable by the conjunction of burned-out buildings and buildings whose windows displayed brightly colored mini blinds, a mix of young men taking engines apart on the sidewalk and yuppie couples landscaping their tiny plots of yard. We had Italian grandmothers who camped on their stoops dispensing gossip and advice to the neighbors; Black grandmothers who marched squads of carefully starched grandchildren off to church every Sunday; and Pakistani grandmothers who fed their hens and illegal roosters while nodding across the fence to me. The buildings were three-story brick fronts. The neighbors talked gardening and insulation, the cost of covering the windows with plastic in the winter and filling them with fans in the summer, and how often the teenage boys stole the garbage can lids. When my mama came to visit all she could say was, "This can't be Brooklyn. This is just like home."

I agreed, but then I told her about all the families in the neighborhood who were lesbian and gay. The conversation messed her up. Nothing was what she had thought it to be. And I knew exactly how she felt.

When I was thirteen years old there were only two things I knew about lesbians: they wore green on Thursdays and had hairy nipples. I learned the first at school when I showed up one Thursday in a green A-line skirt and barely withstood the resulting giggles and whispers. Nobody ever explained the derivation of the rule to me, but everyone seemed convinced of its infallibility. Oddly enough, I too believed it, taking my mistaken transgressions as one more clue in a long list of indicators. I was, after all, notoriously literal minded. Later, after reading about self-fulfilling prophecies in a psychology text, I even considered the possibility that queer people were driven to betray their identities by forgetting what day of the week it was. Nervously, I started paying more attention to my nipples.

I learned the rule about lesbians' nipples from the porn books my stepfather kept under his mattress, the same place I had learned about oral sex and tribadism. The last two had fascinated and excited me even though I wasn't completely clear on how they were accomplished. Where did the hip fit, and exactly what was the tongue supposed to be searching for? It was astonishing how badly that stuff was written. How was I supposed to figure things out when it was always so short on the important details? Still, from book to book, *Satan's Daughters* to *Manhandlers*, one detail stood out: all those lusty dykes had hairy nipples. When you're thirteen, that's something that makes a very big impression.

No one told me that dykes might like to garden, that faggots could hang out on their stoop and discuss recipes, or that both shared a wealth of information on paint chips, child custody laws, and kitchen appliances. At thirteen, limited as I was to rumor and pornographic slander, I didn't have a clue that faggots and dykes could be neighbors. One or two gay couples could have added a lot to my childhood—one or two gay couples stopping by to chat with my mama or sending over some extra fish after a successful weekend trip. I doubt there would have ever been an occasion on which I'd have seen any nipples, but even so, the exposure would have been beneficial. Maybe then I wouldn't have had to spend the six years I did praying to Jesus to somehow make me "normal." Maybe then I wouldn't have cared if I sprouted telltale hairs below my chin.

When I lived in Brooklyn we bought our ladder and window fan at a yard sale held by two gay men three blocks over. We shared our grass clippers with the lesbians who lived a few houses up. Every August I knew the Michigan Women's Music Festival was over when a van or a station wagon pulled up late and spilled out sleeping bags, coolers, and starry-eyed, sunburned lesbians wearing brand-new labrys earrings. Every end of June I could tell it was Gay Pride weekend when we would go down to the subway and smile at our neighbors carrying children, handmade banners, thermos bottles, and soft-soled running shoes. We came home together hours later, while the grandmothers on their stoops nodded and called our names. I watched my lover stop to chat as I started planning for a visit from my friend Marty, who had abandoned her rented farmhouse outside Waycross after somebody fired a shotgun through her screen door. I tried not to think about what could happen any time to all of us—all of us queer and at risk in our neighborhoods.

I had sat up sleepless when we first moved into the house in Brooklyn, trying to figure out how we would get along. Maybe I could have started calling my lover my housemate and crawled back into that proverbial closet, but I really didn't know how to start. The truth was, it was the loss of anonymity that scared me. One of the things I had liked about moving to New York was the sheer numbers there, the great numbers of other queers, and the great mass of anonymous strangers who didn't look twice as I passed by. I knew I was giving up some of that when I agreed to buy a house with my lover. The process of buying a house is only partly an issue of banks and mortgages and assuming joint debts. It is much more a matter of moving into and becoming part of a neighborhood. Everybody wanted to meet the new people on the block and find out who we were and what we were going to do with that tumbledown house and yard.

Whenever we walked the neighborhood we watched the neighbors watching us. We smiled at everyone, said hello, and even stopped to chat. Signing a thirty-year mortgage implied permanence, and we were just as curious about our neighbors as they were about us. I found myself being cross-examined by Old World grandmothers, cruised by friendly Puerto Rican boys, and challenged by a mixed crowd of youngsters who wanted to climb the tree in our front yard. We were called "you two girls" so often, I started emphasizing just how old I was in self-defense.

"I work a lot, I go to a lot of meetings," I told the grandmothers. "You girls gonna put in flowers or vegetables?" they quizzed me. "You gonna paint that building or leave it as it is?"

"I don't have much time for gardening," I replied, then heard myself adding, "but I think I want to grow both tomatoes and flowers."

The grandmothers smiled. We had a common topic of conversation.

We bought our house one sunny May day after my lover finally convinced me we could go to closing without having to sell my bicycle. We spent the time between applying for the mortgage and moving day planning the work we knew we would have to do. There was a lot of rotten plaster to take out, at least one whole wall, a bathroom floor threatening to cave in, a wall of corkboard to be scraped off, and a great many high-gloss hot pink, yellow, and green walls where the paint was badly chipped. This did not include the plumbing or electrical work, or replacing the front door—work that would have to be done by professionals. Our budget was strict: everything we *could* do, we would *have* to do ourselves.

The August day we walked over to our empty house, all our neighbors were on the street. "When you girls moving in?" our next-door neighbor asked. More than sixty years old, with a full head of silky white hair, he had already told us how he had been born on this block. Pat had also let us know where the old capped gas line pipes were under the floorboards, the ones that were left from when gas lamps had provided the only light.

"I remember when they put in electricity," he chuckled. "People worried it might be bad for the children's eyes, it was so bright. Gaslight was soft, you know."

I didn't know and I couldn't imagine. People who lived their whole lives on one block seemed magical to me. I had spent my childhood moving every six months, and my adult life in five states and half a dozen major cities. For me, part of buying a house was about settling down and claiming a place for me and mine, something I had always feared was not possible for a lesbian.

I once packed up and moved in a day after a man fired a gun in our front yard in Florida. I remember being pissed off but matter-of-fact about it at the time. That was part of what I had to expect, I told myself, the price you pay for being different from your neighbors. Even a gay rights bill that would keep you from being evicted wouldn't save you from a crazy man who could shoot you on your doorstep. I had a notion that being a "legitimate" neighbor might—being the kind of person who would sit on the steps and talk to the neighborhood grandmothers about the weather and the tomatoes and the kids who played in the garbage cans. Not being comfortable living in fear or lying about my life and my relationship, I wanted to get people familiar and easy with us before they had a chance to become nervous about us as lesbians.

"Gonna try to be in by Thanksgiving," I told our neighbor, "but we have some work to do before then."

"Uh-huh." While Pat spoke, he dug at the weeds in his little patch of frontyard. "Always do. Takes a lot of work to keep a house up, make it comfortable the way you want it."

Our first look inside the empty house was a shock. We'd known it was pretty rundown. How else could we have afforded it? But once the furniture and curtains and taped-up pictures were gone, the full horror of the water damage, mildew, and cracked plaster was overwhelming. After a few moments I realized I was having trouble breathing and had to keep putting my head out the window to get some fresh air. Meanwhile, my lover walked around with a crowbar pulling off paneling and broken wallboard to get a look at the walls. Clouds of roaches swept out every time she hit a wall.

"I hate bugs, hate bugs!" she kept yelling, whacking a wall and leaping back to escape the many-legged hordes.

"We'll get some bug bombs and kill them off before we get down to the real work," I promised her. I went into the bathroom to try out the toilet. There was a powerful rank odor in the tiny dark room. I turned on the light and stepped carefully into the narrow corner that contained the toilet. Beneath me I felt the floor settle several inches and sway.

"Oh my God," I whispered and stepped back.

"What is it?" my lover asked from over my shoulder. I put my foot out and demonstrated how the floor around the toilet sagged. Then I took a slow breath and made myself grin back at her. "Tell me sweetheart, how do you feel about peeing in the bathtub?"

My lover frowned and sniffed the dank rotting odor in the little room. "No way," she told me, dropping the lid on the bowl. "We'll put a chamber pot in the bedroom."

I laughed. "That's what I love about you. You're so good in an emergency."

That night we lay in bed making lists of the equipment we would need—another crowbar, lots of plaster, wallboard, new tiles for the bathroom, a wide selection of tools and cleaning equipment. I got excited at the thought of a reversible drill with a screw set that would help us pull out screws easily. "This is gonna mean a big trip to the hardware store," I teased, rolling over, "and you know how I get in hardware stores."

"The same way you get in laundromats," my lover giggled, "when you lean your hips up against the dryers, and in subway cars when they get into that steady rocking motion." She stopped when she saw my face.

"What's wrong?"

"I don't know. I think I hurt something."

I tried to roll back over. A fierce pain shot from my lower back down my left leg. I tried to sit up. The pain got worse. I lay back, took a deep breath and worked at relaxing. The pain subsided only a little.

"I must have pulled a muscle or something," I told my lover. "It'll be all right. I'll sleep on the heating pad and ease it out with exercise tomorrow."

I did just that, but the pain got steadily worse. Within a few days, trying to walk brought tears to my eyes and forced me to give up on home remedies and go to a doctor.

"A pinched nerve," the doctor told me cheerfully. "Keep cold packs on your lower back and stay in bed with your knees elevated. Maybe a week, and then you can start getting around, but no lifting, no stress, and no working when you're tired. If you're not careful, this can hang on forever."

No lifting. No work.

My lover looked at me and I looked at her. That weekend we were supposed to start taking down walls. Could you use a crowbar from a reclining position?

It took us two days to figure out the answer. Then I went through our address books and sketched out an invitation on the computer at work.

Dear Friend, the bright purple printing read. *How'd you like to come to a great backyard party, sit in the sun, eat barbecue, drink beer, flirt, dance, and, by the way, tear down a few walls and haul out a lot of old plaster? Come to our Laboring Day party and work out all your frustrations with our sledgehammers and crowbars!*

I spent the days before the party cooking barbecue sauce, beans, chicken, and potato salad, stopping to lie down on an ice pack for fifteen minutes every hour. A dumpster was delivered to the house. I stayed in bed with my knees up on a box, making follow-up phone calls to our most muscular friends. The morning of Labor Day, we hauled food, tools, ice, and charcoal to the house, and I made several big jugs of ice tea with sliced lemons.

It was going to be a scorcher. People were already out on their stoops. "You girls having a party?" the lady next door called out.

"Sort of," I told her.

"Great day for it." She shook her sheet out and hung it off the windowsill. "I'm gonna come down and sit in the sun myself, soon as I get a little cleaning done." I smiled and looked up and down the street. Kids were already tossing balls around, and a couple of small boys were swinging from the side of the dumpster. Several women were leaning on pillows on their windows. Whatever else got done that day, the neighborhood would definitely get a good look at our friends.

"I brought my own crowbar!" It was C.C., first to arrive and eager to get to work. She tugged off her leather jacket and hung it over her shoulder. "Going to be hot," she grinned, nodding to the neighbor next door, who hesitated and then smiled back. Under her jacket, C.C. was wearing the skimpiest T-strap shirt I'd ever seen. Well, it's going to be hot, I told myself, and ran off to the backyard to start the charcoal.

For the next four hours friends dropped in, some bringing their own six-packs and tools. None were daunted by the rotten walls under the paneling. Stacy climbed up on a ladder and started scraping off corkboard. Barbie produced a sledgehammer and began to knock crumbly plaster loose from bricks. C.C. used the drill to remove about two hundred screws from a makeshift closet, while Carol tied up bundles of loose boards and paneling. I ran up with surgical masks to protect people from the dust and kept serving ice tea and beer. C.C. and Stacy kept sending me back down to the yard to rest.

"Sit by the grill and play hostess," my lover insisted. "If you put your back out again, I'm gonna tie you down on an ice pack."

"Yes, Mama," I laughed at her. "I'll just sit here and flirt with every sweaty thing."

They got pretty sweaty, and they came down in packs. I started serving chicken and beans after I had set up the sprinkler to rinse people off. Eve and Barbie showed up for a beer as they discussed rigging up a chute to get the plaster out to the dumpster. After two beers they decided we didn't have the makings of a good chute and went back up to organize a relay line of women moving boxes of plaster rubble down the stairs. By that time there were more than twenty women working upstairs, most stripped down to shorts and tied up T-shirts because of the heat.

"You're getting a lot done," Pat told me across the fence, watching while three friends dragged a broken chair across the side of the dumpster. "Nice you've got so many friends to help."

"Uh-huh," I agreed, and saw the young boys on the far stoop blow kisses to the oblivious dykes in the dumpster. Up and down the street every stoop was crowded. Everyone was watching our house and the women hauling down rubble. I started to get nervous.

"People just love to watch somebody else work," Pat told me from across the fence, and then stared in awe as Barbie swung a forty-pound box of rubble on one shoulder. "Good lord, you've got some strong friends!"

"All right, all right! Everything is under control now!" It was Bruce with his little mustache gleaming with sweat and his face already pink with sunburn. "It only took me two and a half hours, but I finally found this place. Probably won't take anybody else any more than three or four." He kissed my cheek and then smiled at Pat across the fence before running up the stairs, yelling, "Here I come!"

Warm brown arms came around my waist and hugged me from the back. "Frances," I shouted. "I thought you had to work."

"I did. I do. But I've got an hour and I want my own piece of wall and the biggest sledgehammer you've got." An hour later she gave me another kiss, grabbed a piece of chicken and a napkin and left.

"You should do this more often," Abby told me, rinsing dust off her face with the hose.

"Oh, yeah! Every time we buy a house," I assured her and poured a few more glasses of ice tea.

My friend Allen arrived, toting a beach bag with a blanket, various plastic bags, and two bottles of balsamic vinegar. "The secret of a good salad," he told me, producing a bag full of chopped lettuce, red peppers, and black olives, "is in the vinegar. You need a great vinegar to make a great salad, and as little olive oil as possible. I know your cooking, all that greasy barbecue and pork-rich beans. You cook like a white trash dyke, sweetheart. Let a white trash faggot teach you something about seasoning." He handed me one of the vinegar bottles, proclaiming it a talisman for my kitchen, an antidote to factory-made salad dressing. Then he set about mixing the other bottle with the greens. When some of the girls came down for food, he waved an arm and passed out paper bowls of salad and french bread.

"Don't worry," Allen announced in a loud, forceful tone. "I am here to save your hearts. This is the alternative to all that grease."

By late afternoon, all the walls were down and people were picking up loose nails and dragging the last of the rubble down to the street. I stood by a back window and watched dykes heaving heavy boxes while singing along to "My Girl" on the radio. Looking down to the backyard, I could see Bruce and Allen with their feet up, drinking ice tea and avidly discussing the latest books.

"You guys finished?" I yelled.

Allen laughed and loosely flapped one wrist. "Oh no, honey, we're just maintaining the stereotype." Bruce reached over and grabbed Allen's pinky.

"Oh, Mary, such muscles!"

They giggled together and toasted themselves with more ice tea. Barbie, C.C., Stacy, Gayle, and Eve flopped down around them, while Pat accused Carol of having eaten all the beans. I watched from the window, my back aching and feeling tired, but no longer worried. In every backyard I could see up the block, people were hanging out, eating dinner, and watching the scene in our backyard. C.C. came up and hugged me.

"Welcome to the neighborhood," she whispered while I hugged her back.

"Oh, yeah. I think they know who we are now."

Down below, I saw Pat come out to water his azaleas. He smiled at the scattered bodies and then looked up at us. Waving, he shot a spray of water in the air.

"Great day," he called out.

"The best," I called back and hugged C.C. tighter to me. "The best."

All right, I told myself, whatever happens now, you're committed. I watched two little girls running in circles three houses up the street. You're going to be a role model or a legend. I just hope it doesn't turn into a cautionary tale.

I have always wanted to be a good neighbor, the kind of person who talks across the fence and shows up at the block party with a plate full of barbecue. Nor do I see any reason why this kind of ambition shouldn't reside in a woman who is also a trashy lesbian, a political activist, and an honest writer. The problem with my ambition is not across the fence but on the street—the streets full of teenage boys and sullen young men who don't need to see a *Dyke* button to know just who I am. They always know. From the angry children in baseball caps on the dirt road in Tallahassee, Florida, to the sharp-featured teenagers in nylon jackets in Washington, D.C. I find myself thinking about the boys up at Prospect Park who like to follow female couples around whispering "Les-be-friends" when my neighbors in Brooklyn talk about being mugged and their fear on the street.

"Ignore them," the lady next door told me. She was a knowledgeable New Yorker, a fifty-year-old feminist and grandmother, and I knew I should listen to her. It seemed like a Zen project, or one of those mythic stories about how some have grace under pressure and some do not. I always wanted to have a touch of grace. That meant I tried to follow her advice, but walking up to the park and the Grand Army Plaza subway stop felt like running a gauntlet of my own nerves. I tracked down the parents of one boy who threw a rock at me and went to talk to them.

"Oh, he's harmless," the mother insisted. "You know how boys are." I nodded to her, and later said it myself, hanging onto my neighborly aspirations, carefully ignoring the teasing, the garbage and taunts that got thrown at every lesbian who passed by. Give it time, I told myself, and tried to believe that change was inevitable.

"Be friendly and they'll get used to us," I said to my friend Bea. "Let them see we're just like anybody else they know."

"Oh, yeah," Bea responded angrily. "Meanwhile, the television, books, everything around them is teaching them to hate and fear us. You walk up to the park a couple of times a month. I'm here every night and I an't got much friendly feeling left. One of these nights, somebody's gonna get hurt."

A few weeks later, one of those harmless neighborhood boys smashed a window and piled burning garbage on the seats of Bea's car. The parents disappeared into their apartments. The police shrugged and said, "You don't know who did it, don't know it was those boys. Without proof, without a witness, we can't charge anybody with anything."

I walked on that street the next day feeling terrified and angry. A boy stood on the sidewalk watching me and grinning, and though I had not laid eyes on him before, my heart swelled with hatred. I felt so helpless, so isolated and fragile. What could any of us do to protect ourselves? What could we do short of disappearing? Not walk out with our lovers where the neighborhood boys could see? Move away?

"Just keep in mind you're never safe," Bea told me. "Don't start imagining you're just like everybody else. You're not. None of us are. There are people who will beat us, maybe kill us, and not even think they've done anything wrong."

A decade later I remember Bea's warning. I walk up the road in Monte Rio, nod at my neighbors, and keep a careful eye on their boys, soft-spoken teenagers who play with my dog and smile at my son. I've hung out and talked to their parents, shared barbecue, given them books. They made us a baby shower when we first moved in, and went down the list of every queer who lives on the hill. It was a long list. I counted and figured it out: nearly half the households on the hill were lesbian and gay, and most of them have been here for more than a decade.

"Used to be called Heroin Hill," the guy next door told me. He's Mexican, sells antiques, moved here from Los Angeles. "They used to have a phone tree that everybody would call whenever anyone heard pistol shots. It's gotten better over time. Rarely hear shots anymore, and nobody has to walk the kids down to the bus for safety's sake. But out here, it's still true that you're either a good neighbor or you leave."

I smiled at him and joked that it sounded like the frontier. He agreed. "It is. For us, it always is." I looked over the railing of his fence to the noisy lesbians next door who were washing their dog out in their yard. One of them was standing, looking up into the trees, stroking the little beard that covers her chin. She reminded me of my friend who had never gotten over that shotgun blast, who now lives on a lesbian land co-op up in Oregon that runs dogs inside the fences every night.

This last Sunday I took over a batch of barbecue beans and a rich balsamic salad to share with the neighbors. It was a block party gathering for the couple down the street who will be moving soon. We all promised to come help them clean up their new house. I told stories about the house in Brooklyn we tore apart one Sunday afternoon. I still have Allen's talismanic bottle with his signature on the label and his cautionary command, *Get Healthy!*, underneath. I use it as a mantra, an opportunity to try for grace and the attitude

of a good neighbor, a lesbian neighbor who stops to talk to all the
boys on the hill.

Parts of this essay appeared in earlier versions in the *New York Native*
on April 7, 1985 as "Good Neighbor," April 22, 1985 as "Two Faggots,
Twenty Dykes and a Whole Lot of Barbeque," and July 3, 1985 as
"Home Sweet Home."

Not as a Stranger

I didn't read children's books as a child. Though I began to read by the age of five, and read everything and anything that came within my reach, I never read a Golden Book of anything. I read biographies and historical novels from the school library, and paperbacks—science fiction collections acquired secondhand from the Paperback Trader at the shopping center on the highway; worn, used copies of adventure novels that my mother read constantly; and finally, my stepfather's hidden, pristine, expensive but cheaply bound paperback pornography. I didn't get around to Hans Christian Andersen until I went away to college on scholarship, when I immediately decided that the robber maiden in "The Snow Queen" was a coded lesbian character whose love for Gerda was not as innocent as Walt Disney wanted me to believe.

Little that I read before adolescence stayed with me. It was the context I took from novels: far-off strange worlds from science fiction, and with them the hope that I might some night be kidnapped to another planet; astonishing cultural insights from Mama's treasured Mickey Spillane and Ross MacDonald; and vague sexual hunger from my stepfather's lurid accounts of outsized appendages and marathon bouts of strenuous intercourse. I took in everything I read from a state of profound skepticism, convinced that fiction was invariably about imaginary beings. No one I knew or cared about was remotely similar to the characters in books. But I also read with a passionate, romantic conviction that fiction was, at times, about a better world than the one I knew. If that was true, it didn't matter if I saw nothing of my life in the books I devoured. Maybe fiction just hadn't gotten around to my life yet.

When I was eleven one of the elderly ladies in the neighborhood gave me a copy of a hardcover novel. It was the first such book I had ever received, a slightly musty copy of Morton Thompson's 1954 novel, *Not as a Stranger*. I accepted the gift with a grateful but cautious smile. I had never heard of Morton Thompson and didn't know anything about the book. Certainly, I had no idea that book would change how I thought about fiction, how I thought about myself and the poverty into which I had been born. That it would take hold of my imagination and shake me out of the belief that there was no connection between my life and the lives of the people in fiction. A couple of years later I would discover James Baldwin, Flannery O'Connor, Tennessee Williams, and the whole rich worlds of Southern, queer, and critical fiction, but the groundwork for my understanding of those books began with Morton Thompson's far less powerful but genuinely effective portrait of a poor boy trying to grow up in a world that pays him as little attention as it seemed to direct at me.

The characters in *Not as a Stranger* were the kind of people I could see all around me. I believed in them and the story Morton Thompson told about them. I believed in Luke Marsh, the little boy of five or six who knows absolutely that all he wants is to grow up to be a doctor. I believed in his warring parents—his stubborn bitter father and his obsessive mother, constantly telling Luke how she might die any time, drinking his heartbroken tears like wine. When Luke went off to college and medical school, I understood how determined and frightened he was. I had the same ambitions and the same fears. When his mother died and his father went bankrupt, forcing Luke to ask for financial help from people who recoil in distaste at his request, I understood the violence and rage that overtook him. In just that way I had experienced shame and resentment at needing help from people who feared and hated our needs. The injustice of Luke's dilemma was mine. For the first time, a book showed me a part of my life in someone else's story in a way that I could believe.

Not as a Stranger seemed much like Mary Renault's *Fire from Heaven*, a book I found the next year and liked even more. Both were romances about the seemingly predestined triumphs of young boys with large ambitions. What I loved about these books was that mix of the real and the marvelous, the tragic and the hopeful. The mean and bitter parts of life were there in full measure, but they did not stop the heroic dream of meaning and purpose, the sense that even the most difficult beginning could become part of a larger story. At the time I ignored the fact that they were about boys while I was a scared little girl. I pretended it didn't matter, that life for a girl could be just as hopeful and deliberately plotted. I ignored the way both novels made the women characters important only in their relationships to the men who were the real focus.

Then there was the undercurrent of sexual desire, the primacy given to the sudden and unpredictable impact of sexual need. I had not seen that portrayed so frankly before, not in Mama's adventure novels, not in my stepfather's pornography books. It made *Not as a Stranger* seem more important than anything I had read up to then. It took on the power other women would attribute to Mary McCarthy's novel, *The Group*, the first novel where women seemed to find a reflection of their sexual reality. *Not as a Stranger* is not in the same class as *The Group*; it is not a great book. It won no prizes, though it did sell well enough to be made into a somewhat successful bland romance featuring Robert Mitchum, Frank Sinatra, and Olivia deHavilland. The movie concentrated on the romance, how the desperate Robert Mitchum marries the older, hard-working deHavilland and gets through school on her earnings, learning to appreciate her only after an affair with a rich but contemptuous woman. I hated that movie when I saw it years later, with its simplistic moralisms and horrible dialogue. It had none of the power and realism of the novel.

What I remember still of that book is the sense of the power and complications of sexual desire. I believed in the way lust seemed to take over and shape Luke's life, just as I believed in his envy and resentment of his wealthy friends. Sex seemed to me like poverty, the thing not to be mentioned, never to be admitted, but just as implacable and ubiquitous and fearful. As young as I was, I knew all too well how it feels when your body surprises you with desire. I recognized Luke's helpless discovery that his body has needs his mind has not cataloged, the fever that overtook him as he looked up at the lighted windows of the nurses' dormitory. I even recognized the terror and contempt he felt for the woman he married who holds so much power over him. It was a story I had seen all my life, the painful horrible resentment and need that played out in the lives of my cousins and aunts.

Sex was the secret engine driving the stories I had heard—sex and fear—and *Not as a Stranger* made that bluntly clear. When I read the book again, the memory came back to me of what it was that had first captured my enthusiastic nod of agreement—the moment in the story when Luke looks at his rich friend Alfred, who will not loan him money because that would be distasteful, and feels "a spasm of hatred for Alfred, for all of them." Reading the book in the grass near my mama's laundry basket at the age of twelve, and then at thirteen in my aunt's old DeSoto, and again the next year as a guest at someone's swimming pool, I had stopped every time and nodded, Yes. That was how I felt. That was it, that feeling of shame and grief and rage and resentment. Yes. People had looked at me out of Alfred's eyes and I had looked back at them with Luke's. What I saw in those eyes was fear. What I knew was in mine was fear, too, an unbreachable wall of fear constructed around the secrets of this society: class and privilege, entitlement and denial. And sex, that other fearful, terrible, dangerous secret, just as walled off and denied and omnipresent.

I kept that copy of *Not as a Stranger* for close to a decade, hiding it between other books or tucking it in the bottom of a box like one of my stepfather's jerk-off manuals. I kept it until the pages fell out and all I had was the feelings echoing down the years of my life. I was ashamed of how it haunted me, and stubbornly certain it was a piece of the puzzle of how I had survived. Fear and resentment, reality and sex—perhaps Morton Thompson had mined his own life, perhaps not. I never learned anything about him, and it did not seem to matter. What mattered was the weight of what he gave me, a way to see myself and sex and poverty from an angle perversely heroic and stubbornly romantic. If one cannot be James Baldwin or Flannery O'Connor, I decided long ago, it wouldn't be a bad thing to wind up a little like Morton Thompson, to write the kind of book a young girl hides like a talisman to protect and burnish, brightening the memory and lighting up an otherwise dark and secret history.

Sex Writing,
the Importance and the Difficulty

In 1975, with three other members of my lesbian-feminist collective, I went to Sagaris, a feminist theory institute, and began the process of completely changing my life. The two-week-long event took place that summer at a small college in Plainfield, Vermont and brought together about 120 feminists from all over the country, the majority of them lesbians. I signed up for workshops given by some of the "famous" lesbians, then hesitated before taking on Bertha Harris' writing class. Even the militant lesbians among us were mostly unfamiliar with Bertha or her novels, *Catching Saradove* and *Cherubino*. I had bought a copy of *Cherubino* the night we arrived, though, and found it difficult and fascinating. The lush descriptive language had intimidated but intrigued me. I wanted to see what the woman who wrote that book looked like, I told myself. I did not admit until I had actually signed up that I wanted to take her class.

My hesitation derived partly from the fact that I thought of myself as a dedicated politico with an accompanying belief in the importance of feminist political theory over the self-indulgent and trivial pleasures of writing fiction. I was also afraid. In between meetings and demonstrations, between building bookcases for the women's center and writing grants for the childcare collective, I wrote what I knew were terrible poems, and fragmentary stories that I suspected were almost as bad. But as long as I wrote only when inspired by political conviction and in stolen moments after the really important work was done, I comforted myself with the fantasy that if I had time—maybe after the revolution—and could really work at it, what I produced might not be so mediocre. I was terrified that anything I took seriously and worked to perfect would still, inevitably, be inferior. There was another fear, too. For all that I mouthed the general platitudes insisting that every woman's story was important, I found a great many of the stories I read boring.

More than anything else I did not want to be boring.

Bertha Harris was more like a drill instructor than a workshop leader. She was adamant, caustic, and demanding. "For the next two weeks," she told us, "you will call yourselves writers, think of yourselves as writers. You will take yourselves seriously. You will not waste my time."

No, I swallowed and promised myself. God no.

I had gone to Sagaris along with two other women from the lesbian-feminist collective that had become both my chosen family and the way I organized my political work. That we had all been lovers was something we didn't think much about by the time we drove up to Vermont, but it fascinated many of the women we met, including Bertha. I remember her leaning toward me in a cloud of cigarette smoke, her face expressionless but her eyes glittering. "Three of you, mmmm, you should write about that," she told me. The tone of her voice was so husky, I involuntarily blushed. Next to the cosmopolitan and fearless Bertha Harris, I felt naive and timid. Years later I would learn that many of the women whom I met that summer thought me intimidating and overwhemingly self-confident. It was a matter of style. Unsure of myself and desperate to learn, I followed everything closely, stared at people like they were keeping secrets, and concentrated on every reference so that I could look up the names later, research all the implications. When I flirted, I did so awkwardly and abruptly, pulling on the persona of one of my aunts like a safe protective overcoat, but falling into naked confusion whenever anyone flirted back.

Mostly I flirted with no real intention of following through on the teasing banter I had learned as a teenager. Though I looked and behaved like a grownup, I knew I was not really an adult. I was an overgrown adolescent, full of sudden outrageous passions but without the emotional capacity to act on them. I had developed a protective stance to steer me through romantic confusion, separating out my emotional responses from my physical desires. I could and did sleep with anyone, never refused any proposition, and teased so much that I found myself caught in quite a few flirtations where the options were either to be very rude or to shut down emotionally and simply perform sexual acts about which I had no real conviction. I had grown up hearing my uncles and cousins curse teases. I would not be a tease. If dared, I would do anything and never admit how distant and fearful I felt inside.

Flirting and sex had nothing to do with writing, however, nothing to do with remaking the world, the revolution I fiercely believed was necessary to force this country to live up to its ideals. But everything is connected, Bertha Harris announced to us at the opening of one of her classes, and "literature is not made by good girls. If you worry too much about being good, you're not going to write worth a damn."

We were talking about romantic love, a subject Bertha found appalling. She wanted everyone to read Shulamith Firestone so we would know it is not drink and drugs that are the curse of the revolution, it is romantic love. She waved her cigarette in impatience at the absurdity of it all. Romantic love continues the status quo in which we both are victimized and victimize each other. I knew that by *revolution*, Bertha did not mean overthrowing governments or restructuring social systems. She meant writing, making art. These were, for her, the most profound and far-reaching actions we could undertake. I was still suspicious of the use of fiction, but I suspected that her comments were true nonetheless. Dividing yourself up, lying to yourself and the rest of the world, being afraid of who you might really be—none of that could possibly be of any use to the person I wanted to become. Even if I never learned to write worth a damn, I was going to have to take Bertha's offhand comments to heart. I would have to think about this sex and intimacy stuff, and think hard.

At the end of one class, Bertha did the unthinkable: she divided the class into two sections and gave us a writing exercise we would be required to read aloud at our next meeting. "Lesbians over here, straight women over there," she told us. We hesitated, horrified and delighted—horrified because we were all survivors of just such divisions in our community, and delighted because it was such a relief to have the issue be treated so matter-of-factly. A few women looked as if they might argue with the division, but Bertha bowled over their objections by announcing that anyone who wasn't sure what they were could just pretend for the moment. Women blushed, sputtered, giggled, and made a choice. We sat on the floor and determinedly did not look at each other. A few women changed groups.

Bertha stood between the two groups, waiting for everyone to settle down, then she addressed the heterosexuals. "Sex," she said, and along with many of the other women I flinched. "You're going to write about sex. How many of you have daughters?" She nodded in acknowledgment of the few hands raised. "Remember what I said about fear and the forbidden? I want you to write about sex, about sex between a mother and a daughter, you with your daughter." A gasp erupted, followed by uncomfortable laughter. Everyone stared straight ahead.

Bertha moved over to our group with a swagger, her thumbs hooked in the front pockets of her jeans. She cocked her head to the side and smiled charmingly. "You get it easy," she smiled. "I want to see what you can do with language. No euphemisms. No clichés. Write for me about going down."

There was a pause. We stared at the floor. From the back of our group came a tentative voice. "About what?"

"Cunnilingus," someone growled.

"What's that?" This voice was high and uncertain. The reply came, confident and deep-voiced. "Come up to my room and I'll show you." We all laughed together. A small frown line appeared between Bertha's dark eyebrows. "Oral sex," she said in a very clear no-nonsense voice. "Write about it as if no one before you had ever written about it before."

Sitting on the floor looking up at Bertha, I ran my tongue over my teeth thoughtfully and then, realizing what I was doing, blushed furiously. Write about that, I was thinking, how can I write about that? Cunnilingus. Sixty-nine. Muff-diving. Pussy-licking. All the words I knew for the act echoed in my brain. I remembered an impassioned argument from more than a year ago when I had slid down my lover's sweaty belly to push my face between her thighs.

"Worship you," I had whispered to her, and then yelped when she had pulled me up by my hair.

"I hate that," she had hissed at me. "That's what *they* think we do." Her *they* was piercing and contemptuous, evoking every man who had jerked off to the image of dykes licking hungrily at rigid clits. Hurt and frustrated, I had argued that I was no man and I wanted to do it. It had become an issue, subject for discussion in our CR group. Tribadism, oral sex, finger fucking. No one admitted using dildos, wanting to be tied up, wanting to be penetrated, or talking dirty—all that male stuff. Sex was important, serious, a battleground. My lover wanted us to perform tribadism, stare into each other's eyes, and orgasm simultaneously. Egalitarian, female, feminist, revolutionary. Were those euphemisms? Euphemisms for *I can't come like that.*

I thought of all the pornography I had ever read. Male language. Fucking. I liked oral sex as an act of worship, after fucking strenuously, after coming and making her come. Afterward, teasing a clit so swollen my touch is almost agonizing, listening to her moan and weep above me, or performing that act of worship while her fist is twined in my hair, holding me painfully, demanding that I work at this thing, strain with every muscle in my body until my neck and back are burning with pain and I can barely go on, following her every movement, every gasping demand, coming myself as she comes, released from the torment, orgasming on the agony and the accomplishment.

I couldn't write that! I looked at the women leaving the room, laughing and joking, running to tell friends what Bertha Harris had dared to assign us. Oh my God, oh my God, oh my God. Pornography, pornographic, I am, it is. Where had all that come from? Reading my stepfather's porn collection as a teenager, jerking off as motionlessly, quietly as possible. No one must know. Sex is dangerous. What can I say that is a *little* dangerous, not *too* dangerous?

Bertha Harris, my lover and her rigid convictions. My fear. I sat down to write about how my sexual imagination had been shaped by my stepfather's porn books, quoting the titles and making jokes about the language. Half a dozen times I began the piece and tore it up. What I wanted to admit was how conflicted I felt, how the language of those dreadful sexist dirty books both offended and heated me. I wanted to talk about how confused I was about desire itself, what acts seemed sexual, what seemed dangerous, what funny or humiliating or deeply, deeply erotic. Every attempt stalled on my fear. Easier to be funny than honest. Simpler to be confusing than blunt. I wrote and rewrote in a terror of betrayal, wanting desperately the love of beautiful women, all right, the beautiful women who would read me. But each effort was marked by my terror of their contempt. With a tremendous effort, I finally finished a piece that was playful and funny, lyrical and sensuous. I wrote about tender, soft, biscuit sex, how sometimes loving her my mouth would taste of apples and yeast. I couched it all in oceanic metaphors and even admitted my great need to charm the reader/lover. Most of all, I spoke a language of lesbian conviction, differentiating my desire from the rude awful acts of men in porn books. I was not male, absolutely not male. "This is no dance with leader and lead," I wrote, "but coupling after the manner of dolphins who never make love where men can see." Definitely not male.

My story-poem was a great success and a small revenge. When we had the reading, everyone blushed and yelped with appreciation. I read in a sweat of terror, self-consciousness, and pride. My ex-lover smiled at me, and I knew that the next time someone wanted to push their tongue against her clit she would find it harder to refuse them. A small glow of pleasure heated my belly. It was not till the following afternoon, when I was lying alone on the hillside in the sleepy afternoon sunlight, that I thought about what everyone else had read, how many stories had flirted with the fear of telling the truth about sex, how few actually described sex itself. Love stories, grief and memory stories, sensual memory stories, one that played on the words *eating her,* featuring the body of the beloved, newly dead, cooked up as stew and savored—nonexplicit to the point of obscurity. In the brave new world of lesbian-feminist fiction, much of it seemed not so brave after all.

In the context of what everyone else had written my cowardice was not so apparent. But I knew it had guided what I had written and not written. I had been almost explicit about the act, the body, and the desire. I had said the word *labia,* talked about sweat, and referred to the pulsing shout of release that punctuates orgasm. But I had only flirted with the truth, the way I love it when my lover's hands pull my hair, when her teeth rake my skin. I had articulated a gentle seductive language, but I am not gentle in bed, not seductive. In heat, I am abrupt and desperate. What I had not said was so much greater than all the soft words I had used with such care.

What was taboo? In what context? Sex had always been so risky. It had seemed enough just to pronouce myself a lesbian. Did I have to say what it was I truly desired, what I did and did not do, and why? The prospect was terrifying. I left Sagaris full of confusion. I packed up my notebooks and shut my mouth on what I could not admit shamed me. I had believed everything Bertha Harris had said about the process and importance of writing. But if everything was connected, and writing well required the kind of self-knowledge and naked revelation she implied, then writing was too dangerous for me. I could not go that naked in the world. I stopped writing for six months. When I started again, I did it knowing what was necessary. Maybe not for anyone else, but for me, the kind of person I am, writing meant an attempt to sneak up on the truth, to figure it out slowly through the characters on the page. If writing was dangerous, lying was deadly, and only through writing things out would I discover where my real fears were, my layered network of careful lies and secrets. Whether I published or not was unimportant. What mattered was the act of self-discovery, self-revelation. Who was I and what had happened to me? In the most curious way, I have only learned what I know through writing fiction. What I have been able to imagine has shaped what I know and revealed to me what I truly fear and desire.

It is hard to connect one year to the next, one action to the one before it, cause and effect and every act with its necessary and unique reaction. For most of my life I have been too busy to analyze, to understand how this experience produced that piece of work, or that woman precluded those others. But rereading Bertha Harris' *Lover**one night, I understood that when I wrote "Thighs" I was writing in response and tribute to the lover herself, "the sequence of events she executes to just get her own body next to another's," and that when I named the Boatwright family in *Bastard Out of Carolina*—carefully avoiding any reference to Gibson and Yearwood, names that would have had all my South Carolina relatives sitting up to take notice of how I talked about them—I was reaching back to *Lover*'s twins, Bogart and Boatwright. Since I know I would never have written either book without the revelations that followed from those classes with Bertha Harris, it strikes me as completely appropriate that I made such indirect and unconscious references to my first teacher. I had not planned it or even known I was doing it at the time, but all those years I had owed Bertha Harris a debt. She was the one who stood up and dared to say what she really thought, who told

---

*Reissued by New York University Press (New York, 1993)

me to name myself a writer and live up to the responsibility, who reaffirmed my conviction that writing was important.

Some of us have no choice, I am always telling my students. Some of us have to write in order to make sense of the world. Write out your obsessions, your fears, your curiosities and needs. You can decide later whether you will publish or not, I tell them, how much and why. Even as I say this to them, I know I am setting a trap— the same one in which I have been caught. Writing is still revolutionary, writing is still about changing the world. Each of my students who tells the truth about their life becomes part of that process, and every piece they share with me that challenges my own self-exploration pushes me to deeper work. Sex and lies, I believe, are the core of it. You may not be happy as writers, I tell them, echoing Bertha Harris, but you will know who you are and you will change the world.

Exactly.

Puritans, Perverts, and Feminists

All right. I'm going to tell the most embarrassing fact about my sex life, a secret I have kept for years, a tacky secret, a humiliating secret, an altogether unexplainable and deeply closeted detail about my adolescence. No, I am not going to tell about rubber undies, or trained puppy dogs, or even a lesbian's long suppressed oral fixation on phallic objects. The honest-to-god truth is that I spent most of my adolescence—and I'll admit it, even my twenties—jacking off to science fiction books, marvelous, impossible stories full of struggle and angst.

As a girl I read Robert Heinlein's *Podkayne of Mars*, C.J. Moore's *Jirel of Joiry*, the Telzey books by James Schmidt, *More Than Human* by Theodore Sturgeon, and all of the Alyx stories by Joanna Russ. Each and every one of them stayed with me long after I put the books down. Their worlds were the worlds where I went to get away from the one in which I had been born, and those worlds were lush, adventuresome, scary, and deliciously satisfying. I'd buckle Jirel's sword across my hip and wipe the demon's kiss from my lips, mourning the lover I had been forced to murder but borne up by my pride and outrage. I would turn my cat-calm eyes on the huge dangerous creatures that captured me and wanted to use me like the Aliens were always doing to Telzey, and like her I would outplot the bad guys and walk away triumphant in the end. Later there were the Joan Vinge books, C.J. Cherryh, Vonda McIntyre, Susy McKee Charnas, and Elizabeth A. Lynn. I became the child thief captured and flogged in McIntyre's novel, the riding woman cleaning my knife while listening to the runaway slave who had walked to the end of the world, one of those fascinating perverts Elizabeth Lynn seemed to understand so well. I would orgasm to the adventures I conjured up for myself in those worlds, but more important was the constant excited satisfaction of imagining myself so far away and different. Justice happened in those books—justice, revenge, vindication, female bonding, sex—and what seemed to me a more humane, compassionate philosophy of life. I am as much a creature of those books as I am of my family, my region, my sexual desire. I am the wages of pulp.

It is frustrating to me that so many people divide the erotic and the everyday into such stubbornly segregated categories. There is this notion that sex is separable from life, that pornography is not only debased and physically suspect, but easily recognizable. When women become fervently righteous about this subject, I want to ask them about their girlhood fantasies. Maybe they have red-lined their erotic imaginations since growing up, but what made them breathe hard when they were girls? Did they never come home from some silly movie and lay across their beds seeing themselves as the heroine triumphant, or the heroine in danger, or even the villain, the one who traps the hero/heroine and gets all the really good lines of dialogue anyway? I wonder if anybody else saw the movie *Barbarella* and fantasized not Jane Fonda's blank-faced helplessness, or the Angel's muscled torso, but the Black Queen with her spinning knives and ominous eyepatch? It is easy to get people indignant about nasty sexist paperbacks most of the population doesn't want to admit they read anyway. It's a lot harder to get people to think about—and harder still to talk about—the kind of erotic imagination that takes banal movies, hackneyed best-selling romances, and the most clichéd television programs and constructs personally tailored sexual fantasies that are invariably more effective than mass market stroke books no matter how explicit.

It's unnerving to talk about how our sexual imaginations really function, even if our sexual desires are nowhere near those black leather and chrome scenarios our social magistrates would love to outlaw. For feminists, it often seems dangerous to acknowledge the sexual imagination at all. The sexual is unpredictable, irrational, sneaky, and far-reaching. Worse still, it is completely resistant to simple legalisms or clear philosophical categories. Most sexual imagery does not have one interpretation but a range of multilevel impacts depending on context, personal taste, and hidden symbolism. I remember all too well one of my best friends as a teenager, a girl who appeared to have no sexual affect of any kind, who prayed the rosary three times a day, and planned with stubborn methodical determination her eventual admission to a convent far in the southwest. As a Baptist child I found her Catholicism exotic, fascinating, and quaintly perverse, especially the way she talked about it with seemingly unconscious sexual detail. The way she described praying all night, the pain in her knees and the burning ache in her bent neck, the breathless image of the crucified Lord almost stopping her heart with anguish, reminded me of nothing so much as my own late-night immersions into erotic dreams and purifying orgasmic release. None of my oblique sexual hints were picked up on by my friend. I don't think she ever touched her genitals except to hurriedly cover them with cotton underpants. But maybe that was her way of refusing sexual shame, putting all those feelings into the safe, sanitized hands of the Virgin Mary. All things considered, she was probably safer with her than with me.

I didn't comprehend how devious and subterranean the sexual imagination could become until I read the Joanna Russ essay, "Pornography by Women for Women, With Love."* Russ' essay explores

*Magic Mommas, Trembling Sisters, Puritans and Perverts (Crossing Press: Freedom, California, 1985)

an idea most everyone else had been ignoring as intently as they could. She examines the genre of Star Trek fiction, particularly the women's K/S (for Kirk/Spock) fanzines and anthologies. Those often X-rated (by the authors themselves) books and stories are surprising for their homosexual content, although like a good bit of the astonishingly violent Japanese comics, they are written mostly by heterosexual women for other heterosexual women. Many of the K/S tales are about Captain Kirk and Mr. Spock becoming lovers, and they often include a great deal of s/m content. Russ goes into wonderful detail about the erotic component of fantasies, pointing out that their context often denies the actual acts that take place. For example, the stories are full of scenes in which Kirk or Spock is beaten or tortured; then one character winds up caring for the victim with pronounced erotic and romantic feelings. In a few cases, sex proves necessary to save the victim, jarring them back to sanity or kickstarting their immune systems. The Kirk/Spock characters might be shocked or embarrassed by their behavior but unable not to perform those startling acts. The conflict itself became part of the erotic charge, and that was something I understood about my own sexuality, the repulsion/attraction dynamic that can overwhelm and obscure sexual desire. The characters in Kirk/Spock stories get to do things they can never admit they want to do, allowing the authors of the stories the same luxury.

The best thing about Russ' essay is that she looks closely at the stories for what is really going on, that is, to what uses the authors themselves are putting their fantasies. She sees the K/S material as a portrait of love and sex as women might want those acts to look in real life, regardless of whether the acts take place with two men, or a man and a woman. She cites the work of theorists Susan Gubar, Patricia Lamb, and Diana Veith, and examines the coding and transference that is characteristic of most of the fantasies. She suggests that when women science fiction writers write about aliens they may actually often be writing about women. An example can be seen in the K/S sex practices: the boys have anal sex with the ease and lubrication that is actually characteristic of vaginal intercourse. I'm an old Star Trek fan myself, and I loved the whole genre. But I couldn't help wonder why there weren't fanzines that gave us Uhura's adventures with a few Romulan female warriors. Was lesbianism so dangerous it couldn't even be handled symbolically? Maybe Kirk and Spock were somehow both encoded females, a variation on alien dykes!

After reading Russ' essay I began to reconsider what my life as a teenage science fiction fan had really been about. I found myself thinking of the levels of meaning I took from science fiction—not just the straightforward adventures, but the symbolic and political lessons I abstracted. After all, I ate up science fiction books like candy, until I was living more in the worlds of fantasy than in the small Southern town where I was born. Yes, the women and girls in those books had adventures. They had great passions, terrors, successes, and narrow escapes. Their minds were working constantly and almost never in the ways traditional fiction told me women thought. They weren't worrying what the men and boys thought of them; they were worrying about survival. They weren't hassling over whether or not they had to wear makeup; they were fastening on their cloaks and taking off across the stars. I also had lots of books in which one character was getting tortured or injured in order for the other to offer erotic comfort, and most of those had been my favorites before I figured out that I might want to find some interesting exotic creature who would tie me up and drive me out of my mind with lust. When most of the female population was running around in beehive hairdos, sweating over whether it was OK for a girl to call a boy, those books were pretty damn radical stuff.

The women read like dykes to me. They even had sex, real sex, without symbolic shrouding.

One of my all-time favorites was, in fact, a Joanna Russ novel, *Picnic on Paradise*. Not only was the heroine, Alyx, a caustic, sharp-eyed Phoenician thief who spent most of the book making fun of the rich white jock who in any other book would have been the hero,

she kept going off into the bushes with the teenage punk and fucking him. And I do mean the active word: Alyx climbed on top of
that boy and enjoyed herself. She didn't even care if he kept his Walk-
man on while she did it. That was a scene that put my lust-ridden
teenage soul into a tizzy, prodding my imagination in directions that
probably would have greatly surprised Russ' publisher. This wasn't
about coding or veiled references. It was flatly heterosexual but still
seemed to offer tacit encouragement to female sexual desire and female sexual aggression. I thought it applied to lesbians as much as
anybody. Alyx, after all, never struck me as overly concerned with
heterosexual passion. She was into adolescents, girls mostly, but there
was that boy in *Picnic*.

Each and every one of the books I've mentioned became fod-
der for my teenage fantasy life, most of which was definitely sex-
obsessed. The private stories I made up for my own enjoyment
tended toward the creation of slightly scary and definitely inhuman
erotic machinery: androids who would do only what their program-
ming commanded, or machines into which one could fit one's naked and tender flesh without fear of any intrusion by the banally human. The conditioned fearfulness of a terrorized and dependent
girlhood led me away from imagining any actual human sexual contact with other fearful, or possibly dangerous, humans like myself.

I was conditioned to suspend my disbelief with science ficion,
and that meant I could imagine myself in the books. But it was still
a big jump from my tentative and careful fantasies to imagining the
sexual adventures of those marvelous heroines. That I began to do
it at all I credit to the power of the really gifted science fiction writers
who gave me worlds in which little girls did not have to confront
the horrors of my everyday life. Some authors were better for
stimulating the imagination than others, and surprisingly, to me at
least, the best were not always female. Samuel Delaney, for example, gave me the female heroine of *Babel 17*—poet, warrior, and
revolutionary who achieves her most powerful goals through the use

of a particularly powerful alien language.

More importantly, he gave me the short story "Time Considered as a Helix of Semi-Precious Stones." The latter was so significant and emotionally devastating that I read it once and promptly lost the book, an act it took me a long time to realize was in no way accidental. For years I kept telling people fragments of the story in the hopes they would know where I could find it again, but I invariably left out the most personally dangerous details. "Time Considered as a Helix of Semi-Precious Stones" was the first story I read that actually had recognizable, almost contemporary, gay characters. It was also my first explicit gay s/m story. Beautifully written and subtle enough for me to virtually pretend it wasn't implying the kind of relationship it did, the story made me think about my own romantic imagery: the boy, the singer whose body is covered with scars, who cannot be stopped from pursuing his own masochistic destruction as actively as he goes out to sing his poems and insist it is this unjust world that must be changed. No coded homosexual character study, no Sal Mineo portrait in miniature, Delaney's masochistic revolutionary took hold of my heart and showed me my own face—just as queer, just as masochistic, just as driven, and just as stubbornly hopeful. When I finally admitted to myself why I so loved that story, how I saw myself in it, more than my erotic imagination shifted. My everyday human-to-human relationships were altered as well. I began to think that perhaps it might be worth the risk to touch another human being, to allow them to touch me back.

Delaney's works were also revelations to me about what the "life of the artist" might be like. Both the young male masochist in "Helix" and the female heroine of *Babel 17* were poets with a clear concept of who they are as marginal and political artists. When I picked up *Dahlgren*, I found that he had taken that concept and pushed it to the limits of what seemed possible, providing along the way a completely original approach to the traditional messianic myth so popular with science fiction writers—many of whom are startlingly conservative and militaristic. Delaney's poets were anarchists, unwilling to spend their talents striving to control history, other people, or sexual behavior itself. He championed the queer and disenfranchised, created women who were as unpredictable as they were fearless and men who came close to breaking my heart with their vulnerability and stubborn grappling with their own desires. He suggested with every sketch, moreover, the profoundly complicated interactions that mark all sexual exchanges. Delaney's ability to treat queer sexuality is still unsurpassed; for my adolescence, it was a revelation.

I've talked to many women, both heterosexual and lesbian, about their adolescent attraction to science fiction. I've tried to draw them out about the ways in which it affected their concepts of the sexual. It is amazing to me how many women have told me that science fiction is where they put their sexual imagination. One of my old lovers, for example, who never saw any of the soft-core lesbian pulps before her coming out, swears instead by the sexually aggressive and sexually matter-of-fact women she found in science fiction.

"They gave me the idea," she told me, reminiscing about her own adolescent fantasy life. For her, as for me, the hidden message was clear. It didn't have to be the way everybody said it was. It could be different. You might be able to have sex with plants or intelligent waterfalls or friendly machines—or women—and not have it be a social or moral catastrophe. Once out, that's a secret that could change everything, and has.

An earlier version of this essay appeared in the *New York Native* in 1985.

Public Silence, Private Terror

*I urge each one of us to reach down into that deep place of knowledge inside herself
and touch that terror and loathing of any difference that lives there.*

Audre Lorde*

*What drew me to politics was my love of women, that agony I felt in observing
the straightjackets of poverty and repression I saw people in my family in. But
the deepest political tragedy I have experienced is how with such grace, such blind
faith, this commitment to women in the feminist movement grew to be exclusive
and reactionary.*

Cherríe Moraga**

Her voice on the phone was a surprise, not only because the call had
come late in the evening, or even because she was so reluctant to identify herself. She had never been a friend, only an acquaintance, another lesbian whose writing I had admired but whom I'd spoken
to less than half a dozen times in all the years we'd been aware of
each other's existence. There was, also, the too-present memory of
the last time I'd seen her, the way her eyes had registered, stared,
and then avoided mine. I'd recognized in her face the same look I'd
been seeing in other women's faces for all the months since the Barnard Conference on Sexuality (which my friends and I referred to

---

* "The Master's Tools" in *Sister Outsider* (Crossing Press: Freedom, California, 1984)
** Preface, *This Bridge Called My Back*, edited by Gloria Anzaldúa and Cherríe Moraga
(Kitchen Table: Women of Color Press: Albany, New York, 1981)

as the Barnard Sex Scandal)—a look of fascination, contempt, and extreme discomfort. She'd gotten away as quickly as possible, and at the time I had reminded myself, again, that it really wasn't any different from the way straight women used to avoid me back in 1971.

"I didn't wake you, did I?" Her voice trembled with anxiety, and automatically I told her, "No, I don't go to bed this early." I started to make a joke, to try to put her a little more at ease, but I stopped myself. After all, she was the one who had called me; she had to know what she wanted.

But it didn't seem that way. She rambled, made small talk, her voice so soft and hesitant that I couldn't bring myself to grab hold of the conversation, to ask, "Just why was it you called, anyway?" I don't remember now how we steered through it, her fear palpable enough for me to gradually figure out that whatever else she wanted, some part of it had to be about sex. When she finally said, "Well, I thought I could talk to you," I was so relieved she was going to get to the point, it almost overcame my sudden tired anger at her for being one more person to label me that way.

Yeah, you should be able to say anything to me, I thought but did not say. Sex, and her terror, her disgust with herself. I listened to her voice and felt my anger melt to grief. I'd heard that tone before, choked with shame and desperation. She had been doing these things—no, she couldn't say what exactly—but there was no one she could talk to about it. She had tried to stop herself, stop the fantasies, masturbation, stray thoughts. But it didn't go away, either her fear or her desire, and finally she had tried to talk to another woman she was close to, someone she thought would understand. That woman had stared at her, hesitated, and then told her she was sick.

"Sick," she said in a very small voice.

I put my head down on my arm and cradled the phone close to my shoulder, remembering the first time I had heard a voice that small and despairing say the same word. In 1974, I had volunteered to be a peer counselor for a lesbian and gay hot line in Tallahassee,

Florida. Over the months I had talked again and again to people who were sure they were sick, criminal, and doomed—all for desires I believed glorious and completely understandable. But I was a long way from Tallahassee, and nothing seemed as simple as it had back then. Worse, I didn't know this woman well enough to be having this conversation. I didn't know what to say to her. I didn't even know what she had been doing, or imagining doing.

I listened to her, and thought about an old lover whose terror had been huge. She liked to imagine herself held down, unable to reach the mouth that hovered over hers until she had to beg for it— that mouth, that release. I started to tell the voice on the phone that story, how I noticed that when we made love, my lover's mouth worked and worked but never made a sound, how gradually I'd teased her and comforted her, teased her some more and reassured her again, until finally she had let go and roared her passion.

"She was so afraid," I said, "so certain that she was a terrible, sick person. When it all came out, though, there was not that much to it, nothing to match those years of knotted-up silent grief. It's usually like that, you know. We're rarely as terrible as we believe ourselves to be."

Silence answered me and stretched out. I pushed my hair back, waiting, wondering if I was saying the absolutely wrong thing. Maybe she really was doing something terrible, maybe she was even a bit sick. What did I know? Maybe she needed serious help. Maybe her desire was to slice pieces of herself off and feed them to her cat. What good was it for me to tell her about someone she didn't know, someone who, after all, had a desire that was relatively easy to satisfy, that didn't demand much of anyone else or herself except the strength to put it out. What lover would refuse to pin her down and tease her? What friend would call her sick for that?

"I'm not an expert," I finally said, "not a sex therapist. Sometimes I think the only thing I understand is myself, and that not very well—just a few of the ways I've fucked myself over, let myself be fucked over, invited it or cooperated with it." Talk to me, I wanted to say. I can't say anything if you don't give a little.

"I've been putting stuff inside me," she whispered. I just about dropped the phone in relief. All right, what was she putting inside her, and inside her where? But she wouldn't give me that. Quickly it became clear she would not be able to stand having said even that much. I knew that after this phone call she would never speak to me again. She would always feel herself vulnerable to me, imagine I knew more than I did—all her secret thoughts, what she did alone in her bed in the dark—and she would believe I had somehow betrayed her, or would when the chance arose.

I grabbed that phone like it was a lifeline. Did she know there was a group, a lesbian group, she could go to? No, but even as I repeated the address I knew she wasn't writing it down. I could hear her urge to run and hide, recognized with certainty that whatever she did, she wasn't ready to talk to people—not about this tender stuff. Well, did she have any books about sex?

"I'm sure you've seen *Sapphistry*," I said, "but I could loan you some others, or you could buy them if you wanted."

She probably wouldn't want to see me, I thought, but if she had the titles she could get them herself in a store where no one knew her. There was so little to recommend, though. How few feminists write anything useful about sex, I told myself for perhaps the hundredth time.

"Seen what? *Sapphistry?*"

I made myself talk quietly, slowly. What I really wanted was to start yelling—not at her, but kicking furniture, screaming in frustration.

"That's Pat Califia's book from Naiad Press. It's good, very clear with lots of practical information, especially about what's dangerous and what's not."

"Oh."

I caught the recognition in her voice. She'd heard that name before, read some review that had growled indignation about all that s/m stuff and probably reinforced all her own sexual terrors. If she really was pushing something into her cunt or ass, it didn't matter that *Sapphistry* was one of the few books to tell her what was involved in plain and simple terms, that wouldn't play into all the guilt and self-hatred she was carrying. Odds were, the same friend who had told her she was sick had told her all about Pat Califia.

Suddenly, she had to get off the phone. Her cat was getting into the garbage. She thought she heard someone at the door. It was an excuse and we both knew it. Then the phone went silent. I sat holding the receiver until the hum broke into a howl. I put it down and moved to wrap myself around my lover, so angry I couldn't speak, couldn't even say, "It was another one of those terrible phone calls."

I began receiving those late-night phone calls after I got caught up in the Barnard Sex Scandal of 1982. A year earlier I had helped organize the Lesbian Sex Mafia, a group intended for "politically incorrect" women, and began to do public speaking on sexuality, in part to help that organization succeed. In addition, I had started publishing my fiction and essays on incest, family violence, and sexuality. The combination of activities had made me increasingly question what, at that time, was the dominant feminist ideology on pornography. I did all this without thinking too much about the possible results—though I knew it was dangerous to be too public as a pervert or too visible as a feminist who did not think pornography the prime cause of women's oppression. Still, when I found myself accused of being a pawn of the patriarchy, an antifeminist writer, and a pimp for the pornographers, I was surprised and unsure how to reply.

For years I had struggled to share with other women the rage with which I began my work as a lesbian and feminist activist—outrage at anybody telling me what I would and would not be allowed to do with my life. Always this struggle had been equally about sex and class, about shattering the silence imposed on us concerning our terrifying sexual desires and the powerful details of the different ways in which we engage the world. When I helped organize the Lesbian Sex Mafia, I felt very much in that tradition, and for all my uncertainties and fears about what might happen to me and the women who would work with and join such an organization, I was convinced that this was a continuation of the politics I had been engaged in for a decade.

The Lesbian Sex Mafia was to be an old-fashioned consciousness-raising group whose whole concern would be the subject of sex. To be sure that we would remain focused on our own outrageousness, we chose our deliberately provocative name and concentrated on attracting members whose primary sexual orientation was s/m, butch/femme, fetish specific, or otherwise politically incorrect. We drew more women from the lesbian bars than the feminist movement, but we deliberately brought back the principles of CR (using xeroxes of guidelines from 1973 that I found in my files). We insisted that within the group we would make no assumptions, no judgments, and no conclusions. We began by asking each other what it would be like to organize for our sexual desire as strongly as we had tried to organize for our sexual defense.

The failings of the Lesbian Sex Mafia largely recreated the failings of earlier CR groups. With the emphasis on sharing stories, it was hard to move toward taking any group action, or toward a public, political identity. Some members felt frustrated with this, while others wanted the group to concentrate only on meeting the private needs of its members. There were limits on how the latter could be achieved. Integrating new people was extremely difficult, partly because everyone was hesitant and afraid and consequently defensive. The membership tended to focus on individuals who had already come to some state of self-acceptance more than on those who were still completely unsure of their sexual orientation or desires. The kind of fearful young woman who called me might never have come back after an initial orientation, and some women who did come expected the group to provide them with an instant source of sexual satisfaction or adventure. They tended to get bored with all the talk and business. Absolute emphasis on privacy and confidentiality also presented many barriers to public action. The Lesbian Sex Mafia became one more example of public silence, though we intended it to provide a measure of safety rather than another locus of fear.

The most striking failure of the Lesbian Sex Mafia, however, was that none of us predicted the kind of attack and vilification that accompanied the April 23, 1982 Barnard Conference on Sexuality or the speakout on politically incorrect sex we organized to take place the next day. Concentrating on supporting each other and under-standing our own issues, we had not seriously prepared to deal with critics who would be horrified at our behavior as lesbians, never mind queer queers. While the forum fulfilled its intended function as an event at which we could talk about our pleasure, rage, and fear about sex, where we could exchange information with women who, al-though they would never come to a Lesbian Sex Mafia meeting, had equally embattled concerns about sexuality, it proved an extremely painful lesson in how effective and public the terror around sexual behavior could become.

In the months following the speakout, the Lesbian Sex Mafia underwent a complete reorganization. I was distracted by first dealing with an onrush of publicity within the feminist press and then a series of personal crises. One of the most painful of these was the publi-cation of the June 1982 issue of *off our backs*, which described in great detail a sexual encounter between me and two other women in a les-bian bar, using the kind of language I would have expected from con-servative or religious moralists. Over and over again I found myself having to talk to strangers and be stubbornly, bluntly explicit about what I did in bed, what I did not do, and why. The alternative did not appear to be silence but death itself. I was fighting to keep my straight job at a publicly funded arts organization which had received a series of anonymous phone calls demanding that I be fired, while invitations to speak, publish, and edit were systematically with-drawn. By the fall of that year even the Lesbian Sex Mafia reflected the virulence of the onslaught by censuring me for the publicity the speakout had produced. As one of the primary organizers I was held responsible for endangering the confidentiality of members, and instead of protesting, I withdrew my membership. It was not until several years later that I received an apology and reinstatement as a founding officer.

And throughout that year there were those phone calls—quizzical, rude, and painful—from women I barely knew, who somehow felt I had become a kind of public resource to whom anything could be said and of whom anything could be asked. Worse, by far, were the calls and letters from old friends who suddenly had the need to be extremely clear about the limits of their friendships.

Even for those of us with backgrounds as political activists who thought we had some handle on sexual anxiety and its variations in this society, the revelations of shame, fear, and guilt that occurred after the Barnard Sex Scandal and the period of public controversy that was its aftermath—since labeled the Sex Wars—were simply overwhelming. The women who kept talking and working as publicly identified sex radicals, or pro-sex feminists, began to engage in an expansive conversation that was in no way safe but was powerfully revealing. Most of it reminded me of the discussions we had held in the Lesbian Sex Mafia, and convinced me that very few people in our society believe themselves normal, think that their sexual desire and behavior is like anyone else's. Women talked about years of celibacy, self-hatred, rejection, and abandonment by lovers, helplessness after rape or incest, social censure and street violence, family ostracism, and—overridingly—the fear of what our desires might mean. I went through a period of involuntary withdrawal in my relationships that took me right back to when I was first working out my response to childhood incest. It became impossible to let anyone, no matter how trusted, touch me in an intimate way, and for almost a year I became completely nonorgasmic. There was a kind of painful irony in being such a publicly recognized sex radical who could not have sex, and who dared not acknowledge that condition until it was past.

I thought a lot about the early discussions in the Lesbian Sex Mafia as time passed. In spite of all we had done to set up the group to avoid judgments and to provide unqualified support for diversity, there had still been a depressingly persistent need for people to be reassured that they were not sick or crazy or dangerous to those they loved. The strength of the group had been the strength of consciousness raising itself, that frank revelation of the common personal experience and the lies that are uncovered when we show ourselves as vulnerable and human creatures, both needy and hopeful. We had worked at turning our fears and experiences into a source of insight rather than confusion. That we could feel any measure of safety while being so vulnerable had been a constant source of energy and power. Every forbidden thought that was spoken enriched us. Every terrible desire that we shared suddenly assumed human dimension, and our meetings had been full of warmth and laughter. I watched a similar thing begin to happen with post-Barnard organizing and the creation of F.A.C.T.—the Feminist Anti-Censorship Taskforce. We wanted to talk truth about sex, wanted to understand without fear of censure, and most of all, we wanted to know that our lives were neither a betrayal of our beliefs nor a collusion with all we had fought to change in this society. None of us became antifeminists, though many of us were accused of being that, and all of us share a conviction that sexuality is not a distraction but a vital issue in any political organizing. For me, the struggle came down to an inner demand that I again look at sexual fear from my own perspective, without giving in to the impulse to hide, deny, or wall off desire itself.

On the wall over my desk I hang pictures, clippings, and notes to myself. It is crowded with fantasy images, lists, and ideas, even love letters several years old. The picture of the young woman in a black lace dress and feathered hat has been up there almost as long as the samurai woman sweeping her long sword into the sunlight. Each inspires me, though in very different ways. Some days I want to become one or the other of them. Some days I want to write the story of how they become lovers. Other days I can't stand to look at them at all and turn instead to notecards pinned up between the pictures, reading the words over and over to myself, knowing I have not yet exhausted all I need to learn from them, that what I am engaged in is nothing less than my own explication of what it means to be a lesbian, the kind of lesbian I am, in this time and place.

The quote from Adrienne Rich's introduction to the reprint of her essay, "Compulsory Heterosexuality and Lesbian Existence,"* is pinned next to the paragraphs I copied from Barbara Smith's short story, "Home,"** so that the words follow each other and echo an idea that has been worrying me for a long time.

There has recently been an intensified debate on Female sexuality among feminists and lesbians, with lines often furiously drawn, with sadomasochism and pornography as key words which are variously defined according to who is talking. The depth of women's rage and fear regarding sexuality and its relation to power and pain is real, even when the dialogue sounds simplistic, self-righteous, or like parallel monologues.

Adrienne Rich

I knew when I first met her that it would be all right to love her, that whatever happened we would emerge from this not broken. It would not be about betrayal. Loving doesn't terrify me. Loss does. The women I need are literally disappearing from the face of the earth. It has already happened.

Barbara Smith

I keep wanting to take down the card that holds Adrienne Rich's words so that I can file them away and no longer have to think about the fact that it is certainly fear that has dominated the debate on female sexuality, that it is fear that has provoked the shouting, name-calling, and rejection. I am tired of trying to understand why peo-

---

* *Sign*, V, Summer 1980
** *Home Girls*, edited by Barbara Smith (Kitchen Table: Women of Color Press: Albany, New York, 1983)

ple fall into self-righteous hatred, but the card stays up for just that reason: to remember the human dimensions of the debate. The quote from "Home" serves the same purpose, but it also reaches my own fear, going deeper still to a level of desire I have known since I first realized what it would mean to my life to be queer. Home is what I have always wanted—the trust that my life, my love, does not betray those I need most, that they will not betray me.

"You confuse the two," a friend once told me. "When we talk about love, we are not necessarily speaking of sex. When we talk about sex, love is not at issue."

Is that true? I ask myself and read the cards over again. *Sexuality. Sex. Rage. Fear. Pain. Love. Betrayal. Home.* These are the words that have scored my life. I have always been trying to understand myself, to find some elemental sense of a life that is my own and not inherently wrong, not shameful, not a betrayal of those I love most. At thirteen it was the simple issue of just being a lesbian; at twenty it was the kind of woman I wanted to touch and to be touched by; at twenty-five it was the realization of what kind of touch felt like sex to me. None of it has ever been easy. Throughout my life I have felt that I was fighting off some terrible, amorphous confusion about sex itself, what I have a right to do or want, what was dangerous and what was vital, and most fearfully of all, what would make the women I loved literally disappear from my life.

Beneath the quotes from Adrienne Rich and Barbara Smith, held by a pin that positions a picture of my younger sister and her two children, is a line I have written out for myself, the beginning to an article I started long ago and could not finish. *The terrors of sex are real,* it reads. *The awful vulnerability of the individual exposed physically and emotionally—and we are too often betrayed by our own desires or the failures of our lovers.* Betrayal again, I notice, and this time failure. It does not appear that I am so very much different from the woman who called me. We are both stumbling over our private fears, worrying at desire from the downhill side, not speaking to the trust and joy I know we both are seeking.

Grief should not be where we have to start when we talk of sex. But the idea of a life in which rage, physical fear, or emotional terror prevents even the impetus of desire—that is the image that haunts the discussion for me. The thought that we could all be forced to live isolated in our own bodies, never safe enough to risk ourselves in naked intimacy with others, rides me like an old nightmare from my childhood: a dream of silence, cold hands, and suspicious eyes. It was a nightmare I used to believe was common to all lesbians, but one I thought had grown less powerful in our everyday lives. It was the fear behind our politics, a unifying and radicalizing perception that we did not need to voice because we all knew it so well. The experience of having the meaning of our love and desire for women twisted, misused, or totally denied seemed to me central and basic to feminism in the same way that our politics itself was supposed to rest in the actual lived experience of women who must name for themselves their needs, hopes, and desires. But I never wanted fear to be the only impulse behind political action. As deeply as I wanted safety or freedom, I wanted desire, hope, and joy. What, after all, was the worth of one without the other?

Those notes hang on my wall and watch me as relentlessly as the pictures of my lovers, sisters, and fantasy figures. I cannot answer them, or tear them down, or ignore them, because in trying to write about sex, I am always faced with the fear that any conclusion I make will betray someone. If I outline, even if only for myself, a new understanding of how our desire for sex is used against us, some face always stares back unsatisfied. If I demand my right as a lesbian to examine and explore my relationships with other women as sources of both passion and grief, I am flat up against it again. I can imagine faceless heterosexual feminists unable to understand any human relationship not rooted in the dynamics of male-female interaction, as well as the lesbians who will tell me that I am betraying them by putting such information out for perusal and possible use by men or nonfeminists. Even lesbians who will dismiss me because my life is nothing like theirs, the springs of my passions strange or frightening to them.

It is difficult, in fact, for me to frame any questions about sex without getting caught up in endless considerations of the meaning of the acts, sometimes quite astonishing philosophical, political, and spiritual treatments of meaning that I cannot bring back down to the level that interests me most—my everyday life. All the impassioned rhetoric serves no purpose but to lead to greater obscurity if it does not originate and flow from an examination of the specific: how we all actually live out our sexuality. Without that detail, I have concluded, there are no valid generalizations to be made about sex and women's lives except for the central fact that we are all hungry for the power of desire and we are all terribly afraid.

The hardest lesson I have learned in the last few years is how powerful is my own desire to hang onto a shared sense of feminist community where it is safe to talk about dangerous subjects like sex, and how hopeless is the desire. Even within what I have thought of as my own community, and worse, within the tighter community of my friends and lovers, I have never *felt* safe. I have never *been* safe, and that is only partly because everyone else is just as fearful as I am. None of us is safe because we have not tried to make each other safe. We have never even recognized the fearfulness of the territory. We have addressed violence and exploitation and heterosexual assumptions without first establishing the understanding that for each of us, desire is unique and necessary and simply terrifying. Without that understanding, and the compassion and empathy that must be part of it, I do not know how to avoid those acts of betrayal. But it is one thing for me to confront my own fear of those different from me—whether they are women of color, middle-class women, or heterosexuals—and entirely another to demand of other feminists that we begin again with this understanding. Yet that is exactly what I want to do. I want to once again start by saying that as women we don't know enough about each other—our fears, our desires, or the many ways in which this society has acted upon us. Nor do I want to give ground and allow sex to be exempted from the discussion.

As feminists, many of us have committed our whole lives to struggling to change what most people in this society don't even question, and sometimes the intensity of our struggle has persuaded us that the only way to accomplish change is to make hard bargains, to give up some points and compromise on others. What this has always meant in the end, unfortunately, is trading some people for others.

I do not want to do that.

I do not want to require any other woman to do that.

I do not want to claim a safe and comfortable life for myself that is purchased at the cost of some other woman's needs or desires. But over and over again I see us being pushed to do just that. I know for myself how easily I used to dismiss heterosexual desire. Oh, I was kind about it, gently patient, but I used to look at heterosexual feminists with a kind of superior disdain, wondering how long it would take them to realize the hopelessness of their position. Crawling headfirst through the eye of a needle didn't seem to me half as difficult as dragging a man through your life. I took as whole cloth the notion that feminism is the theory, lesbianism the practice, and only a childhood of enforced politeness kept me from preaching that conviction to the less enlightened. I made no connection between such expectations and the kind of pressure to reform myself that had hurt me so badly for so many years.

I cannot pinpoint what changed all that for me, made me see the absurdity of such a theory. I know that a piece of it was my relationship with my sisters. While I could imagine some theoretical stranger deciding that rational lesbianism was the solution, I could not face my baby sister—with her children, her half-tamed boyfriend, and her hard-won self-respect—and try to convince her that she'd be better off in a lesbian collective. Once when we'd stayed up talking almost all night, and she'd told me she thought her fellow was sleeping around, and I'd admitted that yes, that woman I'd told her about had hurt me almost more than I thought I could stand, she had put her hand on mine, squeezed and said, "I know that pain." She was telling me the truth, she understood me, and I knew, too, that all the things wrong in her life would not be solved by her trying to be something she was not.

My understanding of what feminism meant changed even more from reading and listening to the many women who contributed to *This Bridge Called My Back*. It was a matter, then, not only of looking at the personal racism that blights all our lives, but of examining the institutional racism that shapes our convictions of who is or can be *right*, and what it is that we really know as feminists. In a very real sense, *Bridge* gave me a new way to look at my life because it was so full of the lives of women who, while they were very different from me, voiced the same hopes, the same desperate desires to change what any of us is allowed. While addressing the very real ways racism tears at all of us, the writers spoke again and again of joy, of love, of power, of lives shared and things accomplished. They offered a vision that struggle between white women and women of color did not have to be framed in terms of betrayal, that just as Barbara Smith had written, we might "emerge from this not broken." If we could hope for this across the barriers of color and class, why not across sexuality and gender? And if the writers in *Bridge* could make themselves vulnerable while still insisting on a shared vision of feminism, I believed that I had a responsibility to do the same.

Bridge also raised the question of the difference between politics and personal style—a complicated, critical, and painful issue that no one has addressed sufficiently. Part of the power of the writers' voices lay in how different they were from what I had come to think of as the same old, slightly distant, and carefully respectable aura of feminist theory. Here were all kinds of women speaking of their real lives, not abstract generalities, not shielding or obscuring anger or impatience. I thought of all the meetings I had attended, the papers I had read, where the dominant tone was academic, polite, and distant, while the undercurrent was personal and vicious: the urge I had to say, Can we stop a minute and talk about what is really going on here?

When Cherríe Moraga wrote of how, "with such grace, such blind faith, this commitment to women in the feminist movement grew to be exclusive and reactionary," she was talking specifically about racism and the tendency to ignore or misinterpret the lives of women of color. While her words made me look at my own fears, avoidance, and racism, they also enabled me to see that I had the same criticisms of the movement around the issues of class and sex. Moreover, just as I was terrified of addressing my own racism, so, too, other women were afraid of stepping into the deep and messy waters of class and sexual desire. If we get into this, what might we lose? If we expose this, what might our enemies do with it? And what might it mean? Will we have to throw out all the theory we have built with such pain and struggle? Will we have to start over? How are we going to try to make each other safe while we work it through?

My first response to these questions was that it was too hard, too deep, too frightening. It was only when I took my second breath that I began to think of going ahead anyway. We learn prejudice and hatred at the same time we learn who we are and what the world is about, at the same time we learn our fundamental convictions about sex. The real choice is whether we will simply swallow what we are given, or whether we will risk our whole lives shaking down and changing those very bottle-fed convictions.

Essential political decisions are made not once, but again and again in a variety of situations, always against that pressure to compromise, to bargain. I have found that in my slow reassessment of my politics, the most telling factor has been the gap between the rhetoric of lesbian feminism and the reality of my own life. It didn't matter how many times I was told I was oppressed as a woman. That fact did not satisfactorily answer many of the contradictions of my life. Simple answers, reductionist politics, are the most prone to compromise, to saying we're addressing the essential issue and all that other stuff can slide. It is, in reality, people who slide.

Throughout my life somebody has always tried to set the boundaries of who and what I will be allowed to be: if working class, an intellectual, upwardly mobile type who knows her place, or at least the virtues of gratitude; if a lesbian, an acceptable lesbian, not too forward about the details of her sexual practice; if a writer, a humble, consciously female one who understands her relationship to more "real" writers and who is willing to listen to her editors. What is common to these boundary lines is that their most destructive power lies in what I can be persuaded to do to myself—the walls of fear, shame, and guilt I can be encouraged to build in my mind. Like that woman who called me, I am to hide myself, and hate myself, and never risk exposing what might be true about my life. I have learned through great sorrow that all systems of oppression feed on public silence and private terrorization. But few do so more forcefully than the systems of sexual oppression, and each of us is under enormous pressure to give in to their demands.

In the early feminist and lesbian movement days, many women slowly worked out a personal analysis about the omnipresence of silence—the impact on all our lives of the things that must not be said, and the social use of such strictures. AIDS activists extended the analysis until the cautionary Silence Equals Death achieved the status of tautology, self-evident and unquestioned. Looking again at our silences, the sources of our fears, is both a way to see where the greatest damage is being done, as well as an opportunity for coalition and shared understanding. I have seen that when I speak as a lesbian about my own struggles to understand and publicly acknowledge the full meaning of my love for women, straight women nod back at me. I have heard them reveal their own terrible secrets, their own impossible desires. For all of us, it is the public expression of desire that is embattled, any deviation from what we are supposed to want and be, how we are supposed to behave. The myth prevails that good girls—even modern, enlightened, liberal or radical varieties—don't really have such desires.

A decade later, many of my questions from the early 1980s remain unanswered. I find myself continuing to wonder how our lives might be different if we were not constantly subjected to the fear and contempt of being sexually different, sexually dangerous, sexually endangered. What kind of women might we be if we did not have to worry about being too sexual, or not sexual enough, or the wrong kind of sexual for the company we keep, the convictions we hold? I have not found a solution to my own impatience with the terms of the discussion about sex that persists among feminists, lesbian and queer activists, and radical heterosexuals. Not addressing the basic issues of sexual fear, stereotyping, and stigmatization reinforces the rage and terror we all hide, while maintaining the status quo in a new guise.

Instead of speaking out in favor of sexual diversity, most feminists continue to avoid the discussion. It is too dangerous, too painful, too hopeless, and the Sex Wars are supposed to be over anyway. But when women remain afraid of what might be revealed about our personal fears and desires, it becomes clear that the Sex Wars are far from over. When it is easier to dismiss any discussion of sexuality as irrelevant or divisive rather than to look at all the different ways we have denied and dismissed each other, the need to break the public silence still exists.

We have no choice. We cannot compromise or agree to be circumspect in how we challenge the system of sexual oppression. We dare not willingly deny ourselves, make those bad bargains that can look so good at the moment. I think, for example, of all those times we have pandered to this sex-hating, sex-fearing society by pretending, as lesbians, that we are really no different from heterosexuals; and by placing such a strong emphasis on statistics that portray lesbians as monogamous, couple- and community-centered, and so much more acceptable than those publicly provocative, outrageous, and promiscuous queers. Every time we articulate, as feminists, the need for reproductive freedom rather than abortion, talk about our right to control our bodies but do not go on to demand all that that might mean, and speak of morality as if that word did not stick in our throats with the memory of every lesbian ever attacked for the immoral acts we each enjoy, every time, I believe, we are in collusion with our own destruction.

Our enemies are not confused about this issue. In 1993, as in 1982, the preachers, psychologists, and politicians who want us to be the silent, frightened women they can control are not avoiding the issue of sex, the naming of deviants, the attacks on us as queers and perverts and immoral individuals. And it is as individuals that we are most vulnerable to them: individual lesbian mothers fighting for their children, individual lesbian teachers demanding their right to do the work they love, and individual lesbian citizens who want to live as freely and happily as their neighbors, whether they wear leather or all-cotton clothes, keep compost heaps or drive motorcycles, live with one woman for thirty years or treat sex as a sport and are always in pursuit of their personal best. All of us are vulnerable to individual attack. Sex is still the favorite subject of demagogues—they know how vulnerable we are.

I am certain that none of us wants to live with the fear, the sense of loss, betrayal, and risk that I worry at all the time. I know that many of us want what Barbara Smith described in her short story— the ability to love without fear of betrayal, the confidence that we can expose our most hidden selves and not have the women we love literally disappear from our lives. I know, too, that we cannot inhabit that safe ground easily. If we are not to sacrifice some part of ourselves or our community, we will have to go through the grief, the fear of exposure, and struggle, with only a thin layer of trust that we will emerge whole and unbroken. I know of no other way to do this than to start by saying, *I will give up nothing. I will give up no one.*

For my lovers, my sisters, the women who in the early eighties were afraid to speak to or be seen with me, and all those women who called me late at night to whisper their terrors, I make a promise: I promise not to lie and not to require anyone else to lie. I still offer that open book where I hope we can all write out our fearful secrets and sign them or not as we choose, to honor our secrets and break the public silence that has maintained so much private terror.

An earlier version of this essay appeared in *Pleasure and Danger*, edited by Carol Vance (Routledge: Boston, 1984).

Her Body, Mine, and His

Frog fucking. Her hands on my hips; my heels against my ass, legs spread wide; her face leaning into my neck; my hands gripping her forearms. Her teeth are gentle. Nothing else about her is. I push up on the balls of my feet, rock my ass onto my ankles, reaching up for every forward movement of her thighs between mine. Her nipples are hard, her face flushed, feet planted on the floor while I arch off the edge of the bed, a water mammal, frog creature with thighs snapping back to meet her every thrust.

My labia swell. I can feel each hair that curls around the harness she wears. I imagine manta rays unfolding great undulating labia-wings in the ocean, wrapping around the object of their desire. Just so my labia, the wings of my cunt. I reach for her with my hands, my mouth, my thighs, my great swollen powerful cunt.

Her teeth are set, hips are thrusting, shoving, head back, pushing, drawing back and ramming in. I laugh and arch up into her, curse her, beg her. My feet are planted. I can do anything. I lift my belly, push up even more. Fucking, fucking, fucking. I call this fucking. Call her lover, bastard, honey, sweetheart, nasty motherfucker, evil-hearted bitch, YOU GODDAMNED CUNT! She calls me her baby, her girl, her toy, her lover, hers, hers, hers. Tells me she will never stop, never let me go. I beg her. "Fuck me. Hard," I beg her. "You, you, you...hard! Goddamn you! Do it! Don't stop! Don't stop! Don't stop! Don't stop!"

Jesus fucking christ don't stop.

Don't stop.

I have been told that lesbians don't do this. Perhaps we are not lesbians? She is a woman. I am a woman. But maybe we are aliens? Is what we do together a lesbian act?

Paul took me out for coffee in New York and gave me a little silver claw holding a stone. "A little something for that poem of yours," he told me. "The one about the joy of faggots. I've been reading it everywhere." He drank herbal tea and told me about his travels, reading poetry and flirting with the tender young boys at all the universities, going on and on about how they kneel in the front row and look up to him, their lips gently parted and their legs pressed together. Sipping tea he told me, "They're wearing those loose trousers again, the ones with the pleats that always remind me of F. Scott Fitzgerald and lawn parties."

I drank the bitter coffee, admired his narrow mustache, and told him how much I hate those blouson pants women are wearing instead of jeans. "It's hell being an ass woman these days," I joked.

He started to laugh, called me a lech, looked away, looked back, and I saw there were tears in his eyes. Said, "Yes, those jeans, tight, shaped to the ass, worn to a pale blue-white and torn, like as not showing an asscheek paler still." Said, "Yes, all those boys, those years, all the men in tight-tight pants." Said, "Yes, those jeans, the pants so tight their cocks were clearly visible on the bus, the subway, the street, a shadow of a dick leading me on. Sometimes I would just lightly brush them, and watch them swell under the denim, the dick lengthening down the thigh." He stopped, tears all over his face, his hand on his cup shaking, coming up in the air to gesture. A profound sad movement of loss. "All gone," he whispered, the romantic poet in his suede professor's jacket. "I never do it anymore, never.

Never touch them, those boys. Can't even imagine falling in love again, certainly not like I used to for twenty minutes at a time on any afternoon."

I started to speak, but he put his hand up. "Don't say it. Don't tell me I'm being foolish or cowardly or stupid or anything. I loved the way it used to be and I hate the fact that it's gone. I've not become celibate, or silly, or vicious, or gotten religion, or started lecturing people in bars. It's those memories I miss, those boys on the street in the afternoon laughing and loving each other, that sense of sex as an adventure, a holy act."

He put his cup down, glared at it and then at me. Indignant, excited, determined. "But you still do it, don't you? You dykes! You're out there all the time doing it. Flirting with each other, touching, teasing, jerking each other off in bathrooms, picking each other up and going to parties. Fucking and showing off and doing it everywhere you can. You are. Say you are. I know you are."

I said, "Yes." I lied and said, "Yes, Paul, we are. Yes."

She has named her cock Bubba. Teases me with it. Calls it him, says, "Talk to him, pet him. He's gonna go deep inside you." I start to giggle, slap Bubba back and forth. Cannot take this too seriously, even though I really do like it when she straps him on. Bubba is fat and bent, an ugly pink color not found in nature, and he jiggles obscenely when she walks around the room. Obscene and ridiculous, still he is no less effective when she puts herself between my legs. Holding Bubba in one hand I am sure that this is the origin of irony—that men's penises should look so funny and still be so prized.

She is ten years younger than me. . . sometimes. Sometimes I am eight and she is not born yet, but the ghost of her puts a hand on my throat, pinches my clit, bites my breast. The ghost of her teases me, tells me how much she loves all my perversities. She says she was made for me, promises me sincerely that she will always want me. Sometimes I believe her without effort. Sometimes I become her child, trusting, taking in everything she says. Her flesh, her body, her lust and hunger—I believe. I believe, and it is not a lie. When I am fucking her I am a thousand years old, a crone with teeth, bone teeth grinding, vibrating down into my own hips. Old and mean and hungry as a wolf, or a shark. She is a suckling infant, soft in my hands, trusting me with her tender open places. Her mouth parts like an oyster, the lower lip soft under the tongue, the teeth pearls in the dim light. Her eyes are deep and dark and secret. She is pink, rose, red, going purple dark...coming with a cry and a shudder, and suddenly limp beneath my arms. I push up off her and bite my own wrist. It is all I can do not to feed at her throat.

I drank too much wine at a party last fall, found myself quoting Muriel Rukeyser to Geoff Maines, all about the backside, the body's ghetto, singing her words, "Never to go despising the asshole nor the useful shit that is our clean clue to what we need."

"The clitoris in her least speech,"* he sang back, and I loved him for that with all my soul. We fed each other fat baby carrots and beamed at our own enjoyment.

"Ah, the ass," Geoff intoned, "the temple of the gods." I giggled, lifted a carrot in a toast, matched his tone. "And the sphincter —gateway to the heart."

He nodded, licked his carrot, reached down, shifted a strap, and inserted that carrot deftly up his butt. He looked up at me, grinned, rolled a carrot in my direction, raised one eyebrow. "Least speech," I heard myself tell him. Then I hiked up my skirt and disappeared that carrot, keeping my eyes on his all the while. There was something about his expression, a look of arrogant conviction that I could not resist.

"Lesbians constantly surprise me," was all Geoff said, lining up a row of little baby carrots from the onion dip to the chips, pulling the dish of butter over as well. He handed me another carrot.

---

*"Despisals" by Muriel Rukeyser in *The Collected Poems of Muriel Rukeyser* (McGraw-Hill: New York, 1982)

I blinked, then watched as he took one for himself. "I propose the carrot olympics, a cross-gender, mutually queer event," he challenged. I started to laugh as he rolled buttery carrots between his palms. His face was full of laughter, his eyes so blue and pleased with himself they sparkled. "All right," I agreed. How could I not? I pulled up the hem of my skirt, tucked it into my waistband, took up the butter, and looked Geoff right in the eye. "Dead heat, or one on one?"

FAGGOT! That's what he called me. The boy on the street with the baseball bat who followed me from Delores Park the week after I moved to San Francisco. He called me a faggot. My hair is long. My hips are wide. I wear a leather jacket and walk with a limp. But I carry a knife. What am I exactly? When he called me a faggot I knew. I knew for sure who I was and who I would not be. From the doorway of the grocery at 18th and Guerrero I yelled it at him. "Dyke! Get it right, you son-of-a-bitch, I'm a dyke."

I am angry all the time lately, and being angry makes me horny, makes me itchy, makes me want to shock strangers and surprise the girls who ask me, please, out for coffee and to talk. I don't want to talk. I want to wrestle in silence. It isn't sex I want when I am like this. It's the intimacy of their bodies, the inside of them, what they are afraid I might see if I look too close. I look too close. I write it all down. I intend that things shall be different in my lifetime, if not in theirs.

Paul, Geoff—I am doing it as much as I can, as fast as I can. This holy act. I am licking their necks on Market Street, fisting them in the second floor bathroom at Amelia's, in a booth under a dim wall lamp at the Box—coming up from her cunt a moment before the spotlight shifts to her greedy features. I have tied her to a rail in a garage down on Howard Street, let her giggle and squirm while I teased her clit, then filled her mouth with my sticky fingers and rocked her on my hipbone till she roared. We have roared together. Everywhere I go, the slippery scent of sweat and heat is in the air, so strong it could be me or the women I follow, the ones who follow me. They know who I am just as I know them. I have ripped open their jeans at the Powerhouse, put my heel between their legs at the Broadway Café, opened their shirts all the way down at Just Desserts, and pushed seedless grapes into their panties at the Patio Café. The holy act of sex, my sex, done in your name, done for the only, the best reason. Because we want it.

I am pushing up off the bed into Alix's neck like a great cat with a gazelle in her teeth. I am screaming and not stopping, not stopping. Frog fucking, pussy creaming, ass clenching, drumming out, pumping in. I am doing it, boys and girls, I am doing it, doing it all the time.

An earlier version of this piece was first performed in 1989 as part of The Body in Context, a performance and art series at Southern Exposure Gallery in San Francisco. It appeared in *All But the Obvious*, the Lesbian Art Show catalog from LACE in Los Angeles in 1990, and is included in *Leatherfolk*, edited by Mark Thompson (Alyson: Boston, 1991).

The Theory and Practice of the Strap-on Dildo

"**H**ey, girl!" The woman running toward me up the train platform waved one arm frantically while pulling a bright red backpack up with the other. The backpack almost fell down her arm again when she caught me and hugged me tight. "You look terrific!"

I laughed and pushed her away from me a little. All around us people were pausing to stare, then moving on. Sweet Pris looked exactly the same as she had the day she turned eighteen and we first made love. Her hair curled loosely toward her high cheekbones and her blue eyes sparkled brightly. The hips under her loose cotton pants were still narrow, her breasts still barely showing under her Indian print blouse. "Aren't you ever gonna grow up?" I kidded her.

Pris hugged me again and pinched my butt. "You wouldn't notice if I did. You're always gonna see me as that silly girl who followed you around the campus. Look here," she said, and put her fingers up to her eyes. Only then did I see the fine lines that crinkled under her lashes.

"Thirty, girl." She grinned like she was proud of herself. "I'm thirty now, and you better start treating me with some respect."

"OK, lady." I took her elbow and started steering her up the ramp toward the station. "Tell me why you'd make a special trip up to New York City to rendezvous with your nasty old girlfriend."

Pris almost stumbled, and when I looked at her, I saw she was blushing. She shifted her backpack to the other arm and for the first time seemed to notice all the people passing around us. "Well," she said, and dropped her voice to an embarrassed whisper, "I thought you and I could do some shopping."

"Shopping?"

"Yeah, huh...," Pris blushed more brightly. "Well, you know that time we talked about how you and your girlfriend liked to use things. You know, rubber things, you know di-di-dildos," she stuttered. "...Well, Katy and I, we were thinking we'd like to try some stuff. You know...." Pris stopped. Her face was so red she looked like a winter's elf on a Christmas card.

"You want to buy a dildo?!"

My exclamation startled even me. One doesn't say dildo loudly in Grand Central Station; it attracts attention. I had been too shocked to keep that in mind. Pris had always been adventurous, but not about sex. She was one of those lesbians whose repertoire was limited to tribadism, a practice she mostly preferred done through her karate gi pants. Oral sex had been the most outrageous sex act she would consider when we lived together, and she didn't consider that too often. It wasn't that she thought good sex should wait until after the revolution. Unlike many young lesbians I'd known back then, Pris was very matter-of-fact about the positive role of sex in her life. But she always seemed perfectly happy getting off as quickly and efficiently as possible. Of course, I may have gotten that impression from how often we hurried through lovemaking to run to a meeting. Still, I was surprised. If the woman that a third of Tallahassee still called Sweet Pris was thinking about buying something expressly made for sexual use, then the world had, indeed, changed a lot.

The first time I used a dildo was in 1973 when I persuaded the most obviously butch woman I had ever met to take me to bed. Though I was fairly notorious in our small southern town as a radical feminist lesbian and something of a badly behaved "femme slut," I had the notion that this woman was going to teach me more about sex than I had yet managed to learn. At least I hoped so. With her clear grey eyes above sharp cheekbones, carefully ironed blue jeans, and talent for posturing on the dance floor, Marty was the image of the worldly wise older lesbian. From the moment she curled her fingers in my hair and slipped her tongue between my lips, I knew I was in the arms of a practiced seducer. Fortunately, that was exactly what I was trying to find.

"Oh, baby," Marty hissed into my shivering ear with no self-consciousness, and no hesitation. She rolled me easily down on the couch while distracting me by sliding her teeth gently along the edge of my jaw. There was a moment when I found myself admiring how smoothly she got my jeans off and then a moment of distracted fumbling while I pressed myself up against her, then something cold and rubbery pressed between my legs.

I held still. I had an idea what that was and I wasn't sure I liked it. I tried to move so I could see Marty's hand. But just as determinedly, she kept her body positioned to shield her hands while she nipped at my earlobe and growled in sexy excitement. I wiggled again, thinking about stopping her. Maybe we could discuss this?

But Marty had no intention of stopping to discuss the politics of using a male-identified sexual apparatus. Her rubbery appendage ground enthusiastically at my labia while her other hand and her mouth worked fiercely to get my full attention. In a moment she had it; the woman was as good as I had imagined.

"Oh fuck!" I moaned after a while and never even noticed the first thrust of her stiffened hand.

"Girl! Girl! Girl . . .," she began to chant, fucking me the same way she danced, with grating power and sure coordination. I had never felt anything like what she was doing. The only penetration I had ever explored had been limited to a few fingers and yes, a tender zucchini I had once employed as an experiment. The toy in her hand was as far past my vegetable encounter as sex itelf was beyond fantasy. The fact that, in my mind at least, it also seemed slightly forbidden and nasty only added to its power.

"Mama!" I screamed when I came, and Marty laughed in my ear, rocking on her own fist between my thighs, and giving one sharp "Damn!" to indicate her own orgasm. Then she lay still for a moment before hiding her "thing" back under the couch.

"No, no," I complained. "I want to see it."

"No, you don't," she insisted, grabbing my hand to keep me from reaching for it. I wrestled with her playfully and insisted that I did, too, want to see it. The idea scandalized her. It took me quite a while to get my hands on Marty's toy—a toy that turned out to be a large-size glove finger stuffed with cotton. Her ingenuity impressed me but clearly embarrassed her. For her, half the power of her rubber cock lay in its mystery. Sex itself was supposed to be mysterious, and good little femmes didn't insist on seeing, and handling, their butch's dildos.

All my desire to seduce Marty, and the whole world of butch/femme sexuality aside, I had no intention of behaving like a good femme if it meant limiting my own sexual horizons. Marty and I parted less than amiably after she told me I was letting my feminism prevent me from exploring my "womanly" needs. At the time, my greatest regret was that I was losing one of the best sex partners I had ever found. My second regret was that she retained custody of her dick.

Since I truly believed that only older butch lesbians actually had dildos, I adjusted to the idea of doing without one. But within a surprisingly short period of time, in which I talked about my fascination with that mysterious appendage, I found half a dozen other women who used dildos—some acquired on shopping trips up North and others homemade, like the one that had so surprised me. At least two of my lovers used rubber devices they had found in a pet store, something I was reminded of when I learned that dildos in Texas are sold as animal retrieval toys. Most were just as cautious about showing their toys in bright light as Marty had been, and not a few spent a lot of time telling me that the fact that they used such toys did not make them male-identified. It's not the equipment, they insisted, it's what you do with it. I wasn't too sure about that detail myself. After all, I liked the feel of the things. What did that say about me?

Carey was the first woman I found, before 1979, who used a harness with her dildo. She was openly contemptuous of butch/femme sexuality and very righteous about her own feminist credentials. She didn't seem to harbor the slightest fears that she might be male-identified because of the way she liked to fuck. She called herself a feminist lesbian with the emphasis on lesbian and she liked to strap her harness on me as much as she liked to wear it. Sometimes we would even quarrel over who got to wear it first.

Carey had stitched her harness up out of a couple of old belts and carpet thread. She'd etched a labrys into the front piece that held the dildo she purchased from a mail-order supplier. Years later when I saw a "slave harness" in the Pleasure Chest catalog, the first thing I thought of was Carey's hand-stitched dildo harness. The design was remarkably similar and worked better than any harness I subsequently discovered.

The dildo Carey used had come with a harness attached. Three elastic straps trailed from the base of it, one that went down between her legs and two that wrapped around her hips. The elastic had a tendency to snap loose any time Carey became too excited. She'd rigged her belt harness in frustration after getting snapped on the ass every time she or her partner approached an orgasm. The last time it happened, Carey had jumped up and cut the elastic straps off angrily. Taking an old pair of blue-jeans shorts, she'd poked a hole in the crotch with the scissors and then shoved the dildo through the hole. Pulling them on she'd returned to bed, full of pride at her own invention. The makeshift harness had worked wonderfully, except that it completely prevented Carey's partner from getting to her clit. The next day Carey had sat down with her old belts and begun to put together the lesbian equivalent of the wheel. After we started sleeping together I brought her back a better dildo from a trip to Washington, but I could never get her to sew me up a harness of my own. She seemed to have an intuition that I would use it with other women.

I bought my first dildo and harness in New York later that year. The dildo was similar to the one Carey had bought by mail years earlier, and like Carey, I found the harness tended to interfere with passion by coming apart every time I tried to really use it. Worse, it pinched and itched and never seemed to hold the dildo in the position I wanted it. Asking around, I found that many of the women who would admit to using one had the same problem. Only a few of my friends would discuss the subject at all. In 1979, the idea of using dildos was still anathema to most feminist lesbians. *Male-identified* was a bigger insult than ever.

I went shopping for something that would work as good as Carey's homemade delight and discovered the "slave harnesses" sold to gay men in the men's leather shops. Unlike the elastic and rubber belts with the little dildos available from mail-order catalogs—the ones that always reminded me of menstrual belts—these harnesses held up under the most strenuous sex play. Once the steel cock ring that would ordinarily be slipped over a man's penis was removed and a rubber one substituted, the harness would snugly hold a dildo comfortably against a woman's mons venus. A little practice with this harness could even make mutual orgasm a possibility since the back of the dildo in the cock ring rubbed just above the clitoris of the woman wearing the harness.

After I started talking about my discovery, I became an underground authority on such devices. Dozens of my friends asked me to help them buy a harness like mine. What I have been most surprised by is the range of women who use strap-on dildos. Contrary to mythology and my earliest experiences, it's not only butch/femme couples who are into such toys. Nor is it just s/m or leather women. I've even heard from an old friend, a vegetarian and animal rights activist, who uses a canvas harness remarkably similar to the leather ones. She adapted it from a truss she got at a yard sale.

With the wider discussions of sexual behavior in the lesbian community in the past few years, more women have been coming out about their enjoyment of penetration and penetration devices. That doesn't mean dildos have become respectable, but they are far more common. Women who like them take the same care in communicating their desire as lesbians once took in identifying themselves as lesbians. Women who don't even believe in the G-spot will bring the subject up in order to talk about penetration.

It's also not uncommon to find women who collect several dildos of different sizes. My friend Jeanny has five in graduated sizes. "Sometimes the little one's just right, you know. But then there are those days when I feel like I could take anything. It's kind of like the ocean and the tides," she mused, stroking her largest dildo. "Maybe it has something to do with the seasons."

Jeanny also has a number of harnesses, including one that fits her and one that fits her current girlfriend, though she really doesn't like wearing one as much as being fucked by another woman. "It's only fair," she tells me. "You've got to give if you want to get."

"Sounds about right," I agreed. A better statement of egalitarian sexuality I've never heard.

For a moment on that train platform my friend Pris seemed as if she wanted to drop right through the floor. Then she took a deep breath and looked me right in the eye. I remembered how quick she had always been to take a dare.

"That's right," she said loudly, obviously surprising herself. "I want a dildo." She paused and had a look around. "And a harness for it," she added in a slightly lower tone. She kept her eyes level with mine, but her blush didn't fade. A man in a blue business suit bumped her slightly as he tried to pass us. Pris stepped out of his way and her grin returned. "Actually, I want to get two or three— different sizes you know, and at least two harnesses—a leather one for me like the one you showed me in Atlanta, and a canvas one or something for Katy. She's gotten real serious about being a vegetarian lately. Do they make them in canvas?"

The man in the blue suit stared at her incredulously. Pris gave him one of her finest shit-eating grins and put her arm around me again. "Why don't you just take me shopping and show me all those sex toys you're always talking about?"

I gave the man my own friendly nod and smiled into Pris's eager face. "Sure, honey," I told her. "We'll get you the finest strap-on cock New York City has to offer." Neither of us glanced back as we went up the platform toward the street.

This essay appeared in _Forum_ in Spring 1985.

Conceptual Lesbianism

I'm not yet a lesbian, the letter began. Not yet? I passed the page over to my friend Jan. "What the hell do you think this is supposed to mean? You think maybe it's something she hasn't gotten around to, like putting henna in her hair or trimming her toenails? Or maybe she thinks of lesbianism as a trip she's always planned to take—like a day trip out to Coney Island or a really complicated expedition to the Himalayas, or maybe Montana?"

Jan gave me one of those looks that clearly expressed she knew I knew what the woman meant, all the different things she had implied. The letter, after all, had been written to accompany a review copy of the woman's book of poetry. And Jan was right. I could easily imagine the woman sitting down with a stack of magazines and newspapers, or a list out of one of the directories of writers and reviewers, wondering how she was going to get anybody interested in excerpting or reviewing her work. Maybe she had come to my name after hours of work and had been feeling both tired and silly. There had probably been different letters for different categories of reviewers, but I doubted she had sent one off to the *Guardian* that said, *I'm not yet a socialist.* Nor could I imagine such a letter from a male writer wherein he would define himself as *not yet a faggot.* Even the radical faeries and men's movement theorists don't talk about conceptual homosexuality as the goal of a heightened sensitivity. But lesbians have had to confront a world of misconceptions, from our teenage years when they tell us it's just a phase, to the last few years when magazines have prominently featured pretty young white female pairs, and suggested that we're all some variation on k.d. lang, Martina Navratilova, or Melissa Etheridge—somehow establishing a notion in the public mind that lesbians are young, healthy, middle-class jocks who can sing.

Ever since I heard the Ti-Grace Atkinson quote about feminism being the theory and lesbianism the practice, I've been uncomfortable with the odd glamour applied to the term *lesbian*. I use the word *glamour* deliberately, since I believe that what has grown up around the concept of lesbianism is not only an illusion of excitement, romance, and power, but an obscuring mystery. Or, as a nasty lady I used to adore would always joke, "When is a lesbian not a lesbian? When she's a feminist!"

In the early days of the women's movement, many women found themselves struck dumb by the accusation of lesbianism: "Ah, you're all a bunch of dykes!" Some of these women made a practical and moral decision to confront the basis of the prejudice. After the first roll of, "Oh no, we're not," they started saying, "So, what if we are?" Or at least some of them did. While parts of the women's movement did everything they could to disassociate themselves from anything remotely queer, just as they continue to do today, other feminists made a conscious and political decision to identify publicly with lesbians. In doing so they brought to question—in a way they had never intended—what it meant to be queer in this society. I am thinking not so much of the attention given to women like Kate Millett, who came out to wild press coverage and attack, but of women like Ti-Grace Atkinson and Robin Morgan. The former framed sex in social/political terms, and the latter insisted on her right to call herself a lesbian (and not a bisexual) while committed to her marriage, husband, and son.

I was in Tallahassee, Florida, in 1974, a photographer's assistant and community activist trying to be a female version of the happy homosexual I had read about. The conceptual war being fought on the issue of lesbianism had a major impact on my life, though at first all I wanted to know was who was really a lesbian and who was not. But I read Ti-Grace Atkinson, Shulamith Firestone, the Furies Collective, and countless raggedy newletters from Radical Feminists and began to rethink who I was and what I could do as a lesbian activist. Eventually my women's group and I decided that Charlotte Bunch's statement, "No woman is free unless she is also free to be a lesbian," was the perfect way to frame women's struggle for autonomy. It did not matter then who was really queer. It only mattered that we all challenge the boundaries of what was acceptable behavior and what was perverse.

Right.

Unfortunately there seemed to be a discrepancy between my personal life and my politics. I discovered, painfully, that this blurring of the definition of lesbianism led to a few problems: regardless of how hard we tried to pretend that there was no difference between women who slept with men and women who slept with women, there did seem to be differences. For one thing, I noticed that although there were lots of lesbians working to get the childcare center established at Florida State University, there were no heterosexuals working to get the same university to recognize the lesbian peer counseling group. Nor were we supposed to identify ourselves as lesbians when we applied for funding for the women's center itself. Very quickly, in fact, *feminist* seemed to become a code word for *lesbian*, at least as far as the heterosexual population of Tallahassee was concerned. At the same time, saying you were a feminist at the local gay bar made many of the older lesbians nervous. "Yeah, but are you a lesbian?" I was asked, and began to suspect that something more than semantics was being confused.

Then I fell in love. Well, it might have been lust. I never got it all sorted out because the passion of the moment ran aground pretty quickly. Joanna was older than I was, served on the board of the women's center and the local land co-op, raised honey bees and goats, and drove a VW van with a sleeping bag perpetually unrolled in the back. She had long hair but wore it tied back all the time and was never seen in anything but blue jeans, high-topped canvas sneakers, and T-shirts. I found her tremendously sexy and tried to tell her so one night after we'd finished putting tile down on the floor of the newly funded daycare center.

"Hnnnn," Joanna's mouth gaped open and her face flushed a dark rose color. She looked away from me and started picking at the frayed cotton threads on the knees of her jeans. I told myself she was shy and sat quietly, waiting for her to get over it.

"I do like you," she said finally, but her voice was uncertain and strained. We both waited. There's no telling how long we might have sat there if my friend Flo hadn't walked in. Joanna jumped up and announced that she had to go feed her goats. Flo looked at me curiously.

"What's wrong with her?" she asked, once Joanna was gone.

I didn't know. For a few weeks I suffered all the miseries of an early Ann Bannon heroine, mooning over Joanna while she avoided me. She must be in love with someone else, I told myself, and she was: a myopic, shaggy-haired guy out at the land co-op who had the plot of land next to Joanna's.

"I'd marry him, except he don't believe in marriage," Joanna told me finally, months after I had stopped tensing up every time she entered the room. "And I do like you," she said again. For the first time I understood the awkward emphasis on the *do*. We were eating pizza and sipping beer at one of the local student hangouts, surrounded by noisy fraternity boys and the celebrating members of the women's volleyball league. Joanna rubbed at her eyebrows with both hands and peered at me nervously. "Thing is, I just couldn't get myself around to doing anything with you. I mean, I can't even think about it without giggling." She promptly giggled. "I mean, I know I should be able to love you as easily as Charlie, make love to you, I mean." I watched that familiar blush creep up from her neck to her eyebrows. "But it just an't happening. You know?"

I nodded. I was feeling almost as embarrassed as she was. I had never slept with a straight woman in my life, and the thought made my stomach flutter. All I could say to Joanna was that the whole thing had been a misunderstanding. I didn't want to tell her that she looked like a dyke; I didn't know how she'd take that, and I didn't want any of my friends to think I had been pursuing her. Maybe if we had done something about it, the idea wouldn't seem so disconcerting to me, but the notion that my tentative flirting had made Joanna's stomach feel the way mine did at that moment—that was simply awful. I watched Joanna take another sip of beer and lean forward.

"But you know something?" she said. "It certainly got Charlie going. He's been just major enthusiastic since I told him."

I felt my own cheeks flame. "You told him about me?"

"No, no." Joanna looked indignant. "I didn't say who. I just kind of told him there was a woman interested in me. He an't got no business knowing who." I felt a little better at that, but she didn't stop. "But he did like the idea. Only I think he likes it more that I didn't do it than if I had. You know?"

Right.

At Sagaris, the feminist institute held in Vermont in 1975, I ran into a number of women who labeled themselves "political lesbians." They didn't actually have sex with women, or at least not with any great enthusiasm. None of them seemed to think that sex was a priority. They loved women and felt like men were pretty hopeless—at least until after the revolution. In fact, one of them told me, maybe all sex is just too problematic right now. She was pretty much celibate, although she felt that she should still call herself a lesbian. Didn't I agree?

I didn't. I was starting to have serious doubts about this whole concept. All right, in 1975 it was painfully obvious that there were

tactical advantages to having all these woman-identified women running around. It seemed to ease the passage of some women through
the coming out process, as well as providing a measure of safety for
those lesbians who could not afford to be publicly out. It also gave
a major theoretical boost to making lesbian rights an issue for organizations like NOW. I liked the theory of the woman-identified
woman, liked watching women make other women the priority in
organizing for civil rights, liked that even heterosexual women were
beginning to see, on a day-to-day level, that treating other women
badly was no longer socially acceptable. I knew that the issues were
connected, but it still made me uncomfortable. All that talk about
the woman-identified woman was taking the sexual edge off lesbianism, and I was sure I didn't like that.

Political lesbians made the concepts of lust, sexual need, and
passionate desire more and more detached from the definition of lesbian. The notion that lesbians might actually be invested in having
orgasms with other lesbians, that lesbians might like to fuck and suck
and screw around as much as gay men or heterosexuals, became
anathema.

By the late seventies, I was tracking the progress of the spiritual
lesbian, a close cousin of the political lesbian, perfectly woman-
identified and adamant about what was and was not acceptable practice for the rest of us. She wasn't goal-oriented (didn't really care
if she came, just liked to cuddle), didn't objectify other women (never
squeezed her lover's ass and breathed, ''God, I'd love to get my
hands in your pants''), and didn't lie awake nights mourning her
inability to find true love or her constant obsession with sex and the
lack of it in her life. The spiritual lesbian was a theoretical creature
and a lesson to us all, not about what we were but what we must
not be.

This stuff gets confusing. I remember going to political gath-
erings—right now I'm thinking of the matriarchy conference in New
York City in 1979—where lesbians were accorded a kind of rarified
status for their detachment from males, and male-identified precepts,

which seemed roughly equivalent to a state of grace. But much like the state of grace I was taught about in Baptist Sunday school, the one ascribed to lesbians was pretty ephemeral and unsubstantial. It evaporated as soon as one displayed any actual sexual desire, since lust seemed to be evidence of male-identification. At that same conference, I watched one of the speakers become extremely indignant at a lesbian who raised questions from the floor, a young woman whose main affront appeared to be the fact that she was wearing a buttondown shirt and a tie.

"I think we're in trouble," I told a friend standing with me after the woman with the tie walked out followed by half a dozen women easily recognizable to me as not-at-all theoretical lesbians, but she just smiled. "When are we not?" she joked, and she was right.

The theoretical lesbian was everywhere all through the eighties, and a lot of times I could have sworn she was straight. Speaking on college campuses, identifying myself as a feminist and a lesbian but not an antipornography activist, I kept running into young women who knew who the lesbian was. The lesbian was the advanced feminist, that rare and special being endowed with social insight and political grace. I argued that there was a gap between their theory and my reality—that there were lots of lesbians who fucked around, read pornography, voted Republican (a few anyway), and didn't give a damn about the National Organization for Women. The lesbian you're talking about, I would try to explain, is the rage of all women, perhaps, but the lust of few. Real lesbians are not theoretical constructs. We have our own history, our own issues and agendas, and complicated sex lives, completely separate from heterosexuality, and just as embattled and difficult for straight society to accept as they ever were.

I do not believe that identity is conceptual. I am a lesbian and a feminist. I am not a paragon of political virtue, not endowed with an innate sense of feminist principles. My political convictions are hard-won and completely rooted in my everyday life. I can't sing. My hand and eye coordination is terrible; I'm legally blind for driving purposes. I am way past young, not very healthy, born working-poor and fighting hard to acquire a middle-class patina, but seem unable to change any of my working-class attitudes and convictions. I have never been monogamous, except in a de facto fashion these last few years when I just don't have the time and energy for any serious flirting. Contrary to rumor and assumption, I don't hate men. I have never found them sexually interesting, though. I cannot imagine falling in love with a man. Nor do I believe that sexual orientation is something one can construct, that people can just decide to be lesbians or decide not to be—for political, religious, or philosophical reasons—no matter how powerful. I don't know if sexual preference and identity is genetic or socially constructed. I suspect it's partly both, but I do believe that there are people who are queer and people who are not, and that forcing someone to change their innate orientation is a crime—whether that orientation is homosexuality, lesbianism, bisexuality, or heterosexuality. I believe that sexual desire is a powerful emotion and a healthy one. I'm pretty sure that when anyone acknowledges and acts on their desire, it does us all some good—even if only by giving other people permission to act on their desire—that it is sexual repression that warps desire and hurts people.

All of these statements sound very simple, almost trivial, but it is a simple fact that telling the truth, making simple statements of fact about your identity and beliefs—particularly when they don't match up with existing social prejudices—can get people attacked, maligned, or murdered.

Some of the material in this essay first appeared in the *New York Native* on February 27, 1983 in an article entitled "Is the Spirit Willing?"

Talking to Straight People

In 1981, three of us went to Yale. We went as the guests of our friend Jean, who was teaching a class in Issues for Contemporary Women and asked us if we would be willing to come up from the City and be visiting lesbians for her students. Stephanie, Claudia, and I had agreed easily. We thought the idea of being imported lesbians for Jean's class hilarious, an adventure, kind of like being outside agitators from an earlier era. On the train we teased each other about our qualifications for the role, and then nervously addressed the matter of what questions we might be asked and how we should present ourselves.

"You realize we are about to become these people's idea of female homosexuals," Claudia said to me, and for a moment I wasn't sure if she was teasing or not. Claudia, Stephanie, and Jean are old friends, ex-college buddies, while Stephanie and I had known each other for just over a year. We met when we both took jobs at an arts organization in New York City and discovered that we shared the same critical sense of humor and a similar weakness for sarcastic remarks in staff meetings. I met Jean when Stephanie introduced us, and I liked her immediately. She was the kind of tough, no-nonsense individual I admire. Only Claudia was a mystery to me. I could never tell whether she was serious or making a joke. She had a habit of looking me straight in the eye and still implying that she was somehow not quite serious. Perhaps that's because she thinks partly in Portuguese, having grown up in Brazil, the daughter of Christian missionaries.

"Wait until Jean comes out to them at the last class," Stephanie laughed. "That might shake them up, if they don't know already."

"Oh, if only these straight people realized how many of us there are in the world."

"*We* don't know how many of us there are. There might even be a dyke or two in Jean's class, and we'll never know."

"Don't get too passionate about it," Steph warned. "From what Jean said, it's a pretty small class—around a dozen."

"Then they're not going to gang up on us." Claudia looked like she was ready to giggle. "They're going to be scared of us. We're going to be the big, bad lesbians from New York City."

"Not too bad, please." Stephanie looked uncomfortable. "I don't want you telling lies about all the women you wished you'd slept with."

I just smiled. The wrinkle in Jean's plan was the simple detail that Stephanie and Jean have been lovers on and off for years, but when we got in the classroom they were going to pretend just to be good friends. I wasn't sure they could pull this off. Actually, I was nervous about all of them. I'd done this performance before, spoken on feminism and sexuality at everything from Sunday school meetings to juvenile detention centers, but Claudia and Stephanie hadn't, and Jean was a teacher with that attendant aura of untouchable authority. I worried that they were going to become self-conscious or defensive when the questions got personal, and I was pretty sure that people always got personal on the subject of lesbian sexuality.

"What's Jean's position in the school?" I asked. "They know she's queer, right? And she thinks this is a good idea?"

"Jean knows what she's doing," Steph told me. "She's a great teacher, award-winning and all that, and she says this is a really terrific bunch. It's mostly older people getting back into school after working or raising families, lots of women. So far they've done well with Gladys—you know, the lawyer for the sexual harassment program—and Abby, who did a really tough presentation on Black feminism. They're not going to come undone over a few dykes. Besides," she added, "if anybody does get smart, I'll just turn on my Bella Abzug run-em-over act and blow them away."

"Oh, sure," I laughed. Steph looks so sweet and mild-mannered, like a Jewish female version of Clark Kent. It's hard to imagine her switch to superdyke, which is why when she actually does turn on that fast-talking, emotional bulldozer self, she is so effective. I'd seen her reduce kissy-mouthed New York construction workers to open-mouthed stuttering boys.

"Don't worry," Steph kept repeating, "they're going to love us."

"You realize," I had warned Steph when we'd first discussed the trip, "I have been known to say inappropriate things, particularly when I lose my temper."

"You are not going to lose your temper," she told me. "We're just going to talk about ourselves, let them know what lesbians are like as real people."

It had sounded fine at first, but on the train up to New Haven, we reconsidered. After all, Claudia pointed out, there were only three of us to represent all the lesbians in the world. Stephanie nodded, looking suddenly pale and uncertain. "Yeah, they're gonna think whatever we say applies to every lesbian they ever meet. We could really screw up, guys."

Claudia pulled out a notebook and started making lists. "I think we should choose which aspect of ourselves we want to emphasize. I can talk about growing up in Brazil."

"Just don't get off on your parents. This isn't supposed to be about your critique of Imperialist Christianity."

"Well, don't you start going on about all that Yankees don't know about Southerners."

"All right. All right."

Steph took Claudia's notebook. "I think this will be easy. We can exaggerate our personalities a little, not repeat the same stuff, and really make some strong points. How about you be the radical feminist activist, make the political arguments, and I be the romantic barfly?"

"Oh, no," I laughed. "I don't think you know how to do that one."

"I'm as much a romantic as you are. Besides, all they're going to want to talk about is sex and relationships."

"No, it's Yale. They're going to have an analysis."

"Well, I don't care." Claudia looked like she was losing patience with the whole plan. "I'm going to talk about my own life. They need to know that there are lesbians who are still lesbians even when they're not involved in a relationship. Might be an antidote to all that romanticism you two talk all the time."

"Well, don't get tragic." Steph started putting away her list. "We're coming into the station." She looked over at me. "You think it's all right if I play the romantic, the one who's done it all for love?"

"Why not?" I grinned over at Claudia. "What do you think, should I go into detail about how much I mess around?"

"Who could stop you?"

Jean picked us up in her ancient Chevy station wagon with the blanket seat covers. She looked eminently respectable in her dress-for-success pantsuit and betrayed not a shred of nervousness. Giving Steph a quick kiss, she hurried us into the car and off toward campus. "You guys are late," she explained. "We've got to hurry."

"Well, we've talked it all out and know what we're gonna do." Claudia pulled her brush out and started working on her tangled hair. "I've even got a little list. Want to tell them about the time I was let go and couldn't prove they picked me first 'cause I was a dyke."

"Queer jokes," I said. "I want to talk about what it's like to have to listen to straight people's ideas of what's funny about us."

"Oh, God, I'm nervous as a cat. Think I need a drink."

"Oh, let's not play into that. They think we're all alcoholics as it is."

"Come on you guys." Jean was almost laughing, but keeping

her eyes on the road. "You sound like you're scared to death. This is going to be fun."

Yale made the back of my neck go tight. The place looked like a Disney version of a Gothic compound, massive stonework and bushy ivy. "Bet they turn out a lot of lawyers here," I told Claudia. "Business administrators," she said, but Stephanie snorted at us.

"Nothing so predictable." Her hand drew a circle around Jean's head and her own. "We're what you get here, too. Philosophers, language scholars, social workers, English majors, a few women's studies rebels, everything you can imagine—along with the second sons of the rich and powerful."

I looked up as we drove under yet another stone arch. "Where do the first sons go?" I asked.

Stephanie and Jean replied in unison, "Harvarrrrrd!," drawing the word out in a parody of a Boston accent. Claudia and I both laughed, and for the first time, we all relaxed.

The class was almost an anticlimax. There were fewer than a dozen people there, and it was more a conversation than a confrontation. One young woman had brought her sister, who stared at us intensely but said nothing. One of the two men in the class came in late, dressed in a three-piece suit and shiny shoes. He blushed pink as soon as Jean introduced us, and stayed pink until he left. But the two older women kept telling us how happy they were we had made the trip.

"My niece is a lesbian," one of them said with a tentative expression and no little pride. She looked around at her classmates as if she expected them to be shocked. "She lives out in San Francisco and every year she rides a motorcycle in the Gay Pride parade there. This year she sent me a picture to prove it." She passed the photo around and seemed disappointed that no one expressed any recognition—or shock. When the snapshot came to me, I glanced down to see a skinny intense-looking young woman in a fringed leather vest. The girl's hair was shaved close to her head. Her left ear seemed completely encrusted in earrings.

"Quite striking," I said, and was rewarded with a huge beaming smile.

None of us looked as exotic as the woman's niece, and I could see that some of the students were disappointed at that fact. It reminded me of the last time I went home to see my sister. Her little girl wanted to know what happened to the woman I was dating with the purple hair. My mama had showed them a picture of the two of us in the New York Gay Pride march, for which my friend Leslie had bleached and tinted her high, bushy Mohawk. The photo had made Mama laugh at the same time it completely fascinated all the children in the family. "Bring her home," they insisted. "We want to meet the one with the hair." If I had wanted to make them all completely happy, I should have bleached and two-toned my own hair. Neighbors would have probably come around from blocks away, and my nieces would have taken me to school for show-and-tell. Like Jean's students, my sisters' children always seem disappointed that I look "normal."

Reflexively, I started telling that story to Jean's class and saw smiles and nods go around the room. In a moment, everyone was talking. Our careful planning evaporated. Stephanie forgot she was supposed to be the romantic and started discussing political theory. Claudia talked so quietly and so intently about her childhood that all the women in the class were leaning forward to hear her every word. I kept waiting for someone to ask us, "But what do you do in bed?" They were too sophisticated for that, though, which meant I didn't get to pronounce my slow drawl of "Everything!"

They did hit all the other old familiar questions. "Were you ever involved with a man?" "Do you believe in true love?" "Do you want children?" "Do you hate men?" I liked the one about true love, but it was man-hating that got the discussion hot. As soon as it came up, one of the older women snapped, "Oh come on! How can you ask that?"

Claudia waved one hand in the air to get everyone's attention.

"I think that's a myth," she announced. "There is no lesbian in the world that could hate men the way straight women do." She told me later that she was about to add, "They have so much more opportunity," but before she could say anything else, one of the students jumped in. "Maybe lesbians have more room to see men dispassionately, not having to fight them off all the time."

"Oh, you think?" Stephanie looked suddenly flushed. "Most men don't know we're lesbians. Most men think we're just like every other woman they've ever met—prey."

"Oh, come on now." The pink-faced guy in the suit looked almost hurt. "You talk like men act like dogs all the time."

"They do." It was the woman sitting next to him, and her voice dripped venom.

"Exactly." This time it was an equally flushed young woman on the other side of the room.

Jean stepped in. "I think," she said in her soft firm voice, "we might just agree that this is a very difficult time for men and women to have comfortable relationships."

"That's a fact," said one of the women in the print dresses. "Way things are, it's a wonder any of us ever hook up at all."

I looked around the room at all the nodding flushed pink faces, and for the first time in my life began to consider how hard it must be to be heterosexual. To my right, Stephanie and Claudia seemed as if they might be thinking much the same thing. Claudia dropped her chin and stage-whispered to me, "Sure am glad I'm a lesbian." There was a moment's silence, and then the whole room began to laugh in response.

Curiously, the more rational, friendly, and open the discussion became, the more disappointed I was. It felt as if our energy and worry had been wasted. Also, I realized that throughout our surprisingly comfortable performance, Stephanie was very carefully not looking at Jean, and Jean, equally carefully, was not putting any direct questions to Steph. The students smiled and nodded, as if the whole subject of lesbians and lesbianism was interesting but not terribly exceptional. I might have felt the same way, except for the fact that Jean still hadn't told them she was a lesbian, and certainly had no intention of bringing them face to face with the idea of Stephanie as her one-time lover. I found myself trying to imagine a context in which a homosexual community would import a little group of polite well-behaved heterosexuals to debunk all our myths about them. Surely we have some myths about them, I thought, watching a woman still fingering that snapshot of the San Francisco Dyke. But they're not in hiding. We are the aliens in their country, not they in ours, studying them constantly for the simple necessity of our own survival.

When straight people wear their tolerant expressions, I am reminded of Baptist Sunday school sermons from when I was a child in South Carolina. The preacher would talk about hating the sin but not the sinner, a line that has since become a cliché, but one that even back then I did not trust. I remember watching his face, shiny-pink and stern, and knowing that he did not make any such distinction. It was like the conversation I had with a relatively mild conservative lady from Houston. She was looking at the table of feminist journals I was selling and looking at me with the most awkward expression of polite distaste.

"I know," she said, "you must be a fine young woman, and you think you can't help yourself." Her face was very patient, very Christian. "But my dear," she concluded, "I will always think your life is a tragedy."

I couldn't help myself. I leaned forward and deliberately touched her, taking her hand. "I understand," I said. "And it's sad. That's just what I could say to you."

Part of this essay appeared in the *New York Native* on March 8, 1981 as "Three of All the Lesbians in the World."

Femme

"**I**'m in my femme phase," I always tell them. And they look back at me, those women with the muscley arms and indifferent expressions —at the hair swinging on my shoulders, my two-inch glass dangle earrings, and the silver filigree chain around my throat—and, to a woman, they smile. Each is sure she understands just what I mean. I always sip my wine and grin, knowing they understand nothing at all, and for once not really caring. None of them takes note of the garrison belt cinching in my shorts, the thick silver ring on my left little finger, the narrow glance I give them over my grin. These are such polite women, mostly "political" in that way only lesbian-feminists of a certain age can claim to be. They are so soft-spoken that they seem almost nonsexual to me, and half their charm revealed when they prove how wrong I am.

There isn't one among them who understands what I am really saying when I speak in that code, when I swing my hair and talk about how femme I've become.

I used to code it, say, "I like my women tough." I would be down at the women's bookstore sipping seltzer and hanging out before the reading began. Or over at the clinic leaning back in a plastic chair after an hour of fruitless waiting for a doctor. Or in the showers at the gym, squatting down to rest my thighs after trying to prove just how tough I can be. No matter. It was always the same. Someone would joke about the spring atmosphere and how it had triggered new romances. Someone would stare at me intently. Once my friend Leslie actually leaned over and gave me a push. "Everything is so sexual to you," she said.

Uh-huh. She was right. I have always been this way—wanting, needing. But I didn't use to talk about it so explicitly, admit it so readily. I had one of those quiet childhoods, delayed adolescence. I did not become sexually active until I was past twenty and I suffered then from a sense of permanent deprivation—as if all the sexual adventures I never had were out there, taunting me, waiting to take place.

So I do like tough women, butch women, big, confident, strong women. I like to twist and turn and roll my fingers down my lover's hips, pull her open vulva to my mouth and work at it, the art and act of pleasing her. And when she turns to me, I like to scream when I feel the burning heat of her skin on mine. It is then that every part of me opens and sound naturally happens, the sounds not of passion but of joy. Satisfaction. Determined grown-up satisfaction that denies silence, all silences, most particularly the long silence of my girlhood, the denial of a lesbian girlchild who was never meant to survive.

I grew up in a household of contrasts. The women in my family were almost always pregnant, and remarkably outspoken about sex. "He's not worth the trouble it takes to get his pants off," they used to say about one of my uncles, while Aunt Dot, for whom I was named, had a way of nodding in a man's direction and holding her hands out about four inches apart, then pursing her lips to make a mournfully sad sound. It never failed to make the man blush and the rest of us laugh, even the cousins, those of us too young to quite understand.

My cousins, like my aunts, turned up pregnant with remarkable regularity. They'd leave school at fourteen or fifteen to sit on the porch with their swelling bellies and offer advice to us younger ones. "You're going to have to pay for it, sure as shit," they'd say, "so you better goddamn enjoy it while you can."

I wanted to do them proud, enjoy it and pay only what I would have to pay, in the family tradition. But I had no interest in those dangly parts all my boy cousins were so proud to expose. I knew early how peculiar I was, with the sweat that came when one of my cousins put her hand on my inner thigh and stroked and giggled. I dreamed about it for days after, sweating heavier every time.

"Only boys make babies," my cousin told me. "Messing with yourself won't do it. Though maybe you shouldn't do that too much." She didn't say why not. But no one needed to tell me anything about how I shouldn't sweat over my girl cousins. It was known. I found the words in the books my stepfather hid between the mattress and the box springs. The words were there with the pictures and the terror. *Dykes, queers, sex.* They'd beat me up and leave me, fuck me up and hate me. I'd wind up in a mental hospital, never get a job, have to be supported by the family for the rest of time, and anyway, never, never amount to anything. I wanted to grow up to be smart, rich, educated, and independent. I wanted to go as far away as possible from the bare dirt that marked the front yard of every house we ever lived in. Mama nodded, encouraged me, and somehow along the way, sex and bare dirt yards got confused. Mortally confused.

"She'll pay for it the rest of her life," Mama said when Debbie, the cousin who had always seemed so sensible, started staying out late and telling dirty stories. "It's not worth it. Just not worth it."

Sex was dangerous, a trap, trashy as drinking whiskey in a paper cup or telling dirty stories in a loud whisper. Sex was a sure sign of having nothing better to hope for. "You're different," my mama said, her hand on the back of my head squeezing love into my brain, but her voice was sad enough to break my heart.

"Look at her," Mama said. "By the time you're out of college, her kids will be old enough to have kids themselves." It was a fact. It only took fourteen years to grow a girl up big enough to make girls. Hadn't my mama proved that? Twenty days past her fifteenth birthday, delivering me, just another baby girl?

I would not do that, I decided firmly. When my younger sister began giggling and putting her hair up in curls, I went out and got a city library card and pinned my hair straight back close to my scalp. I was never without a book until it became a family joke. When my aunts told dirty stories on the porch, they'd chase off all the other kids but leave me. "Dorothy's not interested," they'd say, and I'd hunch deeper into the pages of my book, pretending not to listen.

Sometimes they talked about women like me. I had one wild aunt who never made babies, who drove a truck and helped out my uncles in the furnace business, worked sometimes as a mechanic out at the air base. She wore overalls and put her hair under a farmer's cap. Sometimes my other aunts would tell stories about her, make jokes about how she was "drying out."

"If you don't use it, you lose it."

A boy in my eighth-grade math class told me that. I laughed at him, wondering if he really thought I needed him to use it. I used it all the time, at least four times a day, once when I woke up, twice before I fell asleep, and as often during the afternoon as I could find the time alone. I made up stories to accompany it—adventures, sea voyages, pirates, the Resistance, being caught and tied up to wait for execution because I would not betray my best friend. I was a member of a secret organization of young girls who lived in connecting caves and corridors beneath the ground. There was an entrance cut into the floor of my closet. We had marvelous libraries, gymnasiums, and underground pools where we swam naked to develop endurance. We made love on the shelves above the pools, not the rough and clumsy grapples of my boy cousins, but long slow kisses and sudden strokes that brought me to shaking happiness in my damp sheets.

I woke up every morning terrified that anyone would know what

I had been imagining. What would happen to me with those girl-to-girl daydreams? I grew more and more frightened. Still, I wrote up one of those adventures and gave it to a girl in English class who said she loved to hear my stories. She had a thin face, but her eyes were such a warm soft brown I thought I could trust her. She passed the story around at lunch and by early afternoon people were laughing at me. My tale had included a sword fight, an escape, acrobatics, and finally the two of us running away to the Amazon River Basin to build our retreat. In science class, a boy took up the map pointer and pretended to spear me in the belly.

"Hey, Butch!" he yelled, and everybody laughed. They had all seen it.

I made it to the end of the day, but didn't go back to school for two more. I lay in my bed feverish. "A spring cold," Mama assumed.

"Drying up," I repeated to myself, lying still, not touching, not letting myself make up any stories. I would will myself different.

I was *different.*

I *was* different.

I didn't need it.

I did not let myself for a year. Cold, dry, not touching. When I woke up sweating and aching, I made myself lie rigid, staring into the darkness until balls of light moved across the ceiling. I read more than ever, developed what my mama called a smart mouth, as well as insomnia. If I couldn't sleep without it then I would not sleep.

That was the year Granny told me how someone had killed my wild aunt. They had found her truck run off the road and her in the ditch without her overalls. There was more to the story, but Granny wouldn't tell it, not even to me. Specially not to me? I wondered. But, of course, I found out. She had been raped. The uncles were not as careful as Granny, and somehow I knew there was more to the story, more to it than murder. If you didn't do it with boys, they might do that to you, something so terrible grown men would hesitate to repeat the details.

Not just trashy then, evil. I was evil, dangerous to myself and the world. So I collected evil women, stories, books, history. I fell in love with Elizabeth I who burned her enemies, the dark queen of France who poisoned hers, the Gypsy girl in the story of the Snow Queen who carried a knife and knew how to use it, and a rough-mouthed cousin who had a line of scars down both arms. Witches, black pools of darkness, endurance. In the fantasy story, Apache girls went out in the desert to lie with their vulvas facing the moon. I opened all the windows, lay down on the hardwood floor where my sisters couldn't see, not really caring if they did. I felt as if I hadn't slept for a year. A fever was rising inside me, heat coming up my throat. The moon pulsed into the room. Looking at it, I could make out the pattern of a face, a lily in the bright burning disk. I reached down and cupped my sex, fingers moving where they had not touched in so long, a tiny cry of grief sounding low in my belly.

Sex then, no matter how dangerous. Sex then, no matter what the cost. Never again, I promised, would I let anyone persuade me to rob myself. I rolled over so my hips could rock against the grain of the wood, my knuckles grate and press, my mouth breathe earth and wood heat. And I told myself a story that began with my aunt going out the door, heading for the Amazon River Basin, and call-ing back loudly to me as she left. A woman came in, then, a big woman with dark, slow eyes and hands as strong as my own. I rocked the wood and told her story, cursed in her name and laughed when she came—weightless as moonlight, massive as the night—to lie down and press her skin to mine.

I can write about years in a paragraph, but the years took years to pass. I spent a thousand years as a young girl, beating on my own thighs and cursing my life, because I was my aunts' niece, the child of my family, and a lesbian who ached to be loved right. I wanted an operation, not the boy-making kind, but a lever in the flesh, one I could permanently switch to off. I longed for immunity, distance, relief—not the end of all sex, but the end of the need, and more than the flesh, the end of the need for love—her hand fearlessly placed in mine, her eyes warm and brown and trustworthy. The need for a woman is insistent, necessary, easily refused but never successfully denied. My need for her has been constant, hungry, and powerful. Her need for me just as powerful, just as insistent, and thank God, just as impossible to deny.

What was it like to be a lesbian before the women's movement? It was to have the most dangerous addiction, risk the greatest loss, defy the most terrible consequences. The moon was not sufficient, and too many of us hated ourselves and feared our desire. But when we found each other, we made miracles—miracles of hope and defiance and love. This is the story that takes years to tell, my hand in hers and her trusting eyes, loose hair and learning to dance at thirty, borrowing and translating all my aunts' old stories, not talking in code, just pulling those butch girls down.

Everything is so sexual to me. Everything is a miracle. I am forty-four, almost the kind of old I intend to be—insistent, startling, sexual, and surprising. I like to use the rough words off my aunts' porches and use them to my own intent. I like to do the outrageous and tell stories about it, make nervous women giggle and giggly women nervous. I am never discrete, never what is expected. I have always loved those tough girls, those women who combine silence and power, but I am in my blossoming still, my long-delayed adolescence, my perfectly femme phase, and only half a mind to tell all I know.

This is the coda.

I have an ambition to be my own adolescent fantasy, to realize the science fiction fable and go back to that girl I was. I want to appear out of a moonlit lotus, find her twelve years old on a hardwood floor, reach down and take her hands, pull her up and tell her the story she has not yet lived. My life, her life, the life of a lesbian who learned the worth and price of sex. I want to call her Little Sister and laugh in a voice she will recognize. Say, sex is delicious. Sex is power. Never pretend that you do not want power in your life. Sex.

I'm going to get there somehow, swing my hair and promise my younger self that the struggle will be worth it.

"Girl," I want to say to her. "Hang on, honey. You are going to like it. It is going to be worth the price, worth the struggle. Child," I want to say, "you are going to be happy."

Sex Talk

A friend of mine used to distinguish between herself and me by saying that she was a *visual* person and I was a *print* person. Her concern was the image, mine was the word. I wouldn't argue. I was always too distracted by the image she presented in her shiny riding boots, pristine white blouses, and black satin tuxedo vests. That woman knew how to dress. Perhaps it was part of her visual nature.

It wasn't until I'd been living alone for a while that I actually began to understand and agree with what she had been saying. In the middle of what I now think of as my third promiscuous period, it became obvious to me that while I might initially be attracted to a woman by the image she presented, I would lose interest very quickly if she didn't have a good story behind the pose. That meant I might flirt very seriously with the sweetheart in the silver-toed cowboy boots, but I wound up in bed with the woman who made the hair on the back of my neck stand up with her stories.

"You got a wicked tongue," I'd always tell her.

"In more ways than one," six out of ten of them would reply. A lesbian cliché, I said to myself, but ignored it and tried to get them talking again.

The problem I found with promiscuity was the numbers. I sacrificed all discriminations of taste in pursuit of an uncertain epitome of experience. And while a great many women seemed to have perfected a good opening line and a couple of winning stories, very few had the talent and aggressiveness I prized, a verbal nature and an imagination as driven as my own, combined with the determination to use it.

Surprisingly, considering the nature of flirtation itself, I could always attract women who were more interested in the stories themselves than any act we might perform together. Those were the ones I went back to find. Over and over, I was with women who wanted to hear my stories as much as I wanted to hear theirs—not only where I'd been and what I'd done, but what I'd never done and always wanted to do.

"Tell me how it would be," they'd whisper, and I'd make up just the story I imagined they wanted to hear. Sometimes I even got it right.

When I left Washington, D.C. I became a dear friend to a woman with whom I had been a passionate lover. Over several years we wrote and exchanged sexy stories to tease and delight each other. On rare occasions when she'd visit New York or I'd go down to D.C., we'd lie naked together and elaborate on the ones we liked the best. Without those stories, I doubt we would have remained so close. Certainly we would never have learned as much intimate detail about each other. The last I heard she was finally working on a novel, unperturbed that I started publishing the stories I originally wrote for her.

Perhaps my most remarkable lover was the one who told you what she was doing as she did it. I don't mean that trash people talk, that "I'm gonna put it to you" stuff, and the nonsense. No, she would go into rhapsodies of description and response, a masslike litany that sounds mundane in retrospect but was wonderfully devastating at the time. Her monologues bore a curious resemblance to passages out of Faulkner or Joyce, full of run-on sentences and breathless puns.

"Your skin, skin. . . I squeeze your ass. . .you push me back so hard

. . .want to bite your neck. . .your neck tastes like smoke. . .salt. . .sour sweaty girl. . .turn around. . .turn. . .oh, don't do that bad, do you?. . . want your hands to?. . .I want your hands here. . .want to twist you around like a tree in wind, in rough water. . .want to taste you under there . . .taste just like Margaret. . .ass was just like that. . .used to bite me if I touched her here. . .used to whine so. . .you whine so. . ."

No, that's not right. I don't quite know how to catch the interplay of touch and language she used. It was poetry, performance poetry of the very best kind, an unrecognized genius only a few of us ever experienced. Trying to capture one of her passages I realized that sex itself is a very fragile experience, difficult to describe, harder to visualize—even for visual people. We have so many clichés in the way, only a few of which have any shared sexual power. That "visual" lesbian I lived with was a deeply serious photographer. For years I watched her struggle with all the ways there were to see lesbians, all the ways to look at lesbian sexuality. She was not so much concerned with whether the viewer would find what she did sexually exciting, although like all lesbian artists she had to face the idea that some men would find anything she might present sexually stimulating, and that bothered her a little. What she sought with her sexual images was a new and powerful way to see her own life and the lives of the women she loved, a vision that did not fall back into triteness or trivialization. What was frustrating to both of us was that in neither the print nor visual mediums could we find the kind of vision we wanted and needed. It was hard to even begin to examine the dimensions of what we didn't have. And then there was the power of the accepted motifs, the dominating and hard-to-avoid clichés of sexuality itself.

"That stuff is out there all the time," she told me, meaning not only mass culture with the commercial imagery that plays with and against sexual desire, but the unacknowledged although still powerful shared assumptions about what is sexual and what is not, what is good and what is tawdry, what is shameful and what is exciting. Even those who want to do something original and important with our work on sexuality have to address the fact that most people think about sex in very, very traditional terms, in scenarios from old movies and bad novels, in the fetishized language of the most sexist pornography. That stuff is there to be used or reframed, but it cannot be ignored.

In 1975, in Bertha Harris' writing class, the most controversial challenge she set us was to write a story about oral sex with another woman without using any of the clichés or pat phrases that were customary in sex writing. It turned out to be a remarkably complicated and difficult task. In an attempt to make it easier, I compiled a list of all the words I wouldn't be allowed to use. On a single page I listed about thirty words for female genitals, another fifteen slang terms for oral sex, and at least fifty humiliatingly explicit endearments. Reading that sheet out loud inevitably resulted in giggles, but it also made me feel vaguely depressed and sad.

Why were all the words for an activity I thoroughly enjoyed "bad" words? Why did so few of them feel sexy to me? I knew the assumptions of the lesbian community—that the language of sex was male-identified and antiwoman—but it seemed to me merely trite. Why was it so hard to come up with ways to talk about sex that also felt sexy?

The experience gave me a renewed interest in sex writing. I expanded my collection of lesbian novels, soft core and otherwise, to sex writing of all kinds—from gay men, heterosexuals, fetishists. I wanted to see how other people put sex into words: straight people and queers, contemporaries and writers in history, political people and self-conscious aristocrats. What I found is that *most* people talk about sex in clichés, as if cliché were the language of sex, as if there were a whole subtext implied in traditional words and actions—which, in fact, there certainly is.

I also discovered that distinction between visual and print viewpoints in the writing itself. Some sex writing seems to be about set-

ting a scene, so much so that the scene becomes all. It is intrinsically about providing a context—costume, texture, fetish—while
offering very little of the internal dialogue of feeling and emotional
response that has been the main thing that draws me in. Stories that
provide some texture and fetish but place the emphasis on a
philosophical examination of the "I" to whom everything happens,
or who observes everything that happens, appear to be almost a
different genre. Of course, the vast majority of sex writing is simply designed to get the reader off quickly and easily. Like junk food,
this sex writing is categorically labeled—one wouldn't want a foot
fetishist to pick up a fist-fucking novel by mistake—and consists of
as little detail and extended dialogue as possible. The characters never
discuss how they got into those situations. The poses and actions
themselves are the sole subjects of concern, along with the minimal
number of exclamatory phrases. It seems to be about minimalist
sex—without emotion, feeling, depth, or context, the raw stuff in
outline form.

I had a friend who worked briefly at writing some of those
books, and she told me it was mass market production on an assem-
bly line basis. She was not given discretion in what she was allowed
to write. Her assignments were more in the nature of "two wife swap-
pers, a leather biker, and a spanking exposé by 4:30." She'd smoke
a joint and get down to it. As encouragement, every thirty pages or
so she would reward herself with a scene she might actually have
found interesting.

"I'd have the wife slap her husband with his dirty boxer shorts
and run off with her therapist's sister-in-law," she told me, "or have
the bikers meet up with a bunch of angry ex-WACs on the way to
the Michigan Music Festival. I bet the readers were pretty surprised," she giggled. "But after a while I just couldn't get it up any
more, couldn't describe one more pouting nipple, one more swollen
cock."

I understood the problem. "You're word oriented," I told her.
"For people like us it's dangerous to overwork the banal. We're in

trouble when those words lose their power."

Over a bottle of wine I recited my old list from 1975. In response, she reeled off a list of her own. "Tacky," we both agreed.

"Disgusting," she told me when I started on the endearments.

"Yuck," I yelped when she began miming with the wine bottle.

"Terrible," she whispered, as she licked the underside of my chin.

"Bitch," I murmured and poured a little wine down the small of her back.

"Oh," she moaned, rolling me over on top of my list.

I think there's something to this idea of a word-oriented sexuality.

Some of the material in this essay first appeared on August 11, 1985 in the *New York Native*.

Believing in Literature

I have always passionately loved good books—good stories and beautiful writing, and most of all, books that seemed to me to be intrinsically important, books that told the truth, painful truths sometimes, in a voice that made eloquent the need for human justice. That is what I have meant when I have used the word *literature*. It has seemed to me that literature, as I meant it, was embattled, that it was increasingly difficult to find writing doing what I thought literature should do—which was simply to push people into changing their ideas about the world, and to go further, to encourage us in the work of changing the world, to making it more just and more truly human.

All my life I have hated clichés, the clichés applied to people like me and those I love. Every time I pick up a book that purports to be about either poor people or queers or Southern women, I do so with a conscious anxiety, an awareness that the books about us have often been cruel, small, and false. I have wanted our lives taken seriously and represented fully—with power and honesty and sympathy—to be hated or loved, or to terrify and obsess, but to be real, to have the power of the whole and the complex. I have never wanted politically correct parables made out of my grief, simple-minded rote speeches made from my rage, simplifications that reduce me to cardboard dimensions. But mostly that is what I have

found. We are the ones they make fiction of—we queer and disenfranchised and female—and we have the right to demand our full,
nasty, complicated lives, if only to justify all the times our reality
has been stolen, mismade, and dishonored.

That our true stories may be violent, distasteful, painful, stunning, and haunting, I do not doubt. But our true stories will be literature. No one will be able to forget them, and though it will not always make us happy to read of the dark and dangerous places in our
lives, the impact of our reality is the best we can ask of our literature.

Literature, and my own dream of writing, has shaped my system of belief—a kind of atheist's religion. I gave up God and the
church early on, choosing instead to place all my hopes in direct-
action politics. But the backbone of my convictions has been a belief in the progress of human society as demonstrated in its fiction.
Even as a girl I believed that our writing was better than we were.
There were, after all, those many novels of good and evil, of working-
class children shown to be valuable and sympathetic human beings,
of social criticism and subtle education—books that insisted we could
be better than we were. I used my belief in the power of good writing as a way of giving meaning to some of the injustices I saw around
me.

When I was very young, still in high school, I thought about
writing the way Fay Weldon outlined in her essay, "The City of Imagination," in *Letters to My Niece on First Reading Jane Austen*. I imagined that Literature was, as she named it, a city with many dis-
tricts, or was like a great library of the human mind that included
all the books ever written. But what was most important was the
enormous diversity contained in that library of the mind, that imaginary city. I cruised that city and dreamed of being part of it, but
I was fearful that anything I wrote would be relegated to unimportance
—no matter how finely crafted my writing might be, no matter how
hard I worked and how much I risked. I knew I was a lesbian, and
I believed that meant I would always be a stranger in the city—unless
I performed the self-defeating trick of disguising my imagination,

hiding my class origin and sexual orientation, writing, perhaps, a comic novel about the poor or the sexually dysfunctional. If that was the only way in, it made sense to me how many of the writers I loved drank or did drugs or went slowly crazy, trying to appear to be something they were not. It was enough to convince me that there was no use in writing at all.

When feminism exploded in my life, it gave me a vision of the world totally different from everything I had ever assumed or hoped. The concept of a feminist literature offered the possibility of pride in my sexuality. It saved me from either giving up writing entirely, or the worse prospect of writing lies in order to achieve some measure of grudging acceptance. But at the same time, Feminism destroyed all my illusions about Literature. Feminism revealed the city as an armed compound to which I would never be admitted. It forced me to understand, suddenly and completely, that literature was written by men, judged by men. The city itself was a city of Man, a male mind even when housed in a female body. If that was so, all my assumptions about the worth of writing, particularly working-class writing, were false. Literature was a lie, a system of lies, the creation of liars, some of them sincere and unaware of the lies they retold, but all acting in the service of a Great Lie—what the system itself labeled Universal Truth. If that truth erased me and all those like me, then my hopes to change the world through writing were illusions. I lost my faith. I became a feminist activist propelled in part by outrage and despair, and a stubborn determination to shape a life, and create a literature, that was not a lie.

I think many lesbian and feminist writers my age had a similar experience. The realizations of feminist criticism made me feel as if the very ground on which I stood had become unsteady. Some of that shake-up was welcome and hopeful, but it also meant I had to make a kind of life raft for myself out of political conviction, which is why I desperately needed a feminist community and so feared being driven out of the one I found. I know many other women who felt the same way, who grew up in poverty and got their ideas of what might be possible from novels of social criticism, believing those books were about us even when they were obviously not. What the feminist critique of patriarchal literature meant was not only that all we had believed about the power of writing to change the world was not possible, but that to be true to our own vision, we had to create a new canon, a new literature. Believing in literature—a feminist literature—became a reason to spend my life in that pursuit.

There are times I have wondered if that loss of faith was really generational, or only my own. I have seen evidence of a similar attitude in the writing of many working-class lesbians who are my age peers, the sense of having been driven out of the garden of life, and a painful pride in that exile though still mourning the dream of worth and meaning. The feminist small press movement was created out of that failed belief and the hope of reestablishing a literature that we could believe in. Daughters, Inc., Know, Inc., Diana Press, *Amazon Quarterly, Quest, Conditions*...right down to *OUT/LOOK*. All those magazines and presses—the ones I have worked with and supported even when I found some of the writing tedious or embarrassing—were begun in that spirit of rejecting the false ideal for a true one. This was a very mixed enterprise at its core, because creating honest work in which we did not have to mask our actual experiences, or our sexuality and gender, was absolutely the right thing to do, but rejecting the established literary canon was not simple, and throwing out the patriarchy put so much else in question. Many of us lost all sense of what could be said to be good or bad writing, or how to think about being writers while bypassing the presses, grants, and teaching programs that might have helped us devote the majority of our time to writing, to creating a body of work.

The difficulty faced by lesbian and feminist writers of my generation becomes somewhat more understandable if we think about the fact that almost no lesbian-feminist writer my age was able to make a living as a writer. Most of us wrote late at night after exhausting and demanding day jobs, after evenings and weekends of political activism, meetings, and demonstrations. Most of us also devoted enormous amounts of time and energy to creating presses and journals that embodied our political ideals, giving up the time and energy we might have used to actually do our own writing. During my involvement with *Quest*, I wrote one article. The rest of my writing time was given over to grant applications and fund-raising letters. I did a little better with *Conditions*, beginning to actually publish short stories, but the vast majority of work I did there was editing other people's writing and again, writing grants and raising money. Imagine how few paintings or sculptures would be created if the artists all had to collectively organize the creation of canvas and paint, build and staff the galleries, and turn back all the money earned from sales into the maintenance of the system. Add to that the difficulty of creating completely new philosophies about what would be suitable subjects for art, what approaches would be valid for artists to take to their work, who, in fact, would be allowed to say what was valuable and what was not, or more tellingly, what could be sold and to whom. Imagine that system and you have the outlines of some of the difficulties faced by lesbian writers of my generation.

As a writer, I think I lost at least a decade in which I might have done more significant work because I had no independent sense of my work's worth. If Literature was a dishonest system by which the work of mediocre men and women could be praised for how it fit into a belief system that devalued women, queers, people of color, and the poor, then how could I try to become part of it? Worse, how could I judge any piece of writing, how could I know what was good or bad, worthwhile or a waste of time? To write for that system was to cooperate in your own destruction, certainly in your misrepresentation. I never imagined that what we were creating was also limited, that it, too, reflected an unrealistic or dishonest vision. But that's what we did, at least in part, making an ethical system that insists a lightweight romance has the same worth as a serious piece of fiction, that there is no good or bad, no "objective" craft or standards of excellence.

I began to teach because I had something I wanted to say, opinions that seemed to me rare and important and arguable. I wanted to be part of the conversation I saw going on all around, the one about the meaning and use of writing. The first literature classes I taught were not-for-credit workshops in a continuing education program in Tallahassee, Florida. When I moved to Washington, D.C. to work on *Quest* in 1975, I volunteered to help teach similar workshops through the women's center, and in Brooklyn in 1980 I joined with some of the women of *Conditions* to participate in a series of classes organized to specifically examine class and race issues in writing. Working as an editor, talking with other lesbian and gay writers, arguing about how fiction relates to real life—all of that helped me to systematically work out what I truly believed about literature, about writing, about its use and meaning, and the problematic relationship of writing to literature.

Starting in 1988 in San Francisco, I began to teach writing workshops because it was one of the ways I could earn rent and grocery money without taking a full-time job and still be able to write as much as possible. But teaching full time taught me how much I loved teaching itself, at least teaching writing, and how good I could be at it. Sometimes my writing classes gave me a great deal more than rent or groceries; sometimes they gave me a reason to believe in writing itself.

If you want to write good fiction, I am convinced you have to first decide what that means. This is what I always I tell my students. They think I'm being obvious at the outset, and that the exercise is a waste of time, as it could be if I did not require that they apply their newly determined standards to their own work. Figure it out for yourself, I tell them. Your lovers will try to make you feel good, your friends will just lie, and your critics can only be trusted so far as they have in mind the same standards and goals that you do.

I have used one exercise in every writing class that is designed to provoke the students into thinking about what they really believe about the use of literature. In the beginning, I did not realize how much it would also challenge my own convictions. I require my students to spend the first weeks collecting examples of stories they can categorically label *good* and *bad*. I make them spend those weeks researching and arguing, exchanging favorite stories, and talking about what they have actually read, not pretend to have read. I want them to be excited and inspired by sharing stories they love, and to learn to read critically at the same time, to begin to see the qualities that make a story good and determine for themselves what makes a story bad. Near the end of the class they are asked to bring in what they think is the best and worst story they have ever read, along with a list of what constitutes a good story, and what a bad one, and to support their ideas from their examples. I tell my students to keep in mind that all such judgments, including those about craft and technique, are both passionately subjective and slyly political.

The difficult thing about this exercise is that young writers love to talk about bad writing, to make catty jokes about this writer or that, but only so long as none of that nastiness is turned on them. It is always a struggle to get students to confront what is flawed in their stories without losing heart for the struggles of writing, to help them develop a critical standard without destroying their confidence in their own work, or what their work can become. I encourage young writers to find truly remarkable work by people like them, writers who share something of their background or core identity, because I have discovered that every young writer fears that they and their community are the ones who are not as good as the more successful mainstream writing community. I prod young lesbians and gay men to find work by other queers from the small and experimental presses. Then I try to make them think about what they could be writing that they haven't even thought about before. They become depressed and scared when it is difficult for them to locate queer stories they believe are really good, but I am ruthless about making them see what hides behind some of their easy assumptions about the nature of good literature. Sometimes I feel like a literary evangelist, preaching the gospel of truth and craft. I tell them they are the generation that might be able to do something truly different, write the stories that future readers will call unqualifiedly good, but only if they understand what can make that possible, and always, that part of the struggle is a necessity to learn their own history.

In one of my most extraordinary classes the exercise worked better than I had hoped when one of the women brought in a "best" selection that was another woman's choice for "worst." The situation was made more difficult for me because her bad story was one I loved, a painful but beautifully written account of female survival after rape in a wilderness setting. It was bad, said my student, because of how well-written and carefully done it was. It stayed in her mind, disturbed her, made her nervous and unhappy every time she went into the woods. She didn't want those ideas in her head, had enough violence and struggle in her life, enough bad thoughts to confront all the time. I understood exactly what she was saying. She was, after all, a lesbian-feminist activist of my generation, and both of us were familiar with the kind of feminist literary criticism that supported her response to the story. But many of the students were younger and frankly confused.

Subjective, I reminded myself then. We had agreed that essentially judgments about fiction are subjective—mine as well as my students'. But the storyteller seized up inside me. I thought of my stories, my characters, the albino child I murdered in "Gospel Song," the gay man who kills his lover in "Interesting Death," the little girl who tries to seduce her uncle in "Private Rituals." Bad characters, bad acts, bad thoughts—as well-written as I can make them because I want my people to be believable, my stories to haunt and obsess my readers. I want, in fact, to startle my readers, shock and terrify sometimes, to fascinate and surprise. To show them something they have not imagined, people and tales they will feel strongly about in spite of themselves, or what they would prefer to feel, or not feel. I want my stories to be so good they are unforgettable, to make my

ideas live, my memories sing, and my own terrors real for people
I will never meet. It is a completely amoral writer's lust, and I know
that the author of that "bad" story felt it too. We all do, and if we
begin to agree that some ideas are too dangerous, too bad to invite
inside our heads, then we stop the storyteller completely. We silence
everyone who would tell us something that might be painful in our
vulnerable moments.

Everything I know, everything I put in my fiction, will hurt
someone somewhere as surely as it will comfort and enlighten someone else. What then is my responsibility? What am I to restrain?
What am I to fear and alter—my own nakedness or the grief of the
reader?

My students are invariably determined that their stories will be
powerful, effective, crafted, and unforgettable, not the crap that so
embarrasses them. "Uh-huh," I nod at them, not wanting to be
patronizing but remembering when I was twenty-four and determined to start my own magazine, to change how people thought
about women, poor people, lesbians, and literature itself. Maybe it
will be different in their lifetimes, I think, though part of me does
believe it is different already. But more is possible than has yet been
accomplished, and what I have done with my students is plant a seed
that I expect to blossom in a new generation.

Once in a while one of my students will ask me, "Why have
there been no great lesbian novels?" I do not pretend that they are
wrong, do not tell them how many of the great writers of history were
lesbians. They and I know that a lesbian author does not necessarily write a lesbian novel. Most often I simply disagree and offer a
list of what I believe to be good lesbian writing. It is remarkable to
me that as soon as I describe some wonderful story as being by a
lesbian, there is always someone who wants to argue whether the
individual involved really deserves that label. I no longer participate
in this pointless argument. I feel that as a lesbian I have a perfect
right to identify some writing as lesbian regardless of whether the

academy or contemporary political theorists would agree with me.

What I find much more interesting is that so many of my gay and lesbian and feminist students are unaware of their own community's history. They may have read *Common Lives/Lesbian Lives*, *On Our Backs*, or various 'zines, and joke about any magazine that could publish such trivial fiction, believing the magazines contemptible because they do not edit badly written polemics and true confessions. But few of them know anything about the ideology that made many of us in the 1970s abandon the existing literary criterion to create our own.

We believed that editing itself was a political act, and we questioned what was silenced when raw and rough work by women outside the accepted literary canon was rewritten or edited in such a way that the authentic voices were erased. My students have no sense of how important it was to let real women tell their stories in their own words. I try to explain, drawing their attention to ethnographies and oral histories, techniques that reveal what is so rarely shown in traditionally edited fiction—powerful, unusual voices not recognized by the mainstream. I tell them how much could not be published or even written before the creation of the queer and lesbian presses which honored that politic. I bring in old copies of Daughters books, not *Rubyfruit Jungle*, which they know, but *The True Story of a Drunken Mother* by Nancy Hall, which mostly they haven't seen. I make it personal and tell them bluntly that I would never have begun to write anything of worth without the example of those presses and magazines reassuring me that my life, and my family's life, was a fit subject for literature.

As I drag my poor students through my own version of the history of lesbian and gay publishing, I am painfully aware that the arguments I make—that I pretend are so clear and obvious—are still completely unresolved. I pretend to my students that there is no question about the value of writing, even though I know I have gone back and forth from believing totally in it to being convinced that books never really change anything and are only published if they don't offend people's dearly held prejudices too much. So affecting confidence, I still worry about what I truly believe about literature and my writing.

Throughout my work with the lesbian and gay, feminist, and small press movements, I went on reading the enemy—mainstream literature—with a sense of guilt and uncertainty that I might be in some way poisoning my mind, and wondering, worrying, trying to develop some sense of worth outside purely political judgments. I felt like an apostate who still mumbles prayers in moments of crisis. I wanted to hear again the equivalent of the still, small voice of God telling me: Yes, Dorothy, books are important. Fiction is a piece of truth that turns lies to meaning. Even outcasts can write great books. I wanted to be told that it is only the form that has failed, that the content was still there—like a Catholic who returns to God but never the church.

The result has been that after years of apostasy, I have come to make distinctions between what I call the academy and literature, the moral equivalents of the church and God. The academy may lie, but literature tries to tell the truth. The academy is the market—university courses in contemporary literature that never get past Faulkner, reviewers who pepper their opinions with the ideas of the great men, and editors who think something is good because it says the same thing everyone has always said. Literature is the lie that tells the truth, that shows us human beings in pain and makes us love them, and does so in a spirit of honest revelation. That's radical enough, and more effective than only publishing unedited oral history. It is the stance I assumed when I decided I could not live without writing fiction and trying to publish it for the widest possible audience. It is the stance I maintain as I try to make a living by writing, supplemented with teaching, and to publish with both a mainstream publishing house and a small lesbian press. What has been extraordinarily educational and difficult to accept these past few years of doing both has been the recognition that the distinction between the two processes is nowhere near as simple or as easily categorized as I had once thought.

In 1989, when I made the decision to take my novel *Bastard Out of Carolina* to a mainstream press, I did so in part because I did not believe I could finish it without financial help. I was broke, sick, and exhausted. My vision had become so bad I could no longer assume I could go back at any time to doing computer work or part-time clerical jobs. I had to either find a completely new way to make a living and devote myself to that enterprise, or accept the fact that I was going to have to try to get an advance that would buy me at least two years to finish the book. Finally, I also knew that this book had become so important to me that I *had* to finish it, even if it meant doing something I had never assumed I would do. Reluctantly, I told Nancy Bereano what I was doing with *Bastard*, and then approached a friend to ask him to act as my agent. I had never worked with an agent before, but all my political convictions convinced me I could not trust mainstream presses and did not know enough to be able to deal with them. In fact, I learned while doing journalism in New York in the 1980s that I was terrible at the business end of writing, rotten at understanding the arcane language of contracts. In some ways my worst fears were realized. Selling a manuscript to strangers is scary.

What most surprised me, however, was learning that mainstream publishing was not a monolith, and finding there not only people who believed in literature the way I did, but lesbians and gay men who worked within mainstream publishing because of their belief in the importance of good writing and how it can change the world. Mostly younger, and without my experience of the lesbian and gay small presses, they talked in much the same way as I did about their own convictions, the jobs they took that demanded long hours and paid very poorly but let them work, at least in part, with writing and writers they felt vindicated their sacrifices. Talking to those men and women shook up a lot of my assumptions, particularly when I began to work with heterosexuals who did not seem uniformly homophobic or deluded or crassly obsessed with getting rich as quickly as possible. I found within mainstream publishing a great many sincere and hopeful people of conviction and high standards who forced me to reexamine some of my most ingrained prejudices. If I was going to continue to reject the ideology and standards of mainstream literature, I had to become a lot more clear and specific about the distinction between the patriarchal literature I had been trying to challenge all my life and the good-hearted individuals I encountered within those institutions.

As I was finishing the copyediting of *Bastard*, I found myself thinking about all I had read when Kate Millett published *Flying:* her stated conviction that telling the truth was what feminist writers were supposed to do. That telling the truth—your side of it anyway, knowing that there were truths other than your own—was a moral act, a courageous act, an act of rebellion that would encourage other such acts. Like Kate Millett, I knew that what I wanted to do as a lesbian and a feminist writer was to remake the world into a place where the truth would be hallowed, not held in contempt, where silence would be impossible.

Sometimes it seems that all I want to add to her philosophy is the significance of craft, a restatement of the importance of deeply felt, powerful writing versus a concentration on ethnography, or even a political concentration on adding certain information to the canon —information about our real lives that would make it possible for lesbians, working-class runaways, incest survivors, and stigmatized and vilified social outlaws to recognize themselves and their experiences. If I throw everything out and start over without rhetoric or a body of theory behind my words, I am left with the simple fact that what I want as a writer is to be able to tell the truth so well and so powerfully that it will have to be heard, understood, and acted on. It's why I have worked for years on lesbian, feminist, and gay publishing, for no money and without much hope, and why my greatest sorrow has been watching young writers do less than their best because they have no concept of what good writing can be and what it can accomplish.

I started this whole process—forcing my students' discussion of the good and the bad—in order to work on my own judgment, to hold it up to outside view. I can take nothing for granted with these twenty-year-olds, and there is always at least one old-line feminist there to keep me honest, to ask why and make me say out loud all the things I have questioned and tried to understand. Sometimes it helps a lot. Sometimes it drives me back down inside myself, convincing me all over again that Literature belongs to the Other—either the recognized institutions or my innocent students who have never known my self-conscious sense of sin, my old loss of faith. They question so little, don't even know they have a faith to lose. There are times I look at my writing and despair. I cannot always make it the story I think should be told, cannot make it an affirmation or anything predictable or easy or sometimes even explainable. The story tells itself, banal or not. What, then, is the point of literary criticism that tells writers what they should be writing rather than addressing what is on the page?

The novel I am working on now seems to be driving me more crazy in the actual writing of it than it ever did when I was trying to get around to the writing of it. I don't understand if it is just me or the process itself, since many other writers I have talked to are noncommunicative about the work of writing itself. Everyone discusses day jobs, teaching, what they read, music, being interviewed, groups they work with, things they want to do when this project is finished.

But over here, I am halfway done with the thing and feel like I have nothing, know nothing, am nothing. Can't sleep, and part of the time I can't even work, staying up till 4:00 or 5:00 in the morning. Thinking. About what, people ask, the book? I stare blankly, sometimes unable to explain and other times too embarrassed. I think about the book, yes, but also about my childhood, my family, and about sex, violence, what people will ask me when they read this book, about my ex-girlfriends and what they will say, about my hips and how wide they have become, my eyesight that is steadily growing worse, the friends who have somehow become strangers, even enemies, the friends who have died without ever managing to do the things they wanted to do, how old I have gotten not recognizing that time was actually passing, about why I am a lesbian and not heterosexual, about children and whether the kind of writing I do will endanger my relationship to my son—allow someone to take him away from me or accuse me of being a bad mother—and about all the things I was not told as a child that I had to make up for myself. When I am writing I sink down into myself, my memory, dreams, shames, and terrors. I answer questions no one has asked but me, avoid issues no one else has raised, and puzzle out just where my responsibility to the real begins and ends. Morality and ethics are the heart of what I fear, that I might fail in one or the other, that people like me cannot help but fail to show true ethical insight or moral concern. Then I turn my head and fall into the story, and all that thinking becomes background to the novel writing itself, the voices that are only partly my own. What I can tell my students is that the theory and philosophy they take so seriously and pick apart with such angst and determination is still only accompaniment to the work of writing, and that process, thankfully, no matter what they may imagine, is still not subject to rational determined construction.

A few years ago I gave a copy of a piece of "fiction" I had written about incest and adult sexual desire to a friend of mine, a respected feminist editor and activist. "What," she asked me, "do you want from me about this? An editorial response, a personal one, literary or political?" I did not know what to say to her, never having thought about sorting out reading in that way. Certainly, I wanted my story to move her, to show her something about incest survivors, something previously unimaginable and astounding—and not actually just one thing either, as I did not want one thing from her. The piece had not been easy for me, not simple to write or think about afterward. It had walked so close to my own personal history, my nightsweats, shame, and stubborn endurance. What did I want? I wanted the thing all writers want—for the world to break open in response to my story. I wanted to be understood finally for who I believe myself to be, for the difficulty and grief of using my own pain to be justified. I wanted my story to be unique and yet part of something greater than myself. I wanted to be seen for who I am and still appreciated—not denied, not simplified, not lied about or refused or minimized. The same thing I have always wanted.

I have wanted everything as a writer and a woman, but most of all a world changed utterly by my revelations. Absurd, arrogant, and presumptuous to imagine that fiction could manage that—even the fiction I write which is never wholly fictive. I change things. I lie. I embroider, make over, and reuse the truth of my life, my family, lovers, and friends. Acknowledging this, I make no apologies, knowing that what I create is as crafted and deliberate as the work of any other poet, novelist, or short story writer. I choose what to tell and what to conceal. I design and calculate the impact I want to have. When I sit down to make my stories I know very well that I want to take the reader by the throat, break her heart, and heal it again. With that intention I cannot sort out myself, say this part is for the theorist, this for the poet, this for the editor, and this for the wayward ethnographer who only wants to document my experience.

"Tell me what you really think," I told my friend. "Be personal. Be honest." Part of me wanted to whisper, Take it seriously, but be kind. I did not say that out loud, however. I could not admit to my friend how truly terrified I was that my story did none of what I had wanted—not and be true to the standard I have set for myself. Writing terrible stories has meaning only if we hold ourselves to the same standard we set for our readers. Every time I sit down to write, I have a great fear that anything I write will reveal me as the monster I was always told I would be, but that fear is personal, something I must face in everything I do, every act I contemplate. It is the whisper of death and denial. Writing is an act that claims courage and meaning, and turns back denial, breaks open fear, and heals me as it makes possible some measure of healing for all those like me.

Some things never change. There is a place where we are always alone with our own mortality, where we must simply have something greater than ourselves to hold onto—God or history or politics or literature or a belief in the healing power of love, or even righteous anger. Sometimes I think they are all the same. A reason to believe, a way to take the world by the throat and insist that there is more to this life than we have ever imagined.

A Personal History of Lesbian Porn

I lucked out a few years back and wound up housesitting one of those cushy manor houses one mostly sees in expensive magazines. It was to be a short but dream vacation, caretaking the swimming pool, tennis court, spacious lawn, and high-sheltering hedges. Early the first morning I decided to start it off right with a before-breakfast swim and went rummaging through the hall closet for towels. There, I turned up a totally unexpected find—a stack of books as high as my ears with the spines all turned to the back wall. I had a quick flash on what they had to be and pulled off the three top titles: *Valley of the Lesbo*, *Midnight Orgy*, and *Make It Sting*. "Uh-huh," I laughed. Well, what other kind of books do people keep in their closets? I decided the sun would dry me well enough and took some books out to the pool instead.

The deal for staying in the house included the responsibility for keeping up the grounds, which meant endless hours of mowing. In short order I developed a schedule that combined marathon nude mowing sessions with sudden dives over the fence into the pool, all the chores interspersed with regular trips to the hall closet. I worked my way from the top of the stack to the bottom, carefully turning the books over to create a reverse stack on the opposite wall. I knew that when I left I'd want the stack to be in the same order I'd discovered—a matter of just flipping the whole pile back over. Eventually I started dragging a few books out with me to the tennis court where I could bake on the tarmac and read through my sunglasses, retiring to the bushes only when overcome by the sun or lust.

The effect of skimming, and occasionally rereading, volume after volume of heavy-duty hard core was to render the whole world slightly sunburned, pink, and oily. It didn't matter that almost all the books were awful—intermittent sexual escapades paced by eight to twelve pages of plot pretense and rare paragraphs of "socially redeeming value"—nor that sometimes I'd lose track of which one I was reading. Suddenly the bushes seemed thicker, the texture on the dogwood trees rougher, the smell of flowers and chlorine overpowering, while my dreams produced men who searched the garden for their detachable genitals and women who sat on the window ledges and slowly licked their greasy fingers. *Sorority Sister Initiation, Anything She Wants!, The Loving and the Daring, Emmanuelle, The Image, Women in Love With Women.* I didn't bother with *King Dick* or *Case Studies of Young Boys and Their Dogs,* but *The Lesbian Seductress* had me giggling for hours after I'd tossed it into the bushes, while *Carol in a Thousand Cities* sent me back to the house for Kleenex and aspirin.

Some titles were familiar to me. When Beebo Brinker made her appearance, cigarette hanging from the corner of her lip, defending her job as an elevator operator to the too-fragile Laura, I had to put the book down for a quick cold swim. I'd read that one my first year in college in the bathroom of my dorm so my roommate wouldn't know—terrified that the other girls would figure out that my one "date" every six weeks was a protective gesture, that my real passions were saved for a dormmate whose close-cropped hair and eternal sneer mimicked Beebo. When that girl disappeared from the dorm one mysterious night full of shouting and confusion, I'd ripped Beebo cover to cover and spread the pages over eight garbage cans and one dumpster. Suddenly, I wasn't reading porn; I was paging my own history.

I was eight when I read my first hard-core paperback. I had found it sticking out from between my parents' mattresses one spring morning when I was going through my mother's nightstand hoping for buffalo head nickels. It had no pictures other than the cover—a drawing of a naked man and woman, their bodies pressed so closely together you couldn't see anything forbidden. I have no memory of the title but a pretty clear memory of the figures' expressions: wide-eyed, lips drawn back, intense. Obviously this was a secret book. I hid it in my shorts, just in case, and ran off to the utility room to read it.

All things considered, it didn't confuse me much. I knew about fucking, not all the details but the general idea. I just hadn't done it on my own yet. I did play with myself. I was pretty sure everybody did, but I was also sure that everybody had to pretend that they didn't. Playing with yourself was dirty and would get you a whipping if your mama or your aunts found out. It was all sex and it was all "funny"—funny-scary or funny like the jokes my aunts were always making. ("He's got a pecker like a week-old banana. Mash on it and it goes soft in your hand.") They'd laugh themselves silly and never explain anything. But from all those jokes and my cousins' teasing, I'd gotten a pretty clear idea that the boy-thing rubbed against the girl-thing while the two kissed intensely. Also, somehow this was necessary for there to be babies, although it didn't make babies. God made babies. Bobbie had told me so, and no way could I believe my favorite cousin had lied to me.

Since I now knew so much, it was plain that there was something strange about the book my parents kept under their mattress. Obviously it couldn't actually be true. For one thing, nobody acted like that. I couldn't imagine Aunt Dot dragging the delivery boy into the pantry and ripping his pants off. Nor could I imagine—not really—the things the two of them would have done then. Put it inside? Inside where? Couldn't be.

Around the same time I was also reading a set of books that did have pictures—a series of Greek myths. Zeus changing into a swan to hang out with Leda, Arachne turned into a spider for pissing off Athena, dragon's teeth sowed to make deadly soldiers. So maybe this book was true like those stories were true which meant the book wasn't real at all, just like fairy stories and horror movies. This meant that I wound up reading *Bullfinch's Mythology* and *My Secret Life* in the same week and concluding that just as a baby couldn't wrestle snakes to death in its crib, a woman couldn't smoke a cigarette with her pussy. Just that easily I made peace with fiction. The stuff wasn't to be worried about either way, and like anything to do with sex, it was not for children to talk about, particularly since books taken from under Mama's bed could only get me into trouble.

Eventually it got more complicated. I remember very well the nature of the fantasies that used to accompany my nightly self-stimulation. They were invariably intense, exciting adventures in which I was always forced to suffer untold agonies for the love of some little girl from the neighborhood or school. In one variation, I would rescue her from some terrible captivity and we would flee together to the snowbound north country. Which meant we had to hug each other close to keep warm at night. At the most she would kiss my sweaty cheek, or I her windburned forehead.

Gradually, though, events forcibly educated me. My stepfather showed me just how terrible sex could be, while with stunning regularity my cousins turned thirteen or fourteen and pregnant—only occasionally to marry. My cousin Bobbie held out the longest, waiting till she was seventeen to actually marry and then get the baby. Meanwhile the aunts went on: bluntly and continually pregnant, rudely and insistently sexual. They weren't like the women in the books I continued to borrow from my parents' room. They were not secretaries or models, shocked when He pulled out that Big Thang. No, they were textile workers and waitresses who knew exactly what that thing was for, who might grab it down under the dinner table and howl when the man jumped back. The books still weren't real, but maybe they were written about city women, television women,

Yankee women—just about as strange as Zeus had always been and Jesus was getting to be.

What the books did contribute was a word—the word *Lesbian*. When she finally appeared (with hair sprouting from both her upper lip and her nipples, bloated, fat, and sweaty) I knew her immediately. She wasn't true, either. She wasn't me, just like my aunt Dot wasn't Leda. But she was true enough, and the lust echoed. When she pulled the frightened girl close after thirty pages, I got damp all down my legs. That's what it was, and I wasn't the only one even if none had turned up in the neighborhood yet. Details aside, the desire matched up. She wanted women; I wanted my girlfriends. The word was Lesbian. After that, I started looking for it.

I worked my way back and forth from the far hedges to the hall closet, from the dirt-layered compost heap to the hall closet. I compared titles, themes, characters, and cover art. It wasn't a simple collection. I turned up a couple of "romance" books with soft cover art, the woman bent back in the pirate's arms, the knight's arms. A quick skim spotted the sweaty pages, remarkably explicit. There was even one Harlequin romance whose heroine was a divorcée kidnapped on page 20—not learning who her abductor really was until page 168. I wouldn't have called it sexy myself, though it was definitely a tease. I became intrigued by just who the collection belonged to—the woman of the house or the man? And who had turned all those titles to the wall?

When ten books in a row were soft-core dyke porn—four of which I'd read before, all dating from the mid-fifties—I started thinking it had to be the woman. But following that were seven heavy-duty men's leather-lust types, including several magazines (*Bikeboy, His Master's Voice, The Leatherman's Handbook*) and one amazing little goody I'll never forget called something like *Pins and Needles*. It wasn't about piercing. In fact, the title had little or nothing to do with the "story." What was amazing about it was the sex-to-plot ratio. A new and detailed act began without fail every three pages. The author hadn't even bothered to pretend to break it into chapters, just sex acts. Somehow, I had never imagined there were quite so many things two to five men could do together.

I wondered if someone in the household was doing a long-term research project, or maybe suffering from gender confusion. Of course, I'm not sure one's taste in porn actually says that much about gender affiliation. I think of the gay men I know who just love those lust-tinged Gothic novels, of lesbians who collect shelves of gay men's paperbacks and magazines. I have, for example, a friend who is notoriously butch—a woman who came out before adolescence, whose friends are exclusively lesbian or gay, and who can name every woman with whom she has gone to bed sober. The joke among her friends is that Pam would sleep in her boots if they weren't so hard on her sheets. Pam reads, in secret, the most traditional sleazy heterosexual pornography you can imagine. When I ask her what about it she likes, she gets defensive. "I get off on it. What do you think, I read it for the stories?"

"But how does it make you feel about yourself? Do you imagine yourself—"

"The man or the woman? Don't be silly. It doesn't have anything to do with me, especially not me in bed. I don't fantasize myself tricking like that. It's just a quick easy come. You know, just shifting into gear and getting off."

I believe her, though I know most people wouldn't. It seems a little like the way I used to read gay male magazines like *Honcho* and *Mandate*. I don't use it for masturbatory material, though it does get me turned on, which is to say that I don't read it in the traditional one-handed manner except for when I bite my nails. I don't imagine myself the lone hitchhiker picked up by the muscled duo, or the young boy watching the bikers groping each other in the shade of the garage. I am not there but the sex is—a sense of extended and exciting possibility. It's true, though, that sometimes when I'm out at a lesbian bar flirting with the bartender, I might very well imagine myself some naive young girl who just hitched in. The sexual imagination connects in very odd ways.

After the leatherman titles, I did twenty fast laps plotting the development of tighter tummy muscles and started measuring my reading in inches instead of titles. Seven inches down from the midpoint I hit the pseudoporn, a spate of books on "sex in literature" and anti-obscenity tracts that just happened to quote liberally from the worst offenders. I imagined the authors enjoying the best of both worlds—exotic titillation and moral superiority. It reminded me of friends who always seemed to throw a lap rug over the television when company came, pretending to be too intellectual, spiritual, or enlightened to need that trash. Just like my friends who keep their bedtime reading off their shelves and under the mattress or tucked in a drawer.

The "pseudos" included psychology and political texts, but all followed the same format: a standard number of pages of ranting or analysis interspersed with brief but intense sections of classic Victorian pornography or remarkably candid interviews with anonymous informants who had thoroughly indulged their rather extraordinary imaginations. Some of the things described didn't sound physically possible. I found myself examining vegetables with new interest and clotheslines with profound nervous excitement.

Could it really be possible to bend the legs back that far?

In her article in the *Heresies Sex Issue #12*, Muriel Dimen suggested that it is time we started to imagine our own sexual utopias. I agree with the politics and intent of that statement, while still woefully aware of the strategic complications of such a task. I am quite convinced that the sexual utopias described by feminists will be called erotica by some, silly by others, and pornography by all too many. Sexual information is both vital and terrifying. Sexual content invariably provokes fear and misunderstanding, no matter who provides it—educators, feminists, pornographers, theorists, or goodtime girls.

For a long time I coded my journals, obscuring not only peoples' names but their acts. I know exactly when I began to do so and when I stopped, retaining only the insulation of substituting initials for names and nicknames. The coding began one afternoon when I came home unexpectedly from the women's center to find another woman from the collective where I lived sitting on my bed reading my journal. I don't know which of us was more shocked, she at being discovered or I at being betrayed, so suddenly naked.

"It was just laying here," she said, and went on to ask me something irrelevant. I answered automatically, not really wanting to deal with the fact that the book could not have been on the bed, that it had been shelved with the earlier ones. She left, and I took my own book, opened it, and began reading with a stranger's eyes. It was terrible: incomplete snatches of doggerel, notes from meetings, dreams, angry ravings, and throughout, real and imagined accounts of sexual adventure. For a moment I felt exactly as if I had just been discovered stark naked in a room of carefully dressed people, all of my undoubtedly pornographic details showing. Had her face been flushed? Had she been getting off on my life, my imagination? What was she going to tell people?

After that, I didn't write more than careful notes, edited versions of things actually said. Very, very gradually a little more crept in—defensive, nervous, questioning—as if I were constantly surprised by the strange turns of my own imagination. Then one day I left that journal in a restaurant. I was an hour shopping, strolling home, and discovering the loss, another hour retracing my steps, terrified and nauseous until the cashier at the restaurant passed it casually back. I went off to the Confederate graveyard to look it through, searching for some clue that it had been examined in detail. Again I read with a stranger's eyes, and again it was shocking. Where was my life? Where was the adventure, the guts of everything? Why had I been so careful, and what had I really been afraid of? That someone might get off on or use my stories in some way? That

I might seem silly?

I didn't like the feel of self-censorship, the rigidity of trying to appear innocent, of curbing my own imagination to myself. After I had come out as a lesbian, begun to work as a lesbian feminist, I had made my own ethic out of public honesty, of forthright insistence on my right to be anything I damn well pleased, especially lesbian. Why then was I working so hard to pretend that I was nonsexual, that I didn't, at the least, speculate on the bed-style of every woman in whom I took an interest?

It also seemed, somehow, a betrayal of my cousins and my aunts—the lusty women of my family, as well as the butchy Beebos who caught my imagination. It was as if I were trying to be the real pornographic woman, one of those startled sleepy-eyed women in paperback, taken by surprise when confronted with the sexual. I gave up the coding and went back to pleasurable raunch.

Just below my knee, the closet stack took another turn: *The Life of Edith Cavell*, *My Story*, and *Man/Woman*. There were a few lesbian classics, including *Olivia* and *Diana*, alternated with some real trashy paperbacks, all subheaded, "the heartbreak of women who lust as men." Here, too, were the psychological tracts and case studies. I read them with nostalgia, smiling at the emphasis on old notions of perversity. Women who walk the street in trousers today have no idea what would have happened to them in those same trousers thirty years ago. Beebo Brinker again, working as an elevator operator so she could dress as she wanted. Funny how Beebo's story is trash while Natalie Barney in riding pants in the parks of Paris was "eccentric and exciting." What will they think twenty years from now of the oral histories of the passing women on file at the Lesbian Herstory Archives? There's no doubt in my mind that the oral histories of working-class dykes and passing women will get far less serious consideration than those of the famous artists and rich eccentrics. Their biographies will probably still be considered pornographic when the rest of us are shelved under literary history.

I was getting angry, irritable. The collection was no longer titil-
lating or a challenge. I didn't care anymore who it belonged to, or
how they would divide it in case of divorce. No doubt the wife would
get the lesbian case studies and the translated French "avant-garde"
novels. The husband would take the stud scorecard genre, the faggot hustlers and the forced transvestites. Just another triumph for
the gender-distinct division of interest.

Five inches from the floor I got the shock of my life. Jutting out
from the narrower books was the unmistakable Daughters Press sil-
houette from my own library of the seventies. The book was *River-
finger Woman*,* a treasure I must have read half a dozen times. What
was it doing with this other stuff? Who thought this was porn? I
opened the pages I knew so well, saw again Elana Dykewoman's
phrase: "this, the pornographic novel of my life." I shoved it back
down, started flipping books angrily, restacking the whole pile. Goddamn, who put that there? I ran out into the sunlight and dove into
the pool in my shorts.

I left the rest of the books unread. When the owners came home,
I was friendly enough. I smiled and showed them the close-cropped
lawns. I did not mention the hall closet or ask any questions. My
dreams those last few days had all been angry argument and confusion, not books turned to the wall but women—speechless, shamed,
my aunts, my cousins, old lovers, angular leering faces and shocked
innocents. I kept thinking about my books, the stories I have only
dreamed of writing. Where would strangers hide my books?

And my biography? What about my pornographic life? From
whose perspective would it be seen? Would I be a case study, light
humor, or another example of pseudoporn?

The ferns had all died back in my apartment. I went through
my underwear drawer and pulled out the paperbacks, sorted through
the small pile buried under the comforter in the corner of the stor-
age closet, and ferreted out the magazines tucked everywhere: from
the kitchen cupboard to behind the towels in the bathroom. I found

---

*Reissued by Naiad Press (Tallahassee: Florida, 1992)

them all and shelved them—middle of the living room, lower left bookcases. From now on, no hiding, no confusion. Anyone who comes to my house can see my porn.

An earlier version of this piece appeared in the *New York Native* in 1982.

Myths and Images

The world of lesbian fiction has undergone a transformation in the last few years, giving me a wealth of new writers and protagonists I can wholeheartedly recommend—Jeannette Winterson's gondolier in *The Passion,* Carol Anshaw's athlete in *Aquamarine,* April Sinclair's furious, charming adolescent in *Coffee Will Make You Black,* Blanche Boyd's witty and dangerously nervous Ellen in *Revolution of Little Girls,* and, of course, Fannie Flagg's thoroughly engaging butch/femme lovers in *Fried Green Tomatoes at the Whistle Stop Cafe.* Unfortunately, I am never satisfied.

When I read my friend Cris South's novel, *Clenched Fists, Burning Crosses,** I was surprised by a character named Moon, a pragmatic lesbian with a history in the civil rights movement, who at a moment of violent confrontation shows up with a baseball bat and the desire to use it. Only a minor character, Moon stopped the book for me—she was so familiar. I have known a lot of women who could have been Moon. One I knew very well indeed, a woman whose right elbow no longer bends easily since it was broken outside a lunch counter in Little Rock. The last I heard of her, she had married another woman in a hand-fasting ceremony, after her bride's ex-husband had sworn to kill them both. They moved to Arkansas, changed their names, and started an aluminum siding business. I

---

*Crossing Press (Freedom: California, 1985)

know telling anyone she sells aluminum siding puts my friend in the realm of the not very exciting. But I think about her a lot, and how much I'd like to write her into a novel: that big white woman who drawled stories like somebody's grandma, every one of them true, every one of them terrifying and enthralling, though for her they were just the matter-of-fact accounts of things she'd seen and done.

I've got a handful of candidates for novels in the back of my head, at least a half dozen lesbians whose lives are totally remarkable and apparently unimaginable to most of us. For years I kept looking in our fictions for the women I have loved in the world, and mostly failing to find them there. Only recently have a few begun to appear—that amazingly butch working-class-never-been-to-college-and-proud-of-it woman I've found in every city I have ever visited.

I kept thinking about an old girlfriend of mine when I was reading Leslie Feinberg's *Stone Butch Blues*,* about the story she told me, the time her daddy went out and bought her a tailored suit, tie, and fedora. Said to her, "Girl, if you've got to dress that way, at least let me show you how to do it right." He put a perfect knot in that tie, gripped her arms so tightly he left bruises, then walked out to get stunningly drunk. She stood there staring at her image in the bathroom mirror, trying to decide whether she should leave before he came back.

"Did you?" I asked her.

"Kind of," she shrugged. "I went over to my girlfriend's place to show her the suit, then came home in the morning to change my clothes for work. He was already gone, but the mattress from my bed was smoldering out in the alley below my window where he'd thrown it with all my stuff. I packed up what he hadn't burned and didn't go home again till two years later, just before he died." She looked me right in the eye and added, "For every good intention

---

*Firebrand Books (Ithaca: New York, 1993)

that man ever had, he had a dozen more that were purely evil.''
I nodded, knowing just what she meant.

I once had a very strained conversation with a forceful and much-respected lesbian editor. She wanted to know why I wouldn't review any of the novels she was publishing. Didn't I understand how important reviews were, how hard they were to get, and, moreover, how important it was for lesbian books to be taken seriously and discussed by lesbians writers? I kept going Uh-huh and Hhhmmm and trying to change the subject. I couldn't bring myself to say that for the most part I didn't even remember the titles of her books, no less the characters' names, and it just wasn't possible for me to write about fiction in which I have no interest.

Still, many of those books that I wouldn't read if I were trapped in a mine sell thousands of copies, so there obviously are lots of women who do find them interesting. A matter of taste, I've told myself, and tastes change. After all, when I was an adolescent I spent six months totally enthralled by western novels, easily rethinking the gender of all the characters. At the time it didn't matter to me who kissed whom. I just wanted to be the gunslinger on the black horse. When kissing did become important, I hunted down every ''lesbian'' character, writer, and implication I could find without regard to whether the work was any good or not. In truth, for most of my life if a book was about a ''lesbian,'' I would read it regardless of quality or interest. That is how I have gone through an enormous collection of extremely tedious fiction and several shelves of frankly grotesque medical studies, indulging an undiscriminating and omnivorous appetite for many years. Faggots and dykes, rubber freaks and transvestites—everything queer fascinated me, and nothing so much as the everyday life and romantic adventures of people in whom I could dimly see myself. I was constantly juxtaposing one set of myths against another: the imagined life of my own possibilities against the unimagined inarticulate world literature denied me.

It makes perfect sense to me that the most popular lesbian novels are romances, love stories in which the major action is when and how (not if) true love will triumph. Love stories seem to also be the most popular heterosexual fiction, and why should lesbians be different in that? Romances cross gender lines as well as categories of sexual preference. Gay men eat this mind candy with only slightly less enthusiasm than dykes, possibly because they have had more of it available to them for a longer period of time.

Unlike any number of literary lesbians I know, I am in favor of mind candy. I think romances, like science fiction, Gothics, and pornography, serve several distinct and vital purposes, not the least of which is to challenge or augment our own mythology. More than simply a mental vacation, genre fiction and romances provide a grounding in a queer version of the contemporary world. We get to see ourselves and our community on the printed page, and that is vitally important. Growing up an obsessive and self-consciously queer reader, I was ravenous for anything that remotely suggested perversity. I needed to know both that I was not the only one, and what all the people who were not queer thought it meant. After all, knowing the cultural mythology about your identity is vital to organizing your own survival. It also plays a part in developing an affirmative self-image—sometimes just by showing how wrong-headed the straight world can be about us.

"Imagine," I announced to a girlfriend after reading Carson McCullers' *Reflections in a Golden Eye*, "how many people think lesbians cut off their nipples with garden sheers." If they think that, they must be wrong about a few other things too, I reasoned. Scrupulously I researched lesbian and gay characters as presented in mainstream fiction by supposedly straight authors. Silliness, I told myself, though every now and again I'd reconsider. What, I wondered, did Carson McCullers intend with that woman who cut off her nipples—a calculated way to talk about denial and the death of the soul?

I still remember the shock with which I discovered *Carol in a Thousand Cities*, the Beebo Brinker books by Ann Bannon, and later, the weepy but entirely believable *Olivia*. Suddenly I was no longer dependent on straight people's ideas about who we were. I entered the realm of willful self-mythology. As a woman who wanted to write, nothing could have been more important than learning I didn't have to spend my life rewriting my imagination to suit a straight world.

I picked up *Rubyfruit Jungle* from a friend in 1973 and felt the world shift around me. Rita Mae Brown wasn't just a lesbian novelist, and her book wasn't just a reassuring romance. Molly Bolt was a completely new way to imagine myself. Goddamn and Hello, I shouted, and went home to reinvent my imagination again. Nor was I the only one who took up Rita Mae as a role model. Overnight, lots of lesbians started writing the politically aware novel of their own lives, which, in fact, is something we've gotten with monotonous regularity since. After a few years I started feeling like Molly Bolt was a lot to live up to, but still easier on all of us than her clones, particularly since most Molly Aspirants were dismally forgettable.

For years I have made a practice of asking people about their favorite lesbian novel, and it is amazing how many people couldn't remember one, or fell back on *The Well of Loneliness*. I never raise the question of how good the work is as literature, only how memorable—and memorable is about mythos. The characters in fiction we remember are the ones around whom we build our ideas of the world. No amount of political analysis will force people to believe in an idea they cannot imagine, or a character in which they cannot see themselves or someone they love. Unfortunately, I am never sure if it is the power of good writing that makes a character real (and thus an idea of how life can be lived), or how close the character comes to ideas people already accept or are ready to accept. Would Molly Bolt have been the same twenty years earlier? Not a chance.

Given all this, I still find myself irritated with a lot of the lesbian and gay novels being published today. I mostly don't believe in the characters, or else I'm not interested in what happens to them.

Why do so many of them talk alike and appear to have gone to the same college, seen the same movies, read the same books, and apparently lived nearly the same lives? Are we so stuck inside the boundaries of what has thus far been presented as the gay and lesbian mythos?

Well, what should we be writing? my students ask me.

Write about people who fascinate you, I tell them. Write about people who move you passionately, ideas and arguments that get you excited. Don't write uninvolved books. Write engaged books, angry, sexy, outrageous, scary, and dangerous books. Don't prop your story up with slogans, or walk your cardboard characters through the last argument you read in a news magazine. Don't write what you think you should be writing. Write what you love. Write about people you can't forget. It's time for books written by people who are in love with their characters and can make us feel that.

As a start, may I suggest someone like my friend down in Arkansas?

This essay appeared in an earlier version in March 1985 in the *New York Native*.

Bertha Harris, a Memoir

The genuine class difference between women exists between those who had para-dise and lost it, and those who never did but think they do.

Lover

She took my breath away. It was 1975 and I was at Sagaris, the fem-inist institute, taking a writing class with Bertha Harris. The big names there were Rita Mae Brown, Charlotte Bunch, Mary Daly (I still have a tape in which Daly differentiates between the lesbian from the neck up—theoretical, spiritual, and good—and the lesbian from the neck down—that bad, sexually distracted creature), Blanche Boyd, and Candace Falk. Not Bertha Harris, whose name many of us had never heard before. But it quickly became apparent to me that this woman simply *was* lesbian literature—outrageous, compli-cated, fascinating, uncompromising.

When Bertha talked about good-girl literature, banal fiction where the woman is saved by the love of a good man (or a bad man, but a man anyway), she called it cock-sucking literature, her voice edged with absolute contempt. Little shivers of awe went through me. I watched her strut back and forth, dressed in black, chain-smoking and obviously nervous. She was constantly in motion, eyes flicking from one woman to another, but when she picked up a book to read aloud she became motionless, impassioned, droll, and fearless. Writing, she told us, writing and the determination to write well, is always a revolutionary act. We all nodded, sure that it was, expecting her to go on and give the same old boring lecture. But Bertha Harris was not boring, and she never did the expected.

"Writers write for three reasons," she told us, "fame, fortune, and the love of beautiful women." When we giggled she looked at us fiercely over the lenses of her glasses. "Sigmund Freud said it first but never mind."

Was she joking? Was she serious? What an idea! Sigmund Freud and me, that dead white man and us revolutionary lesbians. I had to laugh. We all laughed. Bertha just nodded. She had gotten to us. Now, what do you write about, why do you write? Be honest. Be fearless. That is really the only thing you have to do to write. Look at your fear. The thing you fear is what you should be writing about. She quoted Collette on the subject of the taboo. "The things you hesitate to talk about," Bertha repeated in her husky North Carolina accent, "those are the things you should be writing about."

She read from the manuscript of *Lover*, the book she was going to publish with Daughters, Inc., and from her first languid intonations I fell in thrall. Oh the lesbians in that book! Complex, mesmerizing creatures who lusted after the beloved and ached with desire when she left them. Difficult women were described in a language that made them fascinating. The Rosenkavalier, about whom I knew nothing, pursued an ingenue I knew very well. The baby butch who had always despised her own body was seduced by the famous actress and fell into sex like it was a foreign country she had been born to explore. Various female martyrs appeared and reappeared, impervious to torture or the hatred of men, lesbian role models as reimagined by a woman with a completely twisted sense of humor.

It was the humor that got to me. I had no sense of humor, none, and Bertha Harris saw everything through the prism of her own wit. While I presented myself as a revolutionary in a world that was a terribly serious place—the struggle to remake that world awful and unrelenting—Bertha's wry irony mocked my pose. Her saints became a mirror in which I could no longer avoid confronting my own masochism, while her sense of humor took me back to my aunts and the family I had fled and renounced. Playful, passionate, she was the living example of a lesbian who was trying to enjoy her life, not give it over to the revolution. I didn't know whether to organize a committee to reeducate her or give in to my own fascination and try to seduce her. It didn't matter. She was a force of nature.

When Bertha Harris talked about literature, it was like listening to Billy Graham talk about God. Nothing was more important. Nothing was more demanding. The woman did not lecture, she preached. I had grown up with Baptist ministers and gospel music. Hellfire and damnation was the background to my life. Bertha's version was fast-talking, wholly rational, powerfully affirmative, but part of what made it so enticing was the aura of blasphemy that enveloped her. And she had our number cold: we were all good girls. Bad girls by society's standards, lesbians and feminists and social revolutionaries, but determinedly good girls still, afraid of offending each other. Bertha's stubborn fearlessness was almost a taunt.

"Literature is not made by good girls," she told us, "and neither is politics. Great literary artists are not into sisterhood. Great literary artists are fascists. They are bad-assed, aggressive, insistent." Naturally, she expected us to be bad girls, as she was. That most of us hadn't a clue what she was really talking about is something I did not understand until a decade later. It was not merely that she was presenting an uncompromising vision of writing as a revolutionary act, she was speaking from a position few of us had the opportunity to imagine. She had published two novels (lesbian novels, I insisted, and she just smiled) that had been critiqued as Southern Gothic, decadent, difficult, elitist, and queer—meaning not only homosexual, but strange. She was a Southern working-class female writer who created women protagonists who bordered on madness, whose voices were confusingly lush, and who, by the way, spoke mostly to each other. What was inherently lesbian about *Catching Saradove* and *Cherubino* was that their heroines were female lovers, women-focused women, and if Bertha's style was such that you could not tell whether anyone was actually having sex or crawling on their hands and knees through the garden, the lords of literature got the idea clearly enough. The mainstream literary world, as well as the so-called avant-garde and burgeoning feminist critical aristocracy, saw her as a lesbian writer who refused to obey the rules. She had already run into too many people who wanted her to write to please them: feminists who wanted an easily accessible political fiction, lesbians who wanted great love stories or inspirational accounts of coming out healthy in a homophobic world. None of them got what they wanted. Bertha was a true believer, and literature for her was about refusing all categories, all who would shape her writing to their own use. She could no more write agitprop than she could give up women and start raising rug-rats for some macho stud.

She quarreled with everything. "Goddess worship," she sneered, "moon-womb crap," and I watched the mouths of the women around me fall open in shock, or thin out in fury. Talking like that back then was like walking into a convent to make jokes about Jesus. "There is no point in immersing yourself in a great big cosmic moonpie of goddess worship," she went on, "and reverencing the fact that your plumbing makes you bleed once a month, or in running around with your eyes cast up in awe to anyone else at all." I dropped my eyes but couldn't quite rid myself of the awe. I could easily have formed the church (or maybe coven) of the Blasphemous Bertha, but she wouldn't have cooperated. Bertha didn't want followers or worshippers. She wanted colleagues, big bad girls who would throw out the bullshit and get down to the work that would really challenge the world, take on the boys on their own ground and outwrite them.

There is no lesbian literature, she told us. The relevant word was *literature,* real literature that came out of an authentic lesbian culture. She dismissed works in which what took place in bed was isolated from the larger world, books where the lesbian went straight (or died) or adopted men's attitudes (phallic socialization, she called it), or worst of all, books that lied—particularly those lesbian party-line novels portraying lesbian sexuality as a simple thing, all sweetness and light, or a politically determined act. *Lies make bad literature and bad politics,* she said in a conversation with June Arnold in the Lesbian issue of *Margins.* She warned that some thirteen-year-old girl up in Saskatchewan was going to read those books and suffer from those lies. "We've got to tell the truth," she said over and over again. She wanted a politics that was constantly moving and changing, integrated with an esthetics that was also moving and changing. Nothing simple, nothing frozen, nothing handed down from a committee or on high.

Bertha wanted authenticity, our own culture, reality in life and the arts, and for us not to lose our specialness, our badness, our monstrosity, our affront to that appeasing middle-class mind that she knew was incapable of making great art. When we puffed up in outrage at her, she just smiled maddeningly, and many of us walked away determined to show her she was wrong, to find it or write it and prove to her it existed. What she knew that we did not was that the strength of the desire to be good was to be like everyone else, to hestitate to be bad when it really counted, among our own and with each other. The fear of being monstrous, alone, and denied would dog us all, destroy some of us, and bend that culture we all dreamed about into shapes we could not then imagine.

In "The Purification of Monstrosity: The Lesbian as Literature," Bertha Harris warned, "Most lesbians (like everyone else) would rather feel than read, thus achieving their most longed-for goal: to be like everyone else. And that is too bad. Lesbians, instead, might have been great, as some literature is: unassimilable, awesome, dangerous, outrageous, different, distinguished. Lesbians, as some literature is, might have been monstrous—and thus have everything." Lesbian writing that only replicated heterosexual reality was failing to live up to its own potential, getting in the way of that lesbian culture we all needed so badly. This is the standard for greatness, Bertha Harris told us.

She scared us. At least she scared me. It was not so simple as fighting the patriarchy and being courageous on the page; writing was more than craft. The degree of personal fearlessness demanded was enormous and not simple. When Bertha put her hands on her hips, glared out at us, and announced, "Literature is made by people who are absolutely convinced that they are wonderful, who worship themselves," I almost swallowed my tongue. When she talked about wanting literature, I understood. I, too, wanted literature, but I had no conviction of my own worth, none of the arrogance, insistence, and aggression that Bertha ascribed to great writers. I had only begun to figure out who I might be, not who I was, and listening to Bertha I hunched my shoulders and began to wonder if maybe I should just quit trying to write at all. Settle instead for being the lover of someone who believed in themselves like that. It took me a long time to come to the realization that the conviction of self-worth was something I could only develop through writing itself, through the act of creating a fiction I believed in and wanted to defend—aggressively, insistently, and with all the bad-assed determination of someone to whom literature was nominally denied.

Bertha talked about class, and again she took what we expected to hear and did something different with it. Class was a notion which in the early days of feminism got a lot more lip service than examination. Bertha had her own approach. "In terms of class dynamics and psychology, they [great literary artists] are all lower class," said Bertha, "direct, unequivocating, grabby, impolite, always ready for a fight, and with a nose that can smell bullshit a mile away. The ecumenical, appeasing, side-stepping, middle-class mind never ever produces a great work of art, nor a great work of politics." It was a homage and a challenge, another turning over of the expected, and a demand that we embrace the source of our fears. As a working-class escapee still trying to pay off an enormous college debt and work out how to keep my mama from treating me like a stranger, I gulped down Bertha's lauding of what trash might do like a thirsty woman sucks liquid. My middle-class girlfriends heard those words and thought she meant that they, too, could adopt the bad-assed style of the class. I heard those words as a direct attack on my hesitation and fears, a demand that I get my butt in gear and start living up to the tradition.

Dare to be monstrous, she told us in that tone of irony that warned of puns and witticisms to follow. The monster is female, wild, dangerous, a hero and a criminal in one terrifying flesh—an enemy to the cock culture that attempts to reduce everything to heterosexual materiality. *Remember, the central female organ that makes us different and strong and artists is not the womb but the brain.*

Talking about the monster, Bertha scowled and glared and shuffled her papers impatiently. You can do more, she was telling us, demanding of us. Don't settle for being what they think you are. Find out what you can be, and write it out. She did not say, It won't be easy. She did not say, No one will even notice you are trying. She did not say, You will eat yourself up alive, disappear to the world and become something you cannot now imagine. She said, ''Money, fame. . .women.'' But all that has ever mattered is the women.

This essay appeared in the *Village Voice* in October 1993.

Survival Is the Least of My Desires

I was asked to speak about survival. The difficulty for me is that survival is the least of my desires. I'm interested in a lot more than mere survival. And I do not feel old enough or smart enough to be able to tell other lesbian and gay writers how to survive, much less to send everyone out of this place feeling inspired, provoked, challenged, and determined; to convince people that we, as a community, are capable of so much more than endurance. What I do know is that we must aim much higher than just staying alive if we are to begin to approach our true potential.

I am part of a nation that is not secret but is rarely recognized. Born poor, queer, and despised, I have always known myself one of many—strong not because I was different, but because I was part of a nation just like me, human and fragile and stubborn and hungry for justice in an unjust world. I am past forty now. I have known I was a lesbian since I was a teenager, known I wanted to write almost as long.

My age, my family background, the region and class in which I grew up, and yes, my times—the political and moral eras I have come through—have shaped me. I was the first person in my family to graduate from high school, the first to go to college. It is hard for me to explain what an extraordinary thing that was: to be not only the first, but for a long time the only one of my people to step outside the tight hostile world in which we were born. But I went to college in the early seventies, and I had the great good fortune of being there at a time when lots of other working-class kids were also confronting a world in which we were barely acknowledged. That experience spurred in me, as in many of us, an outrage and determination that questioned accepted barriers of authority, validation, rightness. I became convinced that to survive I would have to remake the world so that it came closer to matching its own ideals.

In college, I was involved in civil rights activism and antiwar demonstrations. I became a feminist activist when other people my age were marrying or joining the Peace Corps or starting careers. All those things that they were doing that I did not do shaped my life, what I thought I could do with my life. Understand me, I am one of those dangerous ones. I have never wanted to be rich. I have always wanted a great deal more. I have always wanted to remake the world, and that is a much more greedy, far-reaching ambition than cash. I joined a small nation of would-be revolutionaries, queers and feminists and working-class escapees, dreamers most of us, who wanted a world in which no one was denied justice, no one was hated for their origins, color, beliefs, or sexuality. Though it is rarely acknowledged, people like me have remade this world in the last few decades.

Let me make clear how much has changed in the short span of my life. Although there are few people who think of themselves as revolutionaries anymore, the world has been remade. Look around you. Apartheid is being dismantled and Nelson Mandela walks the streets of South Africa. Until a few years ago, I could not imagine that happening. Russia is a new place, so is China. The communist bogeyman I was threatened with throughout my childhood is gone. The world is no less dangerous, and people are still dying for their origins, beliefs, color, and sexuality, but I find myself full of startled awe and hope. The rigid world into which I was born has been shaken profoundly. *Homosexual* is no longer a psychiatric disorder, and my lover and I actually married each other down at City Hall in San Francisco last spring.

The world is a new place, but it still needs to be remade. We still need revolutionaries. It was more than ten years ago that the first person I knew personally died of AIDS. Last year I lost four more friends, four more of the many who should not have died. This last year my lover's ex-girlfriend turned up in jail after living on the streets for two years, my last aunt followed my mother into death by cancer, and I went through each day without health insurance, knowing that most likely I, too, will die of cancer before I am sixty. Half of the people I know live without health insurance or the certainty of a living wage. The world needs to be remade. The brilliant, talented, young gay men and lesbian writers in my life earn barely enough to pay their rent, much less buy the time they need to write the books I want to read. We live, all of us, in the most impossible conflict, poor because of the work we choose to do, the lies we choose not to tell. Most of us know that sending applications to the National Endowment for the Arts or well-funded grants committees is like throwing a snowball into the sun. Our own organizations—our presses, magazines, bookstores, and writing programs—barely survive. Oh yes, the world needs to be remade.

If we, as writers, are to continue, we need more people of large ambition, people who refuse censorship, denial, and hatred, people who still hope to change the world. Writers who see themselves as revolutionaries, who turn up at demonstrations or envelope-stuffing parties with the shadows under their eyes that prove how many nights they've gotten up, after a limited sleep, to hone their skills and dream on the page the remade world.

I have lived my life in pursuit of the remade world.

When I was twenty-two, I helped organize a rape crisis center. That same year I was involved in starting a feminist bookstore, staffing a women's center, volunteering as a lesbian peer counselor, teaching a feminist anthropology course, editing a feminist magazine, trying to organize a waitress union, and organizing a lesbian-feminist living collective that became my family and home for eight years.

I did all of that before I was twenty-four, telling myself that if only I could give up more sleep I could get so much more done. These days I look around and think we need a few more people willing to give up a little sleep.

Except for the fact that I lived for eight years in that lesbian-feminist collective, I am like most of the other lesbians I know, the women I love. I have always written after everything else was done, in spare moments after filling in at the childcare center, or building shelves for the bookstore, or preparing grant applications, first for the women's center and then the women's studies department and then the magazines. I have worked with four feminist magazines. None of them still survive.

When I was twenty-four I read everything written by lesbians—and when I was twenty-four it was still possible. I rarely dealt with men, rarely contacted my family, was strictly nonmonogamous, wrote bad poetry when I was too tired to sleep, and taught myself, laboriously, to write fiction in short snatches of time stolen from my day job. I edited other people's writing for long years before I published my own. I didn't publish anything until I began to think I might be good enough. And to put it frankly, by my own standards I am still rarely good enough. What I want—my ambition—is larger than anyone imagines. I want to be able to write so powerfully I can break the heart of the world and heal it. I want to write in such a way as to literally remake the world, to change people's thinking as they look out of the eyes of the characters I create.

I am and always have been completely matter-of-fact about being a lesbian. The statements of gay writers who defensively insist that they wish to be seen as writers first and gay or lesbian secondarily, who insist they simply happen to be queer, that being queer has nothing to do with what or how they write; the arguments that take place between those writers and those others who despise the first category, who take their sexual identities as their primary subject and the underlying factor of their esthetic—those loud insistent arguments seem to me mostly intellectual, beside the point, and curiously old-fashioned. I have never imagined that there was any question about my sexual preference, and as a feminist I know that my convictions shape what I write about, what voice I can manifest, and what kinds of characters I will imagine—what I can write at all. I am one whole person, one whole person who is a lesbian and a writer.

When I listened to Edward Albee speak at the second OutWrite conference in San Francisco in 1991, I kept thinking that the times and the ethos that had shaped his concept of who he was—both as a gay man and a writer—were not so maddening as tragic. That it was first and foremost a waste that he had spent so much of his life in a defensive struggle to claim himself and his sexuality in the face of an ignorant and hateful public. Worse, it seemed that fighting so hard for that sexuality had left him bitterly ignorant of how interlinked the struggles for gay rights and human rights are, unable to see how much the struggle for other people's hopes is related to his own. If we are forced to talk about our lives, our sexuality, and our work only in the language and categories of a society that despises us, eventually we will be unable to speak past our own griefs. We will disappear into those categories. What I have tried to do in my own life is refuse the language and categories that would reduce me to less than my whole complicated experience. At the same time I have tried to look at people different from me with the kind of compassion I would like to have directed toward me.

When I think about that generation of writers that Edward Albee is part of, I become more determined to remake the world. I work to make it possible for young queer writers not to have to waste so much of themselves fighting off the hatred and dismissal of an ignorant majority. But to make any contribution to other lives, I know that I must first begin in the carefully examined specifics of my own. I must acknowledge who has helped me survive and how my own hopes have been shaped. I must acknowledge the miracles in my life.

Yes, I have been shaped as a lesbian and a writer by miracles. Miracles, as in wonders and marvels and astonishing accidents, fortunate juxtapositions and happy encounters, some resulting from work and luck but others unexplained and unexplainable. It was a miracle that I survived my childhood to finish high school and get that scholarship to college. It was a miracle that I discovered feminism and found that I did not have to be ashamed of who I was. Feminism gave me the possibility of understanding my place in the world, and I claim it as a title and an entitlement.

But feminism, for me, was not only about sex. Sexual desire was more problematic. When I was very young I imagined that I would have to be celibate. I knew what I wanted from the first flush of puberty. I knew what I wanted to do with those girls in school. And all around me I saw fear and death and damnation. You cannot imagine how terrified I was at twelve and thirteen. I decided I would become a kind of Baptist Nun. That seemed a reasonable choice after my family moved to Central Florida and I snuck off to the gay bar down near the Trailways bus station in Orlando, Florida. I took one look at those women and knew I was in a lot of trouble. I knew, pretty much from the beginning, what was going to happen to me. I knew I was femme, opinionated, bossy, completely romantically masochistic, and that those girls were going to eat me alive.

So the choice was to be eaten alive or to become celibate.

It's a wonder there's a scrap of me left.

It was a miracle that I figured out what it was I enjoyed sexually that did not require my partner to be crazy drunk, violently angry, or to acquire permanent rights to my body just because she knew how to make me come. It was a miracle that I kept on writing fiction for my own satisfaction even when I truly believed in the women's revolution and was completely convinced it would never come about if I didn't personally raise the money for it, staff the phones, and cook the protein dish for the potluck where we would all plan it. Miracles, incidental and marvelous, women and men met at the right time or just past it, but still soon enough to save me from giving up or doing myself more damage than I could survive. I cling to no organized religion, but I believe in the continuing impact of miracles.

Finally, I have to tell you that it was a miracle I did not kill myself out of sheer despair when I was told I was too lesbian for feminism, too reformist for radical feminism, too sexually perverse for respectable lesbianism, and too damn stubborn for the women's, gay, and queer revolutions. That I am here now, writing and speaking and teaching, and living out my own feminist ideals, is astonishing. I have changed nothing. The world has been remade.

I believe in the truth. I believe in the truth in the way only a person who has been denied any use of it can believe in it. I know its power. I know the threat it represents to a world constructed on lies. I believe any trick that keeps you writing the truth is all right, but that some tricks are more expensive than others. The one I have used most often and most successfully is that gambit in which I pretend that I am only one person trying to get down my version of what happened. My writing becomes fiction soon enough anyway. The truth is wider than the details of what really happened in my life.

I know the myths of the family that thread through our society's literature, music, politics—and I know the reality. The reality is that for many of us family was as much the incubator of despair as the safe nurturing haven the myths promised. We are not supposed to talk about our real family lives, especially if our families do not duplicate the mythical heterosexual model. In a world in which only a fraction of people actually live in that "Father Knows Best" nuclear family, in which the largest percentage of families consists of women and children existing in poverty, we need to hear a lot more about those of us who are happy that we do not live inside that mythical model. But I also believe in hope. I believe in the remade life, the possibilities inherent in our lesbian and gay chosen families, our families of friends and lovers, the healing that can take place among the most wounded of us. My family of friends has kept me alive through lovers who have left, enterprises that have failed, and all too many stories that never got finished. That family has been part of remaking the world for me.

The worst thing done to us in the name of a civilized society is to label the truth of our lives material outside the legitimate subject matter of serious writers. We are not supposed to talk about our sexuality, not in any more than the most general and debased terms, our passions reduced to addictions or the subject of poorly thought-out theories of deviance and compulsion, our legendary loving relationships rewritten as the bland interactions of best friends or interlocking systems of dependence and necessary economic solutions.

I need you to do more than survive. As writers, as revolutionaries, tell the truth, your truth in your own way. Do not buy into their systems of censorship, imagining that if you drop this character or hide that emotion, you can slide through their blockades. Do not eat your own heart out in the hope of pleasing them. The only hope you have, the only hope any of us has, is the remade life. It is the only way we will all survive, and trading any of us for some of us is no compromise. It is the way we will lose our lives, all our lives.

The second worse thing done to us is a thing we do to each other. We ask each other to always represent our sexuality and relationships as simple, straightforward, and life-saving. We want to hear heroic stories, legends where the couples find each other in the end and go off into the sunset, with the one distinction that they are the same gender arm in arm and lip-locked into the next dawn. We need our romances, yes, our happy endings. But don't gloss over the difficulties and rewrite the horrors. Don't make it all easier than it is and soften the tragedies. Don't pretend we are not really murdered in the streets or broken in the darkened bedrooms of the American family. We need the truth. And yes, it is hard when fighting for your life and the lives of those you love to admit just how daunting that fight can be, to acknowledge how many of us are lost, how many destroyed, to pick apart the knots of fantasy and myth that blunt our imaginations and stalk our hopes for families in which we can trust each other and the future. But if I am to survive, I need to be able to trust your stories, to know that you will not lie even to comfort.

I believe the secret in writing is that fiction never exceeds the reach of the writer's courage. The best fiction comes from the place where the terror hides, the edge of our worst stuff. I believe, absolutely, that if you do not break out in that sweat of fear when you write, then you have not gone far enough. And I know you can fake that courage when you don't think of yourself as courageous—because I have done it. And that is not a bad thing, to fake it until you can make it. I know that until I started pushing on my own fears, telling the stories that were hardest for me, writing about exactly the things I was most afraid of and unsure about, I wasn't writing worth a damn.

I write what I think are "moral tales." That's what I intend, though I grow more and more to believe that telling the emotional truth of people's lives, not necessarily the historical truth, is the only moral use of fiction. I'll give you an example. The historical truth about the child on whom I based my character Shannon Pearl is that she went on, a child of her culture, and lives that life still, as far as I know, back in Greenville, though the child I remember knew nothing about gospel music. I gave her that life to make a larger story. But what is emotionally true is that she was someone I thought of as squeezed down, her soul like a pearl compressed as tight and white as cold stone. Maybe the "truer" story of her life would be a better one than "Gospel Song," but I give myself the benefit of the doubt. This was the story I could write then, and it is as true as I could make it. Its veracity lies in the complexity of the character, that she is hated and hateful, that she is not a nice but a tragic person. I do not write about nice people. I am not nice people. Neither is anyone I have ever cared deeply about. The truth about our lives is not nice, and acknowledging that allows me to make the people in my stories more whole, to truly honor those I have lost. It's something I am not always able to do as well as I would like. But wanting this in my stories is about wanting myself whole.

Some of my stories that read hard from the outside are much easier in the writing, stories fueled entirely by rage. Anger is easy. Most of my short story collection, *Trash*, was written in rage. If I'd done it more in grief, it might have been a better book, but I needed to work through the rage first. Sooner or later, though, if you keep pushing yourself, you begin writing stories out of more than rage, and they begin to tear you apart even as you write them. Oddly enough, that tearing open makes possible a healing, not only in the writer but in the world as well. It is as if you were opening up scar tissue and allowing new growth. The easiest story for me to write is the one in which I sit down in front of the imaginary image of the one person I have always ached to say something to—my stepfather, or my mother, or my first lover—and I begin the story by saying, "You son-of-a-bitch. . . ." That's easy. I let the anger tell the story. The harder stories are the ones where I begin with grief or the attempt to understand, the stories that start, "I'm sorry," or even, "I was so ashamed," or, "Goddamn, I miss you so much."

I want hard stories. I demand them from myself. I demand them from my students and friends and colleagues. Hard stories are worth the difficulty. It seems to me the only way I have forgiven anything, understood anything, is through that process of opening up to my own terror and pain and reexamining it, recreating it in the story, and making it something different, making it meaningful—even if the meaning is only in the act of the telling. Some things are absolutely unjust, without purpose, horrible and blinding, soul-destroying: the death of the beloved, the rape of a child. Situations some of us know all too well. There was no meaning in what my stepfather did to me. But the stories I have made out of it do have meaning. More importantly, those stories do not function as some form of retribution. They are redress for all those like me, whether they can write their own stories or not. My stories are not *against* anyone; they are *for* the life we need.

It has taken me twenty years to be able to write what I write now, but what I wrote nineteen years ago was just as important. There's an essay by Ursula LeGuin* that I love, where she talks about the importance of women offering their own experience as wisdom, how each individual perception is vital. That's what I believe to be the importance of telling the truth, each of us writing out of the unique vision our lives have given us. It is the reason I urge the young writers I work with to confront their own lives in their fiction. Not that they must write autobiography, but that they must use the whole of their lives in the making of the stories they tell; they must honor their dead, their wounded and lost; they must acknowledge their own crimes and shame, feel the impact of what they do and do not do in the world in their stories. I tell them they must take the business of storytelling completely seriously. I want the stories I read to take me over, to make me see people I do not know as they see themselves —the scared little girl who grew up lesbian, the faggot child who loved and hungered for truth, the young dying unjustly and too soon who talk about death familiarly and make me laugh at my own fears. Each of us has our own bitterness, our own fear and that stubborn tenderness we are famous for. Each of us has our own stories and none of them are the same no matter how similar some of the details. Tell me the truth and I make you a promise. If you show me yours, I'll show you mine. That's what writers do for each other.

Write your stories any way you have to frame it to get it out, any time you can get it done. Use any trick. I want to know what it was that you looked at unflinchingly, even if you did not know what you were seeing at the time. If nothing else works, start by writing that story for me. Imagine me. I was born to die. I know that. If I could have found what I needed at thirteen, I would not have lost so much of my life chasing vindication or death. Give some child, some thirteen-year-old, the hope of the remade life. Tell the truth. Write

---

* "The Fisherman's Daughter" in *Dancing at the Edge of the World* (Grove Press: New York, 1989)

the story that you were always afraid to tell. I swear to you there is magic in it, and if you show yourself naked for me, I'll be naked for you. It will be our covenant.

I tell people that I write mean stories, and I do—stories that tell the truth that I know and only the part I know, because I don't know that much. I know about being queer in this decade, about the grief inherent in losing so many friends, so many memories, so many members of our precious remade families. I have no aunts left to tell me stories, and three-quarters of the young gay men that I worked with and learned to love when I first began to write are gone, along with far too many of the lesbians.

AIDS and cancer have run through my community—not metaphors, but death in wholesale numbers. Sections of my life have disappeared with the ones we have lost, and I feel a great pressure to write the stories that would somehow preserve those times, those people, my friends: John Fox, Mary Helen Mautner, Allen Barnett, Geoff Maines, Vito Russo, Cynthia Slater, George Stambolian, and too many more to list in anything less than a massive memorial. Just my personal friends who have died, the list is too long. How can I not write mean stories? I don't have that child's easy hope for better times that fueled so much of my early stories. I have fallen in love with the hard side, with the women and men made tough by life and loss, who nonetheless have never lost their determined love for their own kind. If I am not mean enough to honor them, then I have no right to the stories.

I need you to write mean stories. I need you to honor our dead, to help them survive. More than ten years ago, I wrote a poem about a lesbian who died in Boston, a death I read about in the paper and knew immediately could have been my own. The death of a woman who "might not have been known to be a lesbian" but who, as I read her poem in public, I learned more and more about until I was certain that not only her death, but her life, could have been my own, and that very likely she, too, would have wanted the mean story of

her life told. I made a mean piece of hope out of telling about her,
because I believe that if I died that death someone would sing my
song, recount my story.

More and more of what I write now I write in homage to those
we have lost. To do more than survive, that is what we need, what
I need from you. I need you to tell the truth, to tell the mean stories, and to sing the song of hope. I need all of us to live forever and
to remake the world. Listen again to the words of my poem and
remember the life it honors, the remade life denied to one of us.

Boston, Massachusetts, many years ago
a woman told me about a woman dead,
a woman who might not have been known
to be a lesbian.

No one is sure they knew that.
The cops didn't say that, they said
she was wearing a leather jacket, blue jeans, worn boots,
had dark cropped hair and was new to the neighborhood,
living in an old brick rowhouse with three other women.
Said she was carrying a can of gasoline.
They did not say why,
a car waiting
a jar of sticky brushes.
Said she was white
her friends were white
the neighborhood was bad,
she and her friends were fools
didn't belong there
were queer anyway.
Said the young rough crowd of men
laughed a lot
when they stopped her,
that she laughed back,

and then
they made her pour the gasoline
over her head.

> Later, some cop said
> she was a hell of a tough bitch
> 'cause she walked two blocks on her own feet,
> two blocks to the all-night grocery
> where another little crowd watched
> going
>> *Shiiiiiit!*
>> *Will you look at that?*
>> *Look at that!*

I read about it in the paper—two paragraphs
I have carried that story with me ever since
wanting more, wanting no one to have to be
those two stark paragraphs.

We become our deaths.
Our names disappear and our lovers leave town,
heartbroken, crazy,
but we are the ones who die.
We are the forgotten
burning in the streets
hands out, screaming,
> *This is not all I am.*
> *I had something else in mind to do.*

> Not on that street,
> always and only that
> when there was so much more she had to do.

Sometimes
when I love my lover
I taste in my mouth

> ashes
> gritty
> grainy

grating between the teeth
the teeth of a woman
unquestionably known
to be a lesbian.*

Keynote address at OutWrite 1992, the lesbian and gay writers conference.

---

* *The Women Who Hate Me* (Firebrand Books: Ithaca, New York, 1991)

Skin, Where She Touches Me

Skin, the surface of skin, the outer layer protecting the vulnerable inside, the boundary between the world and the soul, what is seen from the outside and hides all the secrets. My skin, my mama's skin, my sisters' skin. Our outer layer hides our inner hopes. White girls, tough-skinned and stubborn, born to a family that never valued girls. I am my mama's daughter, one with my tribe, taught to believe myself of not much value, to take damage and ignore it, to take damage and be proud of it. We were taught to be proud that we were not Black, and ashamed that we were poor, taught to reject everything people believed about us—drunken, no-count, lazy, whorish, stupid—and still some of it was just the way we were. The lies went to the bone, and digging them out has been the work of a lifetime.

Death changes everything. The death of someone you love alters even the boundaries of the imagination. The dead become fiction, myth, and legend. The two most important women in my life—my mother and my first lover—are dead. Because I cannot stop talking about them, retelling their stories and making them mine, turning their jokes to parables and their stubborn endurance to legend, I can feel them changing, in my own mind and in the imaginations of those who know them only through me. Writing about them, I have been holding on to them, even as I was when they were alive. Telling stories about people very like them, but not really them, has been a way

225

to save what they and I have lost. But death is more than the closing of a life. Death is the point at which people begin to sum up,
to say what things meant, what the life was about, what was accomplished and what was not. Death is the point at which, if it has not
already been claimed, vindication becomes possible. Death changes
everything.

No matter what I say about my mother or my first lover, you
cannot know if it is true. You cannot go and see them, hear their
versions of my stories. You cannot watch my mama laugh with her
hand drawn up before her mouth to hide her loose teeth. You cannot look into her eyes and see what half a century of shame and grief
did to her. You cannot ask Cathy what she meant when she told
everyone that it was I who was the lesbian, not her.

Two women, as complicated and astonishing as any women can
be, have shaped who I have become. I can look down at my hands
and see their hands touching mine, imagine their voices, things they
said or might have said, things they wanted to do but never got a
chance to. I think sometimes that I have been driven to write fiction because of those I have lost, the first woman I ever fell passionately in love with, and my mother, the first woman I ever understood
to be deeply hurt and just as deeply heroic. I have written stories
about people like them out of my need to understand them and re-
imagine their lives. Better to mythologize them, I have told myself,
than to leave them with their fractured lives cut off too soon.

My mother died of cancer, twenty minutes before I could reach
her bedside, just before midnight on November 11, 1990. She was
fifty-six years old and had had cancer for thirty of them—a hysterectomy when I was a child, two mastectomies five years apart, and finally the tumors in her lung, brain, and liver that she could not survive. For half my life I had been separated from her, unable to be
in her home while she lived with my stepfather, but talking to her
every few weeks, sending her copies of everything I wrote, and always knowing that whatever else was uncertain in our lives, her love

for me was like mine for her—unquestioning, absolute, and painful.

When I was in my twenties, my mother and I had come to an exacting agreement: I would come home very rarely, but not talk about why that was so. The promise I made her was that I would not cause trouble, would not fight with my stepfather or even be cold to him on the phone, that I would cooperate in the family effort to keep the peace. She would not demand more of me. Through all the years, we rarely talked about my stepfather and the violence Mama always believed to have been her responsibility. She had never been able to stop it, and she had never left him. Only toward the end of her life did she begin to ask me to forgive her, and no matter how much I assured her that I loved her and understood what she had done, she never forgave herself.

On the afternoon my mama was buried, my sisters and I went through her photographs with our aunt Nuell, who came the morning after Mama died and stayed with us for the next three days—through the first grief and the awful funeral. We let her take over caring for our stepfather, feeling only a moment's hesitation because we knew her so slightly. She was not one of the Gibson sisters, only our aunt by marriage. She had married Mama's little brother, Tommy, and moved with him to Alabama in the late 1950s. All our lives we had been hearing stories about her but had seen her only a few times. Still, when she got the call about Mama, she drove through the night to be with us for the funeral, and her presence made things easier. It was as if she had taken on the mantle of our legendary aunts, hugging us like we were children, telling us what to do, making it easier to do as she wanted than to argue. She sat down with us to go through the torn and faded pictures as if that were just one more part of being the oldest living woman in the family. Some of the vaguely recognizable faces she knew instantly.

"Your great-aunt," she said, pointing to an almost washed-out image of a woman standing in front of a gas station storefront. "Don't think I ever knew her name, but she was the one moved off to Oklahoma before your mama married your daddy. And oh, this one, this one is Tommy and Jack when they were boys, that's David and Dan, and those—those look like some boys from the air base. Don't know if you're related or not.''

My sister Barbara rolled her eyes over to my sister June. June looked at me. I tried politely to interrupt Aunt Nuell, to ask if she could maybe write down the names she remembered on the photos themselves.

"Oh, I suppose," she murmured, bending over the big pile and pulling out one picture after another. Her eyes were soft and wet. Though she could only remember a few names, and fewer incidents, the impact of the features was unmistakable. "All these people are gone," she said once, in a voice so taut and pained I didn't dare ask more of her.

My uncle Jack arrived the night before the funeral. When I saw him in the morning, his face was awestruck, horrible. He couldn't smile at me, only grimaced, his mouth pulled back and the loose skin of his face falling into folds. The creases running down from his cheeks were gullies, his eyes were peach-pit hollows, black seeds unable to face the morning sun. He stayed out on the grass, refusing to go inside the funeral home or come to the grave site. When I walked over to put some flowers on the casket, I looked back and saw him standing rigid and tall on a little rise near the memorial to the veterans of American wars. The sun glinted off the wet on his face, the face itself so anguished I could not stand to look at him.

He was the last, though one of Mama's sisters was hanging on—Maudy with the colostomy bag hidden under her housedress, her raging temper still flaring at the nieces and nephews who prowled her porch. She had sent a message, a spray of flowers Cousin Bobby had probably arranged.

"Bobby's the one gets things done," everyone told me the last time I visited Greenville. Aunt Dot was still alive then, playing the role my grandmother Mattie Lee had played before her death—

telling everyone's secrets and coaxing you out of yours so she could say she knew everything first. Dot said it was Bobby who got her sister to check into a motel when she was dying of breast cancer, this after some of her children had been caught stealing her painkillers for their own use.

"Little sons-a-bitches," Aunt Dot had mouthed around her false teeth. "Should have drowned those little bastards while they were still small enough for us to get away with it." I had never had a chance to ask Bobby if the story was true, and Mama wouldn't talk about it, just told me that, yes, my cousin had spent the weeks before she died in a motel out on the edge of Greenville where the Highway 85 overpass cut south of the city.

"Now that's a mean story," I had said to Mama. "Worse than anything I've even thought of writing."

"That imply you an't gonna think about it now?" Mama had looked at me with a patient, almost martyred expression. I had flushed with embarrassment, nodding reluctantly, agreeing that I might write about it someday. There were many things we did not talk about, but we both tried never to lie to each other knowingly. Some of what I wrote had been painful for my mama to read, but she had never suggested I should not write those stories and publish them. "I've never been afraid of the truth," she told me after my book of short stories came out. She spoke in the blunt, stubborn tone that meant she was saying something she wanted to be true.

My mama had been ashamed too often in her life, ashamed of things she could not have managed differently, and more ashamed of being ashamed than of the original sins. Shame was one of the things my mama hated, one of the things she tried to root out of herself and us. And shame was the constant theme of my childhood.

"Never back down," my mama taught me. "Never drop your eyes. People look at you like a dog, you dog them." I had laughed and tried to emulate her, to stare back at hatred and stare down contempt. Like Mama, I learned to stand tall when confronted by my sins, to say, All right, so what? Like Mama, I learned to gaze at the world with my scars and outrage plainly revealed, determined not to hide, not to drop my head or admit defeat. It was good training for a child of the Southern working poor, better training for an adolescent lesbian terrified of what her desires might mean, who she might become and what she might learn about herself.

"The truth won't kill me," Mama said, but I wasn't sure I believed her. Truth seemed to me a very dangerous, tricky concept. Was truth only what we agreed it to be, or was there a book somewhere that would show me the real truth, the rules of right and wrong? A complicated system of vindication and judgment hid behind the small truths everyone presented as Truth. "What's going on here?" my stepfather would shout at us some evenings, and we would all freeze and drop our heads, knowing that he did not really want to know, knowing that to tell him the truth about what we were thinking or feeling or planning was the most foolish choice we could make. No, the truth was something to keep to ourselves and protect—when we knew what it was, when we could be sure of anything.

Skin fear, pulling back, flinching before the blow lands. Anticipating the burn of shame and the shiver of despair. Conditioned to contempt and reflexive rage, I am pinned beneath a lattice, iron-hard and locked down. Believing myself inhuman, mutant, too calloused to ever love deeply or well.

My first lover had been beaten by her father. Everybody who knew Cathy had heard how her daddy caught her at sixteen with her blouse open and her hands in her boyfriend's jeans. He called her a whore and threw her out on the street. She repaid him by going back a few nights later to smash the windows in his truck and smear shit on his radiator coils. When she told me that story I smiled, admiring wholeheartedly any woman strong enough to have taken that particular revenge on a truck-loving Southern man. But by the time I met her, Cathy was three years past her revenge, three years of living hand to mouth with one boyfriend after the other, doing heroin when she could get it and shivering sick when she could not. She wasn't charming. She was so deeply scored by anger that there was no measuring where the anger left off and a woman you could love might begin. Most people were afraid of her, and so was I, some, especially when she looked at me and laughed, knowing at a glance what none of the other would-be hippies in our little community had figured out—that I was a lesbian, and the flush on my face was not only self-consciousness but lust.

Why does anyone fall passionately in love? Does the beloved have to know something, have something, be something you do not know, or have, or cannot be yourself? I had no idea. But from the moment Cathy put her palm flat on my breast and her teeth close to my ear, I knew that I could go mad with love for her. She smelled strong and dangerous and marvelous. When she crawled naked into the bed where I had been lying, hoping she would come to find me, her skin was burning hot, scorching mine at every surface. Still, instead of flinching away I pushed up into her, wanting that heat, wanting her more than I had ever wanted anything.

Within our family it was astonishingly difficult to sort out the truth from the lies. If you did not think about things—and there were so many things all of us tried not to think about—you tended to lose track of what you really thought or felt. We had been raised on public contempt and private outrage, been told every day of our lives that there was something intrinsically wrong with us. Our stepfather shouted it at us, the Baptist ministers said it in soft, sad voices, and the girls at school made it plain with their laughter and comments on how we dressed. Mama's response to that chorus was rage and stubborn insistence that we act as if we didn't believe any of it. But we knew that the power of public opinion wounded her too. She was never as confident as she tried to pretend. I could look into my mama's exhausted grey features and see just how painful, how dangerous the truth could be. The truth might vindicate us, but then again it might destroy us. We might as easily find that all those hateful faces turned to us were right and we were damned from birth, helpless to escape the trap that had ground down our mama. It was never simple. It was never easy to know what was true.

I found ever more complicated truths as I grew up. There was, for example, the fact that Mama told me to my face that she was proud of my writing and "didn't give a rat's ass if I married puppy dogs so long as I was happy." But even as I let her hold me close and say it, I knew that the magazines and stories I sent her disappeared into one box or another, that she never showed what I wrote to anyone, not even my sisters, and certainly never talked about it.

Aunt Dot told me once that the thing Mama regretted most about my life was that I had not had a child. "She don't mind you keeping company with women," Aunt Dot said. "She just wishes you would marry some man long enough to make a couple of babies." I had never discussed with my aunt or my mama the fact that I couldn't have children, and even at twenty-five did not feel capable of talking about why that was so, anymore than I had been able, at the age of eleven, to tell them how badly I hurt "down there," or what had really happened to me. Would it have been "the truth" to hold my aunts and my mama responsible for the venereal infection that was never treated when I knew how hard I had tried to hide my pain from them at the time? Before I could be angry at them, I had to get past being angry at myself and dig my way down to who really hurt me, and why we had worked so hard to pretend nothing was happening. No, it was not the truth to say my mama was at fault, not the truth to blame the child I had been, not even the whole truth to blame my stepfather.

I worried it out over years and years, and finally, I broke the silence, not by going home to hold a massive family confrontation, but by writing a story in which I told everything that had happened to that child and the cost of it, the children that child would never have, the break in the family that could never be fully mended. Some days still, I think about how I wrote that story and gave it to my mama to read, and I know that doing that says more about truth and the depth of my own sense of shame than I could ever say in an explicit conversation.

Before Cathy I had thought myself a kind of chrome nun, armored and dispassionate. I had known myself a lesbian, had loved or thought I loved, but I had always felt an icy distance from the emotional excesses and vulnerabilities all around me. I considered myself cynical, wise beyond my years, knowledgeable about the world's cruelties, and a connoisseur of the risks of any kind of physical or sexual contact. I didn't need that, I told myself. I was different. Perhaps I wasn't a real woman, but some kind of alien mutant creature crafted by sexual abuse and natural resilience—a monster.

Cathy was the first woman with whom I fell in love. Every crush, every close friendship, every momentary rush of desire or fear that came before or after was made understandable by what I felt for her, simply because nothing else was as intense and overpowering. Lying in her arms, I felt crazy and willingly so, eager to give my life to make her happy, to suffer if suffering would ease her misery, to shame myself or look silly if that would make her smile. Breathing in the aura of her, that salty smoky taste of soapy skin and bitter cigarettes, made my heart swell and tightened my throat until it ached. Dreaming about her woke me up. Cathy proved to me that I was my mother's daughter, my sisters' equal.

It was Aunt Dot who told me that Aunt Maudy and Uncle Jack didn't speak, that after years of arguing and cursing, pot throwing and blue streaks, Jack had sworn she could die on her own, that he'd "never darken her door again."

"He said that?" I was amused that he'd use that particular phrase, so melodramatic and emphatic.

"Oh, he cursed her to her face same as she cursed him. They've been going on since they were kids. Never could stand each other."

234   Skin: Talking About Sex, Class & Literature

Aunt Dot had smiled then in pleasure, her face wrinkling up like damp laundry pulled out of the bottom of the refrigerator. "Jack's always been a pisser, you know."

I knew. I had always loved that in him, the way he would come in and do anything he pleased, never mind what anybody thought. And I loved the way he moved that long, lanky body, as if there was music playing in his head, blues or rock 'n' roll, his hips jiggling gently or gliding as smoothly as butter melting. My uncle Jack was the man who made it possible for me to understand how women fell in love with men.

That day at the funeral, Mama's loss ached in me as if a central part of my body had been stolen. I had wanted Jack to comfort me, wanted his smile and his charm, his loose way of reaching around and pulling you up into his big, wide shoulders, the spread of his love and confidence. But he looked as if he, too, had been robbed, as if the meat of his confidence, the deepest, richest part of his life was gone, the sweet stuff of him evaporated in the Florida heat.

"Lord," he said once, and I knew all he meant—the curse and the prayer.

"Who are all those people in Mama's photos?" I asked him just before he left my sister's house.

He barely glanced at the pile on the dining room table. "Family," he grunted, "all kinds of family. Flesh and blood sons-a-bitches." His hands were shaking. He fought with Aunt Nuell and my stepfather, refused to sleep in Mama's house another night, even on the floor as he had the night before. The shadows under his eyes were more cruel than the grey in his hair. "There's lots of dead people in there," he said, pointing at the pictures, "people you girls should have known but didn't. And damn it, it's too late now."

"Better watch out for me," Cathy was always saying. "I'm Fedayeen." And then she would toss her dark hair and bare her teeth in a fierce almost-angry smile.

"You're Arab?" I asked her once, naively.

Her answer was sudden and harsh. "No, I'm a Nigger. Can't you tell?"

The people standing around us laughed, and I quickly backed away in confusion. At the time, I had no idea if Cathy was Black, Arab, Cuban, or just another mean white girl making fun of me. No one I knew made jokes about color. No one talked about it, except to announce occasionally that they were not racist crackers like their parents, and to insist somewhat nervously that they got along fine with all the Cubans who had moved into Central Florida.

"Yeah, right!" Cathy would bark, laughing.

"Liars and cowards," she would sneer at half the people we knew. She had an unfailing instinct for people who could be teased into betraying their prejudices, girls who would back up and withdraw if they thought she wasn't just like them, boys who were reduced to tears when she would not tell them if she was really a colored girl.

"Look at me," she insisted once when we sat up talking into the early dawn. I smiled and told her she was pretty, but she held my hands and insisted. "No, really look at me."

So I did. I looked close, very close—at the dark mass of hair that sprang out from her head like a great cloud of electrically charged wool, the smooth tanned skin only a few shades darker than my own, the fine scar at the outside of her left eye, the mouth that was always pulled back as if she were about to sneer or curse. Her eyes were black and angry, but as I looked closely I realized that she might have been afraid.

"You see?" she demanded. But I shook my head, not knowing what she wanted me to see, not knowing what I was willing to admit I did see.

"They all think it. They look at me and wonder if I'm not some Black bitch from the projects getting over on them. So I say it before they can whisper it to each other. I say it so they have to think about how they're gonna talk to me, how they're gonna behave. I say it so they can't pretend nothing. I make them think about who they are."

"But what about who you are?"

"Yeah, what about it?"

I looked at her hands, the fingers curled into the palms, the knotted fists pressing down on her thighs so hard the knuckles stood out pale and sharp. My words surprised me. "You're just about the scariest person I've ever met," I told Cathy, and waited for her anger to flare. Instead she looked almost pleased.

"Yeah," she agreed. "Damn right."

"The way you talk about your mama is extraordinary," women would tell me, and I would blush, knowing that sometimes they meant not "extraordinary" but "strange," that I talked about my mama with the passion of a lover, obsessively, proudly, angrily, tenderly, insistently. I knew, too, that what it sounded like was not what it was, that I did not want to possess her but to free her. The touch of my mother was always a reminder that she was caught in a trap I could not have survived one day more than I did.

Write me a love story, my girlfriends asked. Write a political story, the women in my consciousness-raising group told me, and I wondered what that would be. Should I use words like *patriarchy* and *male madness* and *class oppression?* I tried. But every time, I found myself stopped, the words sour and mean.

What I began with was the story of my mother's life, my mother as a girl of fourteen, dropping out of school and pregnant with me, proud and stubborn and ashamed. I began with my mother's family—my family—the Gibsons and Yearwoods and Campbells and Hendersons. "Poor white trash," we had been called when I was a girl back in Greenville, "dirty fucking trash." When they were saying it to our faces there was no need for anything but the curse.

As I began to show people what I was writing, I kept the stories about my family back. It was too complicated to explain the mix of pride and shame, easier to write about being a lesbian and figuring that out, about falling in love or not, or about politics, the sim-

ple politics of having grown up female in the South. I hadn't a clue
how to write the complicated story, the story of growing up female
in our particular family, the daughter of the youngest of the Gibson girls, that trashy family where the boys all went to jail and the
women all made babies when they were still girls themselves. My
mama was one month past fifteen when I was born, her attempt at
marriage annulled by my grandmother before anyone knew I was
on the way. I worked my way back to that story, knowing it was the
one I needed to tell to be able to write. I had to believe in the use
of writing, and the primary use was to reject hatred, simple categories, shame. The first rule I learned in writing was to love the people I wrote about—and loving my mama, loving myself, was not simple in any sense. We had not been raised to love ourselves, only to
refuse to admit how much we might hate ourselves.

*Skin hunger. Sometimes it seemed that my skin ached like an empty belly.
The fine hairs below my navel seemed to reach up, wanting to touch something. My mouth would open when I slept and my tongue would push
at the air, reaching, reaching. I would wake from dreams of rising like
yeast into an embrace that welcomed and satisfied that hunger, an embrace I wanted desperately.*

When Cathy called me a dyke, she made it sound like something
to be proud of. She was gripping my fingers tight and laughing into
my neck. Her whole body was stretched along mine, open and easy
and warm against me. "You're such a tough dyke," she growled,
and heat went all through me. "So tough," she repeated, in a softer,
breathier voice, and in that moment I understood all the teenage boys
I had seen blush and preen under a girl's teasing. I felt for all the
world like a teenage boy, proud and nervous and anxious to please.
I wanted to make her smile. I wanted to make her proud of me. I
wanted to lie forever with her strong hand cupping my shoulder and
her whisper against my neck.

"I love you," I said. But she only shook her head.

Write funny stories, my mama told me. That's what people need and want to hear. Mama told funny stories all her life, charming strangers out of quarters across a diner counter, teasing a little more time out of bill collectors, coaxing a discount out of repairmen or car salesmen, and always, and most important, distracting my step-father out of his rages so that his hands would fall less heavily on her daughters. My mama used charm, funny stories, and that seemingly easy confidence to fight off a world of hurt and deprivation. It dismayed her that her daughters grew up angry, that all of us grimaced when she would have smiled, that none of us had her way with a funny story—and even more terrible was that we did not want it. Of all the things about our mama that we were supposed to find shameful—the poverty, lack of education or steady work—the only thing we hesitated to admire was the ingratiating, desperate charm that had eased her life.

"Mama's something, an't she?" my little sister would say, tempering admiration with uncertainty. I would agree, knowing that this was not a simple statement but a host of contradictory ones. Write mean stories, my sister dared me one night. "Go ahead and tell the world what really happened," she taunted, then just as fast as she had spoken the words, she withdrew them. "No, better not." I knew what she was thinking. I too have that voice inside me, the one that murmurs continually. *Maybe we shouldn't say anything,* it whispers. *Maybe if we are real quiet, the world will leave us alone.* If I told as much of the truth as I knew, what would happen? The world would know what he had done, who we had become to survive him. People would think I was a lesbian because he raped me, a pervert because he beat me, a coward because I had not killed him, and worse: I still went home like a well-trained puppy dog keeping my head down and never challenging him.

Sometimes I look into my little sister's eyes and I see those warring demands: the one that wants to take somebody by the throat and choke out answers for all the grief she has survived, and the other, that wounded figure, still a child wanting only to be left alone. Sometimes I don't have to look at my sisters to see that expression. It is in the mirror surface of my own pupils.

We had been brutal with each other. *Smart-mouthed sluts, whores, bitches.* He had called us those names so often, we used the same words on each other. But it is his voice I hear in my dreams, like a wave of burning liquid breaking over me. "Think you're so good, think you're so special, you're nothing, nothing." Dark, dark wave of curse and contempt. "Stupid bitch."

He never called me a dyke, but my sisters did, and from them it was unbearable. They seemed to believe that my being a lesbian meant I was not sexual at all. Like everyone else, they thought that lesbians were women who were afraid of sex, which was something that only happened with men. Only in the last few years have my sisters begun to see me as both a lesbian and sexual in the same way they are—complicated and romantic and prone to entangled, difficult relationships. I have lived with the same woman for six years now, introduced her as my partner, had a child with her, adopted that child, and loved her more than I can sometimes understand. It is this relationship, so like their marriages, this woman, so like their husbands, that has begun to be real to my sisters. Only recently have I glimpsed how important it is for me to have that shared sense of the quality of daily life, the same sense of meaning in what we do sexually. More than just tolerance.

The worst thing either of my sisters ever said to me was spoken one evening on a wave of fury and whiskey, resentment and jealousy, all of it peaking a few hours after he had raged and screamed what a slut she was. "He don't have to worry about some man stealing you away from him, and it an't as if he gave a shit about women." I wanted to kill her for saying it, even while I knew she had it right. My stepfather, who considered women dogs, probably thought about it just that way—that I was his meat, and as long as no other man had me, I still belonged to him. When I had finally straddled a man's hips and settled myself down on a man's cock, I realized it was only partly an experiment to prove to myself I could do it if I wanted to. I never imagined telling my stepfather, who got no access to any of my life, but I made a point of letting my sisters know.

What Mama taught us was to keep our heads up and refuse to *act* ashamed. She could not teach us how not to *feel* ashamed. She didn't know how to do that herself. No one in our family did. What they knew most deeply was the power of rage and silence. Don't tell nobody nothing, my aunts would have insisted if they had lived. Telling the truth is too dangerous, too expensive. I know I am the child of my family on the days when I hear their voices echoing inside me, telling me to keep my mouth shut and give no one a weapon to use against us, those days when I cannot help but think that they were right.

"You're the real thing," Cathy told me once, though I hadn't a clue what she meant. I did not know enough to realize how rare it was for one woman to pursue another unafraid. I could only imagine the kind of romance I had read in paperbacks. Before Cathy, I thought I was the only woman in the world who so desperately wanted sex with another woman. But Cathy's desires were so sudden, so explicit and so powerful, I would flush every time I imagined her skin touching mine. I would go home from Cathy to my mama's house, drunk with pleasure.

"I'm in love," I wanted to say to my mama, but I would see something, some tremor in her hands, and I would stop. It was not the fact that I was in love with a woman; it was my mama's life, the madness that love had thrown at her, the violence, the grief, and the shame.

"Goddamn, your mama must have been crazy about your stepfather!" my friend Marge told me after reading some of the stories in *Trash*. Oddly, that was the first time I really thought about it. Had

Mama ever been genuinely happy with my stepfather? Way back, had she loved him with a girl's love, full of hope and faith? Before he started storming through the house breaking doors and waving his fists in the air, before he began to beat us, before we grew into teenagers and he cursed us with every breath, before he started acting like a crazy man all the time, sitting in the living room with his hands moving rhythmically inside his loose shorts, or going for weeks not speaking to anyone, and when he did, talking only about how we were driving him crazy, how it would be our fault when he killed us all, killed us in the night after we'd pushed him too far, the way he was always threatening? Had there been a time when my mama had been safe to feel love for that man?

I tried to remember when our home had not been a madhouse, when my stepfather had not been that scary, scary man who careened through my childhood. It seemed to me things had deteriorated slowly over the years. In the beginning the beatings had been spankings that went on just a little too long or were a little too harsh. Always there had been a reason, one he would force Mama to admit. I broke a glass and hid the evidence. One of my sisters stole change left on the dresser. Another lied about where she had been playing. Little things became enormous, evidence that we were bad, like his beatings were evidence that he loved us. Everyone spanked their kids, everyone had to if they wanted them to grow up right. When was a spanking too much? When did it become a beating? How could you know? How could my mama know? She couldn't even ask anyone. How was she supposed to be able to tell? How were we?

Hadn't he loved her? Hadn't there been a time when everyone knew that he loved her? For my own life, I tried to remember and understand if that had been so.

I had never really believed my mama would die.

That had been the worst nightmare of my childhood, an omnipresent fear that Mama would disappear, and with her the shelter and protection she gave us. I lived in terror not only of our stepfather's rages, but of being left to face the world's contempt without my mama. The fear was not fantasy. Death stalked the women of my family. My granny died just after turning fifty-nine, and only one of my aunts lived long enough to qualify for social security—Aunt Dot, who still managed to die at sixty-three. Cancer went through us like a fire leaping from one to the next, my mama, my aunts, my cousins.

I have been a student of cancer for half my life. I lost friends to it a half dozen times over, and I was the one Mama talked to at the first mastectomy. I was the one who persuaded her to continue the chemotherapy after the second mastectomy and the recurrence that followed. I brought her books, articles clipped out of magazines, pages of testimonies from other survivors. I even went back with her to Greenville to visit her sisters, reading her a prose poem I called "Deciding to Live" on the way. Mama and all of us, we practiced positive thinking, living our lives as if cancer were not something we all dreamed about, nightmares in which people disappeared before you could get home to see them again.

When the call came and my sister Barbara told me that no, it wasn't that viral infection, this time the cancer was really back—for a moment I prayed it was just another terrible dream. But I was staying in a cabin up in Vermont, and to take the call I had to walk a quarter of a mile to the phone. I did it at a run, my nervous system flaring the whole way.

Barbara cried and asked me please could I get home quickly.

I sat down in the dirt, cradled the phone between my shoulder and my ear, clenched my hands together, and said to my sister, "It's all right. Just tell me everything." When I hung up, I found I had rubbed a blister under the ring on my left hand. I took off my ring and called my lover. Alix was waiting for me. Her voice was deep and reassuring. She said, "It's all right. Just tell me everything." All around me the ashy scent of a New England fall drifted through the trees. My mama was dying. I was a thousand miles away. After a few minutes I stopped crying and we started to make plans.

Alix took a leave from her job, and in two days we were both in Orlando sitting at my mama's kitchen table eating biscuits she had insisted on baking. She had a few days free before she had to check into the hospital and start chemotherapy, or decide not to do it at all and get ready to die.

"There's a tumor on my lung," she said, a cigarette in the ashtray in front of her. I let her explain everything Barbara had already told me, watching her face tighten and then relax as she talked. "It's going to be all right, baby," she said, laying her hand on mine. "I'll go in, they'll make these tests. Ten days from now we'll know a lot more. It's going to be all right."

Mama kept smiling at Alix, flirting lightly the way she had done with every woman I ever brought home. Mama looked good, a little thin and tired, but better than I expected. She would start chemo on Thursday and radiation soon after, and maybe it wasn't as bad as they said. Maybe she could fight it off again. She certainly didn't look like a woman about to die as she smiled at me, hugged Alix, and went to pull another tray out of the oven. I took a deep breath and held on to Alix's hand.

Mama was, at that moment, less than a month from her death.

There is delight in this. The skin flushes and shines. Heat rises and the fine skim of curls beneath my navel lifts. When I laugh, my skin sings, a music of blood and bone in perfect meter, a body that has learned the worth of endurance, passion, and release. Put your hand here. Hear the echo of my mama's pulse, her laugh, her songs. While I live and sing she does not die.

It got so bad so fast. I was never sure of all the ways that my love for Cathy had begun to break down. I told myself it was mostly about drugs.

"Don't start telling no lies about me," Cathy complained once when I was talking about applying for a job with the Social Security Administration, talking about how Cathy, too, could get better work, how I would help her pass the exams offered now and then for county jobs. Cathy was having none of it, but she was stoned on something, as she was almost all the time then. I looked at her, not knowing what she had taken, only knowing that it was no use to talk at all when she was in that condition, but I couldn't stop myself.

"Why?" I demanded. "Why do you do it?"

"'Cause I have to," she told me. "'Cause it stops the noise in my head, and it's the only damn thing that does."

I stood there, not moving, while she walked away. I knew what she meant. I knew that noise. It was in my head too, that constant dragging fearful chorus of uncertainty and confusion. But I had never used drugs to stop it. The only time that noise in my head had ceased was when I lay spent in Cathy's arms.

We stayed for three weeks. We went with Mama to schedule the radiation and afterward to look at the free wigs they offered cancer patients. Mama teased about shaving her head, but blushed when the woman helping her commented on the ink stains the doctors had left on her neck.

"Be careful not to wash those off," the woman said.

"What does she think? I've got cancer, I'm not stupid," Mama whispered at me when the woman stepped away. Both of us grinned then, united as we always had been in dealing with the world of bureaucratic strangers.

It was one of the last good days we had, for the chemo seemed more brutal than any she had survived before. Was she weaker than I had imagined? The doctor wouldn't say much, and Mama couldn't. "It'll be all right," she kept murmuring, even while the chemicals flowed into her arm and her skin turned yellow-pale and her cheeks sank in to leave the bones standing out plain and sharp.

I sat with her in the hospital, told her stories, and hummed old tunes whose words I no longer remembered. Mama's hands would clench at mine occasionally while her mouth opened and closed, and her eyes moved constantly under the translucent membranes of her eyelids. With my sisters at work and Alix running interference with my stepfather, I tried to keep Mama distracted while the nausea rocked her from side to side in the bed.

"Be careful," my mama whispered to me that last week while she was lying in her hospital bed. Her words were like an echo caught in the folds of my brain, the one phrase she had been repeating all my life. *Be careful, baby.* Things that might not be dangerous for other people were terribly dangerous for us. And if I knew that to be true, and I did, how could I ever be the person I wanted to be? What chance did I have to understand enough to write what I wanted to write? And whose story do I tell, hers or mine? There was no certainty, no reassurance.

"I loved it when you came up to visit me at Fire Island," I whispered to Mama one afternoon when she seemed weaker than ever.

With her eyes closed, she smiled and whispered back, "All those beautiful boys, and that hat."

I pulled her palm up to my mouth and kissed it. Her eyes opened then and looked at me. The pupils were dark. Her smile had disappeared.

"Baby," she said in a voice even softer than her whisper. Moisture appeared in the fine lines at the corners of her eyes. Her pupils looked strange, the irises cloudy, her expression confused. "I never meant for you to be hurt," she said. "I thought I was doing the right thing."

It was as if she had hit me. I jerked back and almost dropped her hand, then grabbed it fiercely, pressing it to my neck. Ancient habit took over and my voice dropped to a husky undertone, something no one standing more than a foot or so away could hear. I said, "Mama, there is nothing to forgive. You were not the one who did anything wrong."

"I should have left him." Her head turned on the pillow while her mouth worked and she worried her lips with her teeth. "But every time I thought I would, something happened." Her hand in mine shook, the fingers broke free and grabbed my wrist. "Something always happened."

"I know." I said it softly, looking into her eyes. I said, "I know, Mama. I know. Don't do this. There's no use to it. You did what you had to do."

"All those years," she said. "At first I just wanted to protect you, then I wanted a way to make it up to you. I wanted you to know you were never any of the things he called you." Her face was wet, no discrete tears coursing along her cheeks, just a tide of grief slowly slipping down to her chin.

My stepfather almost always came with Mama when she visited me. Each time I just barely managed, tight-lipped and stubbornly silent, or polite and carefully noncommittal. But in 1984 when they came to New York, he put his hand on my arm and my eyesight went black. I leaned over and vomited on the sidewalk. I could not stop retching until I was in a taxi moving away from him. That time they left the next day.

The following year they came back. Mama was sick again, one of the chemo years. I took her out to Fire Island with her old friend Mab, who tried to flirt with the gay men in the Ice Palace, and kept asking me if it was really true that they were all of them homosexual.

"Such beautiful boys," Mab said. She had mothered half a dozen sons through four marriages and never saw any of them anymore.

"Yes," I agreed, and did not smile at the hungry, lonely way she watched those beautiful boys.

Mama lay on our rented deck in a lounge chair, face turned away from the sun. My stepfather joined us on the third day, and I walked down to the beach to throw up in the ocean. "We'll leave," Mama told me. I started to cry. It was like cancer, that throwing up, the body suddenly betraying me, not letting me go on pretending nothing was wrong. He would reach to touch me, and years of practice, years of hatred would keep my face still and expressionless. But now my stomach battered at the back of my throat, refusing to allow any compromise, robbing me of my last chances to see my mother. They left before sunset, Mama looking at me over the side rail of the ferry with a rigid, pained expression.

I had bought Mama a sun hat with a hot pink ribbon. She put it on at an angle, waving at me. My stepfather told her to take it off loudly, said the ribbon was a "faggy pink." On either side of him two tall gay men stood, as muscled and powerful as football players. At his words, they reached over his head to put their arms around each other's shoulders. Ramona laughed. Mama just looked at me. My stepfather flushed dark purple, so dark the veins on his neck stood out in pale relief. I looked down at his hands and saw they had become fists. I was thirty-six years old. The last time he beat me with those hands I was sixteen. Twenty years. I said the words, but no one could hear me over the sudden roar of the ferry engine. I looked into his face, his empty eyes. My nausea receded, and the boat pulled away from the dock.

I was never sure how Cathy died, did not know what to believe of all the stories that went around afterward. The rumors swore it was an overdose, and I could believe that easily enough. What was certain was that her family had not wanted to pay to have her body shipped back from Arizona, where she had died, but when a collection was taken up everyone insisted her mother contributed a share. There was a memorial service, one attended by a few people who had really known her—the handful who had somehow gotten clean or weren't in jail at the time.

"You should have been there," the ones who had known us together told me when they saw me. "You could have spoken for her," they said, and I just shook my head. For years after I would wake up thinking about it, what I would have said if I had gone back to stand up in front of those people who had seen us as friends rather than lovers. Could I have said anything equal to the grief of her loss? Had there been anything I could have done to mute the roar in her head?

My sisters and I divided Mama's pictures among us. I took away a pile of her snapshots—faded, torn, stained sepia-toned images of her brothers, sisters, cousins, family—people whose faces we had not recognized, even those Aunt Nuell had been able to name. Strong-faced women with high cheekbones and dark eyes looked out from most of Mama's photos, all of them clearly related. Like Joan Crawford or Barbara Stanwyck, I thought, when I held one up to see it better in the light of the lamp my sister June set up on the dining room table. They had favored dark lipstick, thick, arched eyebrows, and engaged the camera directly. Most of the extended family pictures were from the forties or early fifties, while the mass of snapshots of us were taken before and just after 1962 when we moved to Florida. The Florida pictures all seemed to have been shot at the beach, and many featured Mama lying back like a bathing beauty with us playing at the edge of the water behind her. I could barely stand to look at those, and let my sisters take most of them.

I kept the old pictures, particularly the ones of Mama and her sisters, and in the months after Mama's death returned to them again and again. Aunt Maudy and Aunt Dot were in most of the photos, gazing from Barbara Stanwyck's eyes, clenching Joan Crawford's jaw. Mama, younger and more beautiful, had Grace Kelly's chin and eyes. Looking away and down, she seemed posed for the vulnerable line of her neck and the soft slope of her cheek, slightly mysterious but not traditionally pretty. *Film noir* heroines, I thought, every time I shifted through the pile. I kept fingering the snapshot that made my young Aunt Dot look like Maureen O'Hara with that full dark-red hair framing her strong features. Not tragic, though. Flirtatious. She crossed her arms below her breasts and stared at the world forthrightly and unafraid, denying my memories of a stooped, squinting woman with thin grey hair and hands that always lay loosely in her lap. I had known my aunts were strong, determined women, but I had never imagined them as burning, hopeful girls. I had always thought Aunt Dot a woman without vanity, wearing the same housedresses year after year, shunning makeup and laughing at how fat she had grown with her nine children. But the pictures proved that even she had been different as a girl, making herself up to heighten her resemblance to a movie star. Maybe it had been like that for all the sisters, for a year or two in their youth, trying to look like those strong-willed fantasy heroines, not realizing yet what real strength was, their stubborn capacity to endure all that fate would throw at them.

Cathy taught me that I was just like everyone else, capable of emotional and erotic obsessions, deeply needy and hungry for affection, and as talented as my mother and sisters at falling in love with someone who could break my heart. My love for her proved to me that I was female and feminine in the most traditional sense, foolish and damaged and hopeful. That knowledge, the human insight I gained from discovering myself passionate, capable of great joy, vulnerability, and love, had been astonishing. The outrage and despair I experienced in so desperately loving a woman who did not need me as much as she needed the needle in her arm was simply appalling. It took me years to see that falling in love with an addict who did not trust love in any way was a part of proving that I was not a monster, not the sexless creature I had imagined. Cathy showed me that I was humanly fragile. I found in myself the heroine of every heartbreak song I had ever laughed at but played again. I was not completely calloused. My skin was as thin as anyone's.

When I was eleven years old I loved my mama more than my life. When I was twenty-six I was so angry at her I could not even speak to her on the telephone. When I was thirty-six I could no longer pretend that my stepfather, her husband, had not broken me, body and soul. Years between and after, I bargained for every quiet moment she and I could steal. I was forty-one the year Mama died, and sometimes I was angry, sometimes not. We had gone past bargains and lies, past talking about it or not, even past agreeing on what had happened and what had not. I no longer needed that, if I ever had. All I knew was that I loved my mama and that she had always loved me, and that most of what was strong and healthy and hopeful in my life was possible because of her.

Our lives are not small. Our lives are all we have, and death changes everything. The story ends, another begins. The long work of life is learning the love for the story, the novels we live out and the characters we become. In my mama's photos is a world of stories never told: my stolid aunt a teasing girl, my sisters with their mouths open to laugh, and hidden in the pile, a snapshot of me at twenty-two, dark and furious, with Cathy's pale face solemn over one shoulder. Disappeared, anonymous, the story we might have told then remade. She has become legend, I human in grief, and full of the need to grab what I can and hold on, to remake death and begin another tale.

I wear my skin only as thin as I have to, armor myself only as much as seems absolutely necessary. I try to live naked in the world, unashamed even under attack, unafraid even though I know how much there is to fear. What I have always feared is being what people have thought me—my stepfather's willing toy, my mother's betrayer, my lover's faithless tease, my family's ultimate shame, the slutty, racist, stupid cracker dyke who doesn't know what she is doing. Trying always to know what I am doing and why, choosing to be known as who I am—feminist, queer, working class, and proud of the work I do—is as tricky as it ever was. I tell myself that life is the long struggle to understand and love fully. That to keep faith with those who have literally saved my life and made it possible for me to imagine more than survival, I have to try constantly to understand more, love more fully, go more naked in order to make others as safe as I myself want to be. I want to live past my own death, as my mother does, in what I have made possible for others—my sisters, my son, my lover, my community—the people I believe in absolutely, men and women whom death does not stop, who honor the truth of each other's stories.

Promises

My son Wolf, eighteen months old and fearless, loves nothing more than running off under the redwood trees down the hill from our house. The puppies chase after him barking joyfully, determined to catch the ball he waves above his head. I follow behind, just far enough back to give the baby a sense of freedom, not so far back that I can't rescue him when he falls over his own stumbling gait. "Mama!" Wolf shouts, and I find myself laughing. Hearing him call me Mama is almost as unimaginable as living in this landscape of rolling hills, redwood trees, and January camellias blooming as if it were spring. There is a river down the hill, a California river with a rocky bottom, docks, and summer bridges put up in May and taken down each October. It is beautiful and strange, as far from my childhood as I am. Even near the ocean, where this river pulls in marsh birds and fishermen, there is no swampland like the one I remember as a girl—a landscape so ripe, flowers burst out of the brown and black-spotted muck, promising vindication even as it threatened our white cotton socks.

My mama and stepfather took their one and only true vacation when I was eight, driving us south to the coast below Charleston for a week away from work and school. We spent a week on Folly Beach and another guesting at a bedraggled trailer loaned to us by one of the men who worked with my stepfather. The trailer was parked on a tiny plot just a quarter of a mile from the ocean, surrounded by another century's rice plantation property, flat damp grounds thick with mossy gnarled oaks and an impossibly dense lattice of old growth grasses. Our uncle Beau, Mama's brother, joined us with a tent draped in mosquito netting and a truckload of fishing gear.

"We'll catch enough fish to pay for the trip and then some," Uncle Beau swore. He sent my stepfather back to the highway for a load of block ice and dug a pit to keep it a while. My sisters and I baited hooks and hauled buckets of water up to hold the fresh-caught fish. Mama stretched out on a plastic foldout lawn chair with a John D. MacDonald mystery.

"I want you to know right off," she announced. "I'm on vacation. I an't gonna clean no fish I personally an't gonna eat." The men just laughed. My sisters and I were scandalized, and immediately began to beg to learn how to clean fish.

The men caught very little as it turned out. The fish were plentiful but wise. It didn't matter to us girls. We had stopped paying any attention. We took off on our own, walking the raised dirt platforms that marked the old rice fields and inspecting the locked-down wooden frames used to direct the tides into the various rice fields still intact. The remains of the plantation were laid out like a giant chessboard, designed so we could walk the border of each rough square, cleared enough that we could see the snakes sunning themselves in the grass before they heard you coming. Where the deeper water entered, the trees stood like the legs of fossilized Clydesdales, spindly and fine at the top, wide and swollen at the base. Where the trees parted, the grasslands went on for miles, stretching to the sea, here and there spotted with islands of maple and straggly palms, ringed with slow-moving creeks and rivers. We raced each other along the dikes and ate peanut butter sandwiches in the shade of stunted pines. Startlingly beautiful white birds called out as we passed, osprey, ibis, egret, ducks, and wood storks. Some lifted their enormous wings and swung up into a sky so blue and pure it made my heart hurt to stare into its reaches.

Mama told us that Indians—Cherokee even—had lived in those swamps once, and runaway slaves and poor whites had come there, the latter fleeing sheriffs who would have locked them up for debt. All of them passed through carefully, leaving no mark, and that was what we were to do—carrying out everything we carried into the swamp. We peered through screens of ferns and wild rice grass, and played at being runaways hiding in the tall clumps of grass. We tied our hair up in handkerchiefs, put rubber bands around the cuffs of our jeans to keep out the bugs, and brought back gifts of wildflowers and broken shells for Mama to admire. We would have brought her lily pads, but pulled free of the water they stank and shriveled. Instead, we searched out glittery feathers from those big white birds.

Back at the trailer, my stepfather and Uncle Beau had cursed their luck with fish, given up and gone off to get a bucket of spiced shrimp from one of the highway stands. Mama had put her paperback down and was lying quietly, staring up into the clear blue sky. "You come here," she called to us, sitting up and pulling me close to her hip, a story already shining in her soft brown eyes. I picked leaves out of my sisters' curls and listened to Mama while watching the sky myself.

"This is where things begin," I heard myself say. Mama sighed with pleasure and agreed with a quick affectionate hug. The sound of my uncle's truck growled off in the distance.

"We'll come back," Mama promised. But we never did.

The last time I went home to South Carolina, my cousin B.J. drove me around Greenville in her faded green Buick. We headed out to the western edge of the town, avoiding the new butterfly overpasses that channel traffic to the Interstate. Our goal was to locate a house we both remembered well, a two-bedroom wood-frame cottage, memorable for the peach trees in front and back. There, I had turned a sullen thirteen, listening to the music playing at the old Rhythm Ranch dance barn half a mile away. There, B.J. had fallen in love while staying with us, spending her evenings curled up on the kitchen floor with the phone pressed to her ear so that her boyfriend could whisper his own lyrics and promises. We had talked about that house the night before, the way that place had marked us both. We remembered that it had been set on the far side of a huge open field choked with high grass and patches of blackberries. Near there, past the peanuts and the pines, the wetlands began—acres of swampy forest, thick with short pine and stunted dogwood, muscadines hanging in sheets off dark trees, and birds rising in clouds from the intermittent stretches of grassland. It had seemed then that the wild places were close in and mysterious, opening off the backyards of the widely spaced old rented houses. Now my youngest cousins live in apartments and condos, drive out to the country only on weekends, and couldn't spot a muscadine if their lives depended on it. When B.J. and I talk about the old days, they smile and turn the television up louder.

"There were all those trees," B.J. kept saying, as we drove past one suburban blacktop after another looking for that house. Acres of tract houses, barren of trees or blackberry bushes, confused and saddened us. Earlier, we had driven past the old Greenville County high school. It was stark and mostly boarded up, the two-block stretch of dirt playgrounds pressed down to a concrete finish. The windows not covered in plywood were shattered and gaping. We had circled it twice looking for the road where, at one time, the school buses would come in to turn around. Both of us were growing tired and frustrated.

"I know it was around here somewhere." B.J.'s voice was strained and bewildered. I leaned my cheek against my palm and pushed my hair back out of my eyes. "Things change," I told B.J. as we drove away from the school. I was remembering a morning when I had missed the school bus and walked the two miles from my house. Once there though, I had spent the day hidden under the extensions—temporary classes set up in mobile units on blocks. All afternoon I had watched the sunlight move across the banks of win-

dows, turning them to mirrors that reflected the warning lights at
the railroad crossing and the occasional passing clouds. At 3:00 P.M.
I had skipped the bus and walked home again, cutting across the
peanut fields on the other side of the railway line and arriving home
as my mama was turning up our driveway. She had smiled at me
and handed me a wrapped package of leftovers from the diner where
she was working the dayshift. I had taken the package with a guilty
smile, expecting that at any moment she would recognize my crime
from something in my eyes. But she had seen nothing, and no one
had called. It was the first time I ever skipped school, the first time
I ever lied to her, if only by my silence. Not being discovered changed
everything, and after that I skipped school whenever I wanted, wan-
dering in the woods and swamps, finding a peace and comfort out
there that was not possible in our cramped and moody house.

"Do you remember when we'd all drive up into the hills?" B.J.'s
voice was pensive.

"With Aunt Dot and Uncle Bill?"

"Yeah. In the back of the truck with watermelon on ice in tubs."

"And buckets to gather berries for Dot to make pies later."

"She never made pies. Didn't have enough berries left by the
time we got home to flavor a cobbler."

"Well, think how many of us there were. Berry-eating kids leave
little behind."

"But everything was so close and beautiful."

"Yeah."

Is it memory that feeds us as we grow older? Is it memory that
houses all our dreams? The landscape of my imagination is all memory and passion, the wetlands where I wandered as a child, the hidden places where I birthed my stories, widened my vision, plotted
my escapes. That we were poor made no difference in that beautiful place. The flowers bloomed for us as thickly as for others, the

breeze came in at evening and cleaned the heated atmosphere. We could run out into those woods and know that hope is everlasting. What feeds children who never run there, never discover anemones under rotted waste, or startle birds so beautiful they hurt the heart?

B.J. and I drove back to the school and worked our way out for a third time, tracing where the old railway line had been torn up and buried, the highway that intersected just below where the Rhythm Ranch had stood alone in an open parking lot of rutted dirt.

"You remember the music?" B.J. asked me once, and I laughed in reply.

"Bass guitars playing off-key and drunken men singing heartbreak songs."

"Honey, don't hurt me more than I can stand."

"Yes, Lord. They don't make music like that no more."

"No, Lord. Thank God, they don't."

Her hand slapped the steering wheel hard, but I remembered following her in the evening to hike up the road toward the Ranch. We would huddle there and listen to that music drifting out over the grass, the lure of the grown-up world irresistible. Broken-down old trucks parked end to end next to rebuilt sedans and ancient convertibles with ragged canvas tops. Half-drunk musicians were always wrestling near the back door beside the stage, trading drags off cigarettes and curses for the poor wages they were paid. Men and women would come out to stand under the cedar trees that edged the parking lot, hugging and whispering, telling lies we could almost understand. Sometimes, they would sneak off into the woods so close to the lot that leaves drifted down into the backs of the trucks.

Honey, don't hurt me more than I can stand.

None of that remained. Twenty years had obliterated the county roads. Where the woods had once been wild, now there were only manicured lawns and quick-stop milk stores. Shopping centers stood where there had been a landscape a child could explore but never exhaust. Set off by arc lights and hurricane fencing, a discount center and a massive concrete parking lot had replaced the dance barn. We stopped at a shiny new Biscuitville for a Coke and spoke to the waitress who told us, yes, she remembered the Ranch from her girlhood, and yes, it had been right there.

"'Bout where the delivery vans park now," she told me.

I looked back and narrowed my eyes to remember the cedars with pickup trucks pulled up underneath, stooped men in cloth caps passing paper bags and laughing softly under the sound of steel guitars. Bullfrog voices thudding in the night, night birds screaming, the sky so close you could almost smell the stars.

"Progress," the woman said, and I nodded. B.J. wiped her eyebrows with her thumbs and shook her head. She had been a girl in love here. I had been a terrified, stubborn child. None of that was left, and neither of us knew how to speak about what we felt losing the landscape of our memories.

"It's like it was another world," we told each other driving away. "And now it's gone. You'd think something so good, people would save a piece of it."

There is a smell that has stayed with me all these years, a haunting smell of dusty moss, damp, split cedars, stagnant creeks, and salt-flavored evening breezes, that dreamlike landscape below Charleston, the wild open land around Greenville. In Charleston this past fall I smelled that landscape again, the landscape of memory and dreams. I had been sick for a week when I arrived, still sweating out a fever, but determined to see what a handful of stubborn people were trying to save from progress and neglect. At the ACE Basin Project I visited the same land where my mama had once told stories, where my uncle had laughed at the unpredictable nature of fish, where my sisters and I had run off into the wild to see whatever hid there. Unchanged, lush and safe, those old rice plantations still lay sheltering birds and wild grass and childish dreams.

"I thought all the places like this were gone," I said to the friends I saw there.

"Would be if we didn't work to keep them," I was told.

Exactly so, I agreed, and looked back twenty years to the landscape where I had been a girl.

Now I live in Northern California, close enough to the coast to bicycle over in the evening. Salt comes in from the ocean and stirs up the long grass, draws my eyes back toward the redwoods beyond the low hills. It is not the landscape of my childhood but always brings that memory back to me. If I close my eyes I can remember a place where the water was almost sweet, standing brackish around sunken trees and the half-buried nests of wood storks. The approaching twilight brings back the smell of shallow water darkened by tannic acid, mud-stained tree roots, and glistening full-bellied frogs. Live oak, sycamore, and palmetto shelter fern and Spanish moss. Ash trees and maple stand out against the occasional hickory and dogwood. Honeysuckles, daylilies, and anemones throw up brilliant sprays of cool glossy green and hot bright color. Sometimes, where the river meets the ocean, I experience again that waking dream. I become again eight years old, running with my cousins, canvas shoes squeaking in the muck, and the sounds of the shoes pulling free echoing the frogs and crickets and fast-moving night birds. The sky above us filters pink and purple. Ducks and wood storks lift their wings over the still water of the deeper marsh. Squirrels, rabbits, raccoons, and their predators push through the brush. A car radio plays softly in the distance, and the smell of unfiltered cigarettes drifts down with the music. Aunt Dot calls our names with weary patience. In a while, my uncles come stumbling back out of the night with buckets of bullfrogs and deep grunting laughter. By then we are all lying around on blankets eating from bowls of buttermilk and cold cornbread, watching the stars blink out above us, listening to my aunts whispering gossip and lies. It is a dream full of safety, love, sheer physical pleasure, and the scent of a ripe and beautiful landscape, a landscape that has all but disappeared. Only for the duration of the dream does it become again painfully real. If that landscape were not safe somewhere, would my dreams survive? Could my stories live in a world where children never ran free in that place where all my hopes were first shaped?

When my son runs down the hill through the trees, shouting for Mama and laughing as freely as only a baby can laugh, I cup my hands in stubborn hopefulness, making to him the promise my mama could never keep to me. I will make this place safe for him, bring him back to this landscape throughout his life, this wild country of beauty and hope and mystery. Each time he calls for me from those trees in the dusk, I promise again. Each time praying I can keep my promise.

This essay will appear in *A Geography of Hope,* a benefit collection for the Last Great Places Project of the Nature Conservancy (Pantheon/ Vintage: New York, 1994).

Other titles from Firebrand Books include:

Artemis In Echo Park, Poetry by Eloise Klein Healy/$8.95
Before Our Eyes, A Novel by Joan Alden/$8.95
Beneath My Heart, Poetry by Janice Gould/$8.95
The Big Mama Stories by Shay Youngblood/$8.95
The Black Back-Ups, Poetry by Kate Rushin/$8.95
A Burst Of Light, Essays by Audre Lorde/$8.95
Cecile, Stories by Ruthann Robson/$8.95
Crime Against Nature, Poetry by Minnie Bruce Pratt/$8.95
Diamonds Are A Dyke's Best Friend by Yvonne Zipter/$9.95
Dykes To Watch Out For, Cartoons by Alison Bechdel/$7.95
Dykes To Watch Out For: The Sequel, Cartoons by Alison Bechdel/$9.95
Exile In The Promised Land, A Memoir by Marcia Freedman/$8.95
Experimental Love, Poetry by Cheryl Clarke/$8.95
Eye Of A Hurricane, Stories by Ruthann Robson/$8.95
The Fires Of Bride, A Novel by Ellen Galford/$8.95
Food & Spirits, Stories by Beth Brant (*Degonwadonti*)/$8.95
Forty-Three Septembers, Essays by Jewelle Gomez/$10.95
Free Ride, A Novel by Marilyn Gayle/$9.95
A Gathering Of Spirit, A Collection by North American Indian Women edited by Beth Brant (*Degonwadonti*)/$10.95
Getting Home Alive by Aurora Levins Morales and Rosario Morales/$9.95
The Gilda Stories, A Novel by Jewelle Gomez/$9.95
Good Enough To Eat, A Novel by Lesléa Newman/$8.95
Humid Pitch, Narrative Poetry by Cheryl Clarke/$8.95
Jewish Women's Call For Peace edited by Rita Falbel, Irena Klepfisz, and Donna Nevel/$4.95
Jonestown & Other Madness, Poetry by Pat Parker/$7.95
Just Say Yes, A Novel by Judith McDaniel/$9.95
The Land Of Look Behind, Prose and Poetry by Michelle Cliff/$8.95
Legal Tender, A Mystery by Marion Foster/$9.95
Lesbian (Out)law, Survival Under the Rule of Law by Ruthann Robson/$9.95
A Letter To Harvey Milk, Short Stories by Lesléa Newman/$8.95
Letting In The Night, A Novel by Joan Lindau/$8.95
Living As A Lesbian, Poetry by Cheryl Clarke/$7.95
Metamorphosis, Reflections On Recovery by Judith McDaniel/$7.95
Mohawk Trail by Beth Brant (*Degonwadonti*)/$7.95
Moll Cutpurse, A Novel by Ellen Galford/$7.95
The Monarchs Are Flying, A Novel by Marion Foster/$8.95
More Dykes To Watch Out For, Cartoons by Alison Bechdel/$7.95
Movement In Black, Poetry by Pat Parker/$8.95
My Mama's Dead Squirrel, Lesbian Essays on Southern Culture by Mab Segrest/$9.95

New, Improved! Dykes To Watch Out For, Cartoons by Alison Bechdel/$7.95

Normal Sex by Linda Smukler/$8.95

The Other Sappho, A Novel by Ellen Frye/$8.95

Out In The World, International Lesbian Organizing by Shelley Anderson/$4.95

Politics Of The Heart, A Lesbian Parenting Anthology edited by Sandra Pollack and Jeanne Vaughn/$12.95

Presentingßßß Sister NoBlues by Hattie Gossett/$8.95

Rebellion, Essays 1980-1991 by Minnie Bruce Pratt/$10.95

Restoring The Color Of Roses by Barrie Jean Borich/$9.95

A Restricted Country by Joan Nestle/$9.95

Running Fiercely Toward A High Thin Sound, A Novel by Judith Katz/$9.95

Sacred Space by Geraldine Hatch Hanon/$9.95

Sanctuary, A Journey by Judith McDaniel/$7.95

Sans Souci, And Other Stories by Dionne Brand/$8.95

Scuttlebutt, A Novel by Jana Williams/$8.95

Shoulders, A Novel by Georgia Cotrell/$9.95

Simple Songs, Stories by Vickie Sears/$8.95

Spawn Of Dykes To Watch Out For, Cartoons by Alison Bechdel/$9.95

Speaking Dreams, Science Fiction by Severna Park/$9.95

Staying The Distance, A Novel by Franci McMahon/$9.95

Stone Butch Blues, A Novel by Leslie Feinberg/$10.95

The Sun Is Not Merciful, Short Stories by Anna Lee Walters/$8.95

Talking Indian, Reflections on Survival and Writing by Anna Lee Walters/$10.95

Tender Warriors, A Novel by Rachel Guido deVries/$8.95

This Is About Incest by Margaret Randall/$8.95

The Threshing Floor, Short Stories by Barbara Burford/$7.95

Trash, Stories by Dorothy Allison/$9.95

We Say We Love Each Other, Poetry by Minnie Bruce Pratt/$8.95

The Women Who Hate Me, Poetry by Dorothy Allison/$8.95

Words To The Wise, A Writer's Guide to Feminist and Lesbian Periodicals & Publishers by Andrea Fleck Clardy/$5.95

The Worry Girl, Stories from a Childhood by Andrea Freud Loewenstein/$8.95

Yours In Struggle, Three Feminist Perspectives on Anti-Semitism and Racism by Elly Bulkin, Minnie Bruce Pratt, and Barbara Smith/$9.95

You can buy Firebrand titles at your bookstore, or order them directly from the publisher (141 The Commons, Ithaca, New York 14850, 607-272-0000).

Please include $2.00 shipping for the first book and $.50 for each additional book.

A free catalog is available on request.